Daily Seeds

::from women who walk in faith::

Daily Seeds

::from women who walk in faith::

edited by Anita Lustrea, Melinda Schmidt & Lori Neff

MOODY PUBLISHERS
CHICAGO

Editor: Jocelyn Green
Interior Design: Ragont Design
Cover Design: The Dugan Design Group
Cover Image: iStockphoto #4515583 Photographer: Nikola Bilic

Library of Congress Cataloging-in-Publication Data

Daily seeds from women who walk in faith / edited by Anita
Lustrea, Melinda
Schmidt & Lori Neff.
p. cm.
ISBN 978-0-8024-7561-9
1. Christian women--Prayers and devotions. 2. Devotional calendars. I. Lustrea, Anita. II. Schmidt, Melinda. III. Neff, Lori.
BV4844.D34 2008
242'.643--dc22
2008025689

We hope you enjoy this book from Moody Publishers. Our goal is to provide high-quality, thought-provoking books and products that connect truth to your real needs and challenges. For more information on other books and products written and produced from a biblical perspective, go to www.moodypublishers.com or write to:

Moody Publishers
820 N. LaSalle Boulevard
Chicago, IL 60610

1 3 5 7 9 10 8 6 4 2

Printed in the United States of America

To my amazing husband, Mike Murphy, who wholeheartedly believes in my mission to communicate freedom to women and to help them live out of the fullness of who God created them to be. It's also dedicated to my son John. He and I have spent many hours laughing together and searching for the perfect diner, drive-in, or dive! And to my mom and dad who encouraged me, from an early age, to seek out God's best for my life.

Anita Lustrea

To my mom, Helen Correa, who I remember reading her worn copy of the classic devotional *Streams in the Desert* each day, along with her Bible and marked-up prayer list. Now in the throes of dementia, she wouldn't remember that, but I do! Thank you, Mom, for your legacy in modeling the importance of connecting to God's Word, the inspiring reflections of His disciples, and an unwavering faith in prayer.

Melinda Schmidt

To the listeners of *Midday Connection*. I process every phone call, email, and letter that we receive from you. I celebrate with you, grieve with you, and pray for you every day. It's my prayer that this offering will be an encouragement, help, and challenge to you as you grow closer to Jesus. And to Mom and Dad, for your constant encouragement to "go for it." Most of all, to my best friend and husband, John. Thank you for your love, support, and encouragement to be who God created me to be. I love you more than I can express.

Lori Neff

Acknowledgments

This project would not have happened without the nearly 75 friends of *Midday Connection* who said "yes" as soon as they were asked to contribute to this project. All are busy women with plenty already on their plate. We are thrilled to be associated with such a who's who of Christian women in ministry.

We also want to acknowledge the many listeners to *Midday Connection* who, through their emails, helped birth the idea for this book. They listen daily and give regular feedback that helps us know what issues we need to revisit.

We acknowledge the sacrifice our families made as our eyes were glued to computer screens and manuscripts, ignoring all else.

Finally, we are so thankful for the work God has done in each of us, and how He's used a few select women to mentor and encourage us along the way. Many of those women have shown up in this book, some have not. We want to make sure we especially thank Janet. She has given hours of counsel and soul care and encouraged us on our journey to live out of the fullness of who God created us to be.

Warmly,
Anita Lustrea, Melinda Schmidt, and Lori Neff
Midday Connection

Introduction

The daily emails we receive at *Midday Connection* tell of the enormous pressures on women today. We live in a desperate, complex world and the struggles confronting women sometimes seem insurmountable. At *Midday Connection*, we are committed to providing daily radio programs that speak to the seriousness of the issues we hear about on a regular basis—issues like sexual abuse, extreme debt, eating disorders, adultery, sexual addiction, friends or relatives who are in prison, broken friendships, domestic violence, depression, failing marriages, cancer, prodigal children, physically or mentally disabled children, and the list goes on and on and on.

Then there are the everyday issues like how to maintain sanity with two toddlers underfoot, how to discipline teenagers, keep the house uncluttered and clean, how to be chauffer, bill payer, grocery shopper, cook, and laundry lady while still finding time alone with God.

If you've picked up this devotional, you are probably a busy woman. We've never met one who isn't. You are probably looking for a way to connect with God and find daily refreshment. We want to help you make that connection and go deeper in your relationship with God. Have you ever watched someone trying to get to the heart of a piece of fruit, especially a piece that needs to be peeled? There is nectar dripping from fingers, wrists, and sometimes even elbows. We try to lick every drop, not wanting to lose a bit of goodness. It's all worth our broken nails and juice-stained clothing.

What we desire we will fight for despite the messiness and effort. Peeling back the layers and straining to stay with the endeavor does, however, come with a cost. As we work at the thick skin of the pomegranate, a lovely fragrance encourages us to press on to the promise of treasure within: the seeds that deliver the coveted taste and nutrition.

It's our hope that you will find in the pages of this book some seeds of encouragement that focus on many of the issues mentioned above. We know you'll make some new friends as you read from the various contributors to this devotional. These are women we know and trust. They love God, and, like us, they have a heart for women. They've all been guests at one time or another on *Midday Connection* and we've seen them really connect with our listeners.

In the pages of this book, you'll join a group of women who are encouraging other women like you to go deeper with Christ, discovering their own call to live as the woman God has uniquely created them to be. Will you walk with us for a year? Better yet, will you walk with Jesus for a year? Start reading, and let us know how you're growing. Send us a quick email at midday@moody.edu.

May we all live out of the fullness of who God created us to be!

Warmly,
Anita Lustrea, Melinda Schmidt, and Lori Neff
Midday Connection

Anita Lustrea

This means that anyone who belongs to Christ has become a new person. The old life is gone; a new life has begun!
2 CORINTHIANS 5:17 (NLT)

The beginning of a new year comes to all of us with a clean slate. That's one of the reasons we like a new year, for its possibility of new beginnings. The good news is that God is the God of second chances whether it's a new year or not.

For some, New Year's Day doesn't have the feel of a new beginning. It's more of the same. A continuing battle with cancer, or more praying for a prodigal child, or more of wondering where God is in the middle of my pain. So how do we turn it into a new beginning when it feels anything but? I think we have to be purposeful about our focus. We have to take on the attitude of gratitude and remember that we are new creatures in Christ, that the old life is gone and the new life has come.

Take a look at Moses, David, Abraham and Sarah, and Zechariah and Elizabeth. The list of biblical characters that received new beginnings goes on and on. Why would we think we aren't eligible? Need a new beginning? Open up the channels of conversation with the God of the universe. He's there waiting to listen and waiting to speak. You can begin again!

Take some time today to journal about what you'd like to see happen this year. How you'd like to see God move. Reflect over the past year and write down what you're grateful to God for.

Nancy Kane

Not that I have already obtained all this, or have already been made perfect, but I press on to take hold of that for which Christ Jesus took hold of me. PHILIPPIANS 3:12 (NIV)

A recent survey polled more than three hundred thousand people to find the Top Ten Most Common New Year's Resolutions. Among them were: exercise; stick to a budget; pay off debt; and enjoy more time with loved ones.

While these are admirable goals, the reality is that 70 percent of the population never achieves their resolutions and one in five fail within the first six months.

I wonder if part of the reason we fail in attaining our resolutions is the focus of the resolution itself. We are led to believe that if we just set the right goals and are really determined we will achieve the lives we always wanted. I wonder if our resolutions are just another feeble attempt to secure our own happiness and to get control of what seems to be out of control lives.

The apostle Paul indicated one of his resolutions when he wrote, "I press on toward the goal to win the prize for which God has called me heavenward in Christ Jesus" (Philippians 3:14 NIV). Paul had already experienced what the outcome of a life spent in self-serving goals would get him. He encountered Christ on the Damascus road and knew from then on that everything he had ever strove for was nothing in comparison to intimacy with the Son of God.

Maybe we need to simplify our resolutions. While getting in shape and eating right are good things, they pale in comparison to what we really can have. As we are frantically trying to live "successful" lives we are missing the One that has guaranteed without fail; He can make our lives into something that exceeds our wildest dreams.

François Fenelon, a sixteenth century saint, went to the heart of the matter when he wrote, "To love God is only one way . . . to take not a step without Him and to follow with a brave heart wherever He may lead." May this be our one New Year's resolution.

Glynnis Whitwer

For by him all things were created: things in heaven and on earth, visible and invisible, whether thrones or powers or rulers or authorities; all things were created by him and for him. He is before all things, and in him all things hold together. COLOSSIANS 1:16–17 (NIV)

My first (and last) step aerobics class started out fine. Then the teacher had us do a fancy, fast step. With our hands on our hips, we jumped and pointed our feet faster and faster.

For the briefest of moments, I felt like a graceful Irish step dancer on Riverdance. My feet were flying. Then I made a tactical error—I looked down. When I did, my arms flailed in circles as I tumbled to the ground, embarrassed.

I should have kept my eyes on the instructor. That would have helped me keep in step with her. And as a beginner, I really wasn't ready to step that fast. But I wanted to keep up with all the other women in the room.

What an accurate correlation to how our lives get out of balance. To keep my feet underneath me, I need to keep my eyes on Jesus, the center of my existence. As I pattern my step to His, my life takes on balance. As I align my priorities to His, I find a graceful flow to my life. Once my eyes are firmly on Jesus, I won't try to keep up with those around me. My pace will be set according to my abilities and what God is calling me to do.

I learned my lesson about trying to move faster than my feet would take me, and I know I'll never be an Irish step dancer. Now, I'm happy slowing down when necessary—at least I'm still standing.

Identify an area of your life that seems out of control or out of balance. Decide if you need to reduce your commitment in that area or other area. Chose to do only what you are able to do, and still maintain balance in your life.

Brestin

But if we walk in the light, as he is in the light, we have fellowship with one another, and the blood of Jesus, his Son, purifies us from all sin. 1 JOHN 1:7 (NIV)

As a young mom, I was addicted to soap operas. I asked the Lord to set me free. He told me to start choosing the light—which meant dying to the darkness. At first, turning them off was painful, but in time, I found the soap operas boring. I was caught up, instead, in Christian radio. One day I realized, "Dee—you are free."

Do you want to be set free of the chains of sin? The secret is in the little letter of 1 John.

But the first time I read through John's first letter, it scared me. He says a *true* child of God will obey Him (1 John 2:3), will not hate his brother (1 John 2:9), and will not "shut up his heart" when he sees his brother in need (1 John 3:17 NKJV). I thought, *I know I don't always obey, love, show mercy. Am I not a true child of God?*

But reading it again, I knew that couldn't be what John was saying—for he makes it clear that none of us is without sin (1 John 1:8). So—what *is* he saying?

I'd challenge you to do a study of the word "complete" in 1 John. John is writing to believers, telling them the secret of overcoming sin. Every time you respond to the Spirit to love, to obey, to choose the light—then *His love* and *His light* becomes more complete in you. John Stott put it like this: "Our love and our hatred not only reveal if we are in the light or in the darkness, *but actually contribute* to the light or darkness in which we already are."

It is also true, John says, that each time we choose the darkness, Satan gains a foothold. But greater is He within us, John reminds us, than he that is in the world.

Miriam Neff

Do not boast about tomorrow, for you do not know what a day may bring forth. PROVERBS 27: 1 (NIV)

Widow, the title I never wanted. The group no one wants to join. A mere five years ago, Bob and I had a different plan for this day. But here I am, part of the fast growing demographic in the United States. Eight hundred thousand join our ranks annually. We are noticed by new home builders and are a lucrative niche for health and beauty products. We are invited to dinners by financial planners and surveyed by designers for home features that will convince us to sign on the dotted line.

Paradoxically, we lose 75 percent of our friendship network at the same time even in our Christian network. Sixty percent of us experience serious health issues in that first year. One-third of us meet the criteria for clinical depression in the first month after our spouse's death, and half of these remain clinically depressed a year later. Most experience financial decline.

If someone had described this scenario to me five years ago, I would have stated emphatically, "It can't be so! In the community of believers we support each other. We walk together on the journey." I now live much of the reality of those statistics.

Can anything good come out of this adventure? Absolutely. Just as I did not know this day was coming, I did not know how incredibly God would meet me where I am. I know now that when He says He cares for the widow, that we are close to His heart, He means it. His comfort on a lonely night cannot be matched. His peace when looking into the unknown is unexplainable.

Bob and I did not plan for this. But God knew, and He can be trusted. That's enough for me to say that this is a good day.

Before the day is over, call a widow and tell her you thought of her today.

Shauna Niequist

There is a time for everything, and a season for every activity under heaven . . . ECCLESIASTES 3:1 (NIV)

When my friend Annette moved away from Grand Rapids, back to California, Ecclesiastes reminded me that there are seasons for each thing, and that life is a series of beginnings and endings, and most of all that it's okay—good, even—to mourn.

Annette and I mourned together as the day of her move came closer and closer. That last month, I think, we saw each other every day, and cried together many of those days. We remembered the births of our sons, five months apart, and all the dinners and all the baby clothes and maternity clothes we passed back and forth, and all the walks and weekend trips and last-minute lunches and breakfasts at Gaia and the Real Food Café, all the honest conversations, all the times we laughed till we cried.

On the afternoon that we actually had to say good-bye, we hugged in her driveway, icy wind whipping past us, crying, laughing, and we made it a quick good-bye, a good-bye for now, but when I got back into the car, I sobbed, both thankful and heartbroken.

Now that she's gone, I'm trying to love that season, and let this new season be different. I feel thankful every day for the years that Annette and I lived two blocks apart, and I hold them in my heart as one of God's best gifts to me.

These days she and I are working hard to create new rhythms for this new season of our friendship—emails instead of morning coffees while the boys nap, flights instead of walks, long distance phone calls instead of stopover visits.

There is, certainly, a time for every season, and especially when my heart is aching with loneliness, those words are a balm.

Have you ever mourned the end of a season? Have you been tempted to avoid the pain of mourning? Is there anything in your life right now that is ending that might need to be mourned?

Jill Briscoe

It was the same in the days of Lot. People were eating and drinking, buying and selling, planting and building. But the day Lot left Sodom, fire and sulfur rained down from heaven and destroyed them all. It will be just like this on the day the Son of Man is revealed. On that day no one who is on the roof of his house, with his goods inside, should go down to get them. Likewise, no one in the field should go back for anything. Remember Lot's wife! Whoever tries to keep his life will lose it, and whoever loses his life will preserve it. LUKE 17:28–33 (NIV)

"In light of my coming again" said Jesus, don't worry about "the stuff in the house." Paul puts it another way: "The time is short. . . . From now on . . . [let] those who buy something [be] as if it were not theirs to keep; those who use the things of the world as if not engrossed in them For this world in its present form is passing away" (1 Corinthians 7:29–31 NIV).

So often it's the "stuff in the house" that distracts us from the command to "hasten the coming of the Lord," isn't it? How easy it is, especially for us women to hold our possessions tightly rather than lightly!

Think about all that Lot's wife had seen of the hand of God at work in blessing and protection. Despite God's goodness to her, she had pitched her tent toward Sodom, a child of compromise. She wanted a "tent with a view" and the "stuff in her house" mattered more to her than the promises of God.

Chloroforming her conscience and forgetting all that she had learned in Abraham's family, she was continually looking back over her shoulder to the good life. Such a worldview leads inevitably to immobility and leaves our lives a monument to compromise.

Ask the Lord to focus your eyes on Him and not look back. May we be waiting and working for Him when He returns.

Lori Neff

There is an appointed time for everything. And there is a time for every event under heaven—A time to give birth and a time to die; A time to plant and a time to uproot what is planted. A time to kill and a time to heal; A time to tear down and a time to build up. A time to weep and a time to laugh; A time to mourn and a time to dance. ECCLESIASTES 3:1–4 (NASB)

I tend to be serious and easily feel the weight of the sad, heavy stuff of life. There are a lot of legitimately serious things in life—AIDS, orphans, war, poverty, tension in relationships, as well as the daily concerns in our lives . . . it can be very heavy.

I met with my church small group one night when I was feeling weighed down from a load of concerns. One woman surprised the group with an impromptu celebration for our newly engaged friend. As we laughed and celebrated the wonderful occasion, I was struck by the beauty of the moment. How easy it would have been to let that moment pass us by! We could just as easily been preoccupied with the difficulties in each of our lives. My party-throwing friend told me that she has decided to find something to celebrate every day. She has chosen to celebrate—even during difficult seasons of loss, sadness, illness, and pain. With so much desperate suffering around us, we cannot survive with just a steady diet of heaviness. We need to laugh and celebrate the small (or large) gifts God gives to us every day. Will you join me in the pursuit of celebrating every day?

Leslie Vernick

Finally, brothers, whatever is true, whatever is noble, whatever is right, whatever is pure, whatever is lovely, whatever is admirable—if anything is excellent or praiseworthy—think about such things. PHILIPPIANS 4:8 (NIV)

By nature, I'm a pessimist. I always see the glass half-empty. I've been told to think more positively, but sometimes that can be dangerous.

For example, several years ago my husband and I visited Las Vegas on business. Being curious, one evening we went to a casino and I parked myself near a high stakes black jack table. In a short time I saw one gentleman lose twenty thousand dollars thinking positively.

As this example illustrates, positive thinking can be just as deceitful and deluded as negative thinking can be. God warned the prophet, Jeremiah, not to deceive the people with positive words like the false prophets were doing. He said, "They dress the wound of my people as though it were not serious. 'Peace, peace,' they say, when there is no peace'" (Jeremiah 8:11 NIV).

God never tells us to think positively. But he does tell us to think truthfully. He tells us to focus our mind on things that are good, beautiful, pure, and lovely even in the midst of difficult life circumstances. God knows how we think and what we think about affects our emotions and our body. Medical research is discovering this important truth. Our thought life can make us physically and emotionally ill.

If you lean toward seeing the cup half-empty like I do, you may find it difficult to notice the positive things. Begin today to look for what's good in your day instead of what's bad. Focus on what's lovely in your spouse or child instead of what you don't like. Daily write these things down in a praise and thanksgiving journal. Before long, if you practice this discipline, you will find yourself feeling happier with yourself, others, and life.

Kendra Smiley

Come to me, all you who are weary and burdened, and I will give you rest. MATTHEW 11:28 (NIV)

My husband, John, and I took a mission trip to Santa Cruz, Bolivia, a few years ago. We were scheduled to speak on parenting to several groups while we were overseas. In addition, we were to spend a great deal of time at a mission school. In preparation for the trip we asked the principal of the school for a list of things that were needed. Then I went shopping and packed those things in our suitcases.

We took the maximum number of bags—two pieces of carry-on luggage, and four suitcases that we could check when we arrived at the airport. Each of our "check-on" bags could weigh fifty pounds. Because we were taking books and a large assortment of school supplies, we knew that we'd be using every single pound. I moved our bathroom scale downstairs so that I could weigh the suitcases as they were packed.

When we finally checked in at the airport, all of our bags, including those we would carry on, reached the maximum weight. The attendant dragged the suitcases off the scale and immediately tagged them as "Heavy!" In fact she put two tags on more than one bag! "Heavy! Heavy!" What a relief it was to fly back home with a much lighter load!

Have you considered the baggage you are carrying through life? Do you have unresolved issues that are burdening you and making the journey of life more difficult?

The Lord desires to help you "unpack" and lighten your load. If you are weary and burdened, come to Jesus and He will give you rest. That's the Next Right Choice!

Beverly Hubble Tauke

Esau ran to meet Jacob, and embraced him . . . and kissed him. And they wept. GENESIS 33:4 (NIV)

Old Testament matriarch Rebecca was Machiavellian before Machiavelli, luring son Jacob into a scheme to betray his brother Esau (Genesis 27). Bamboozled out of family fortune and status, Esau turned homicidal rage against his twin.

Despite his own blunders, Esau's ultimate triumph over agonizing family betrayal is instructive. Maturing with marriage and fatherhood, he pursued a successful vocation. Diverting energy from rage and revenge to purpose and productivity, Esau gained capacity for personal and relationship healing. Emotionally embracing estranged Jacob, Esau exhibited a heart not only ready to forgive and reconcile, but eager to protect his repentant brother emotionally, physically, and financially (Genesis 33).

Current research shows that Esau's positive mental focus, responsibility for himself, development of competencies and capacity for empathy are traits of victims most likely to repair broken relationships. The same secrets of spiritual, emotional, and relationship vitality were prescribed millennia ago:

• Mental focus on the good and virtuous invites God's peace (Philippians 4:8–9)

• Astute judgment of others requires personal responsibility first (Matthew 7:1–5)

• God's forgiveness of us is linked to our forgiving others (Matthew 6:14–15)

Forgiveness does not exclude moral accountability or confrontation of derelict behavior, as Jesus showed when exposing the moral laziness of his own beloved disciples (Matthew 26:36–40). But grudge addicts who use moral debt to control or bludgeon their offenders often become toxic themselves, morphing into the very villains they so resent.

Just as Esau, you can see old wounds heal and broken relationships mend with a touch of your mercy and grace. Is it time to offer an open heart to someone who has wounded you?

Joanne Heim

Therefore, as God's chosen people, holy and dearly loved, clothe yourselves with compassion, kindness, humility, gentleness and patience. Bear with each other and forgive whatever grievances you may have against one another. Forgive as the Lord forgave you. And over all these virtues put on love, which binds them all together in perfect unity. COLOSSIANS 3:12–14 (NIV)

"What should I wear today?" is a question I ask myself every single day. And I bet it's something you ask yourself everyday too. In fact, it's something all women ask themselves and spend quite a bit of time thinking about. (I suppose men ask it too, but they may not care as much about the answer as we do!)

Who knew that the Bible had the answer to that age-old question? Here it is: In response to being chosen and holy and dearly loved by God, this is what we should wear: compassion, kindness, humility, gentleness, patience, forgiveness, and love.

Go look up each of these words in the dictionary and spend some time thinking about what they mean and what they would look like if you put them on. Then write out Colossians 3:12–14 and hang it up in your closet or on your bathroom mirror where you'll see it every morning.

Just like the outfit we put on each morning, we must clothe ourselves with these things each and every day. We put them on—just like we put on our favorite jeans.

These character traits aren't part of us naturally. We weren't born with them; they don't get put on once and stay put. They come from God and we have to make the choice to put them on. Every single day.

So what are you going to wear today? Because without these things, it doesn't really matter what outfit we choose or how great our shoes look. We may look cute on the outside, but God is looking at our hearts—wanting to see if we're going to wear what He picked out for us.

Joy Jordan-Lake

And whatever you do, whether in word or deed, do it all in the name of the Lord Jesus. COLOSSIANS 3:17 (NIV)

When I published my book *Working Families* on navigating kids and career, I found myself in the troubling position of appearing like The Expert on how to time one's education, childbearing, and promotions so that no offspring would suffer separation anxiety, and so that my own profession and my husband's continued to charge ahead at full speed while money was never an issue. Right.

The radio interviewers often seemed to be waiting with pad and paper to record The Answers that would solve all our twenty-first century work-and-family concerns, and make us all rich and famous—and flawless parents.

"But, um," I confessed, "I wrote this book precisely because I *didn't* have all the answers. I asked other women and men how *they* cope or even to thrive. I wanted to know what they'd given up where, and how they knew when to back off of what." And then I told stories, both from my own life and from those far-wiser souls I'd interviewed for the book.

The hosts seemed enthralled by the stories—but also deflated that they wouldn't be given a definitive list of how-to's in a one size fits all. One day, as I complained to a friend of this, she shook her head. Becca herself has three children and, among other work, founded a ministry with former prostitutes. "People ask me how I maintain balance in my life," she said, "I tell them, '*Balance*! What *balance*? It's about holding on to God.'"

Exactly. Because a life of faith is never about DayTimer formulas. Instead, all we do, no matter how that looks season to season in our homes and places of work, in our playgrounds and in our boardrooms, we would do everything—changing dirty diapers and preparing PowerPoint presentations—all for the glory of God.

How can you focus today not on some elusive perfect balance in your life, but on holding on to and listening to God?

Nancy Anderson

Create in me a clean heart, O God, and renew a steadfast spirit within me. PSALM 51:10 (NASB)

If your marriage is less than blissful, and you feel like giving up, I can tell you from personal experience: marriages can be raised from the dead. My husband, Ron, and I had one of the worst marriages I've ever seen, but now, we really love each other—even like each other. You can too. Are you willing to begin anew?

You're probably thinking, *Why should I be the first to change?* or *Why do I have to do all the work?* The answer is simple: God will work with whoever is available and give that person the strength to change. Are you available?

You already know that you can't change your mate, but you *can* change your own behavior. The word "change" indicates a transformation, which is a metamorphosis; the word *metamorphosis* begins with the two letters *m* and *e*. Change begins with me.

Maybe you're saying, "But, Nancy, you don't know how selfish my husband is." You're right, I don't know your situation, but I'm assuming that you chose to marry him, so he must have some wonderful qualities too. Unless your husband is abusing you or your children, you can choose to be satisfied in your marriage.

Look for the best in your husband, not at his faults. It doesn't matter who plants the first seeds of restoration and forgiveness, because you'll enjoy the harvest—together. It might be hard to start, but if you don't, and your husband won't, then who will?

My husband and I have learned that fighting and blaming won't work. Commanding and demanding can't work. Surrender works. So surrender your heart to the Lord and ask Him to work in you and through you. He will accomplish more than you could ever do on your own.

Melinda Schmidt

Trust God from the bottom of your heart; don't try to figure out everything on your own. Listen for God's voice in everything you do, everywhere you go; he's the one who will keep you on track. PROVERBS 3:5–6 (MSG)

It was Sunday afternoon and I munched on a ridiculously expensive miniature Chicago deep dish pizza at a deserted airline gate. Watching planes filled with passengers, I thought, and all those people have stories. An ambulance left one of the planes and sped across the concrete—I'll bet they never expected that car ride today.

And the other passengers—which ones would be gutting out one more business trip, and who were they leaving behind? Perhaps some of the men had to leave young moms who were going to miss dad's presence each night to give them a break from the kids. Would those dads and moms trust God to see them through the week?

Would men and women ask God for the courage to take on the tasks . . . and the temptations . . . of the week ahead? Would daughters look to Him for patience and wisdom as they settled their widowed dads into new living situations? At the end of the week, which folks would tell stories of God's faithfulness?

In your busy days ahead, what's one spiritual action you will take to strengthen your trust in your heavenly Father, knowing it is His delight to sustain you and meet your needs and help you cope (a Scripture verse, time each day to express your needs to Him and find His present hope)? What's one lifestyle change you can make to alleviate stress this week (a break for exercise, rest, community)? Write it down.

Carolyn Castleberry

A man's pride will bring him low, but a humble spirit will obtain honor. PROVERBS 29:23 (NASB)

Let's be honest. One of the most frightening, humbling issues we deal with every day is money. We freely talk about relationships, work pressures, social anxieties, but speaking about money challenges with friends and fellow church members is strictly taboo. Once you realize that God is also Lord of all resources, you can begin to rest in His security. We can also become better stewards of our finances by asking a lot of questions. Really! Especially humbling questions like, "Hey, I just don't understand this stuff. Will you please explain it to me one more time?"

In *Women, Get Answers About Your Money: Because There are No Dumb Questions about Personal Finance*, I tell my own story about going through a financial crisis, and in meeting with an "expert," I found myself too intimidated to ask the dumb questions. Or should I say too prideful? You see I have a business degree and had hosted a national business radio show and I was supposed to have all of the answers, right? Unfortunately, not for my personal life, and the broker I met with gave me one of those looks like, "don't worry your little head over all of this … I'll take care of your savings for you." You can probably guess the end of this story. Thousands of dollars lost, a serious humbling, but I learned that questions are the beginning of knowledge. Humility is also the beginning of financial wisdom.

Meet with a financial counselor, at your church if they are available, and ask at least five dumb questions! Remember, the humble will inherit the land and will delight themselves in abundant prosperity (Psalm 37:11 NASB).

Nicole Bromley

Then the woman, seeing that she could not go unnoticed, came trembling and fell at his feet. In the presence of all the people, she told why she had touched him and how she had been instantly healed. Then he said to her, "Daughter, your faith has healed you. Go in peace." LUKE 8:47–48 (NIV)

The woman mentioned here in the Gospels was desperate. She longed for healing and relief from years of suffering. Throwing fear and reputation aside, she approached Jesus, and through His touch and her faith she was freed from bondage. The same is available to us. Whatever our pain may be, whatever our past may look like, the only way to find true peace and comfort is to lay it all at Christ's feet.

It can be frightening to bring out from hiding the pain we hold deep within. The healing journey is difficult. But Jesus doesn't expect us to go this road alone. He desires to walk with us. He wants to carry our burdens and take our pain. More than anything, Jesus wants us to choose Him as our Healer—the only One who can free us from our suffering.

May today be a day marked in history for you—a day in which you would choose Jesus as Healer. May you come in touch with your own need for healing and restoration. The Lord is inviting you to get real before Him and to willingly place your burden at His feet for healing. And when you do, our Lord and King says, "Your faith has healed you. Go in peace."

Write about your deepest hurt and place it at the Lord's feet for healing.

Erin Smalley

I will bless them and the places surrounding my hill. I will send down showers in season; there will be showers of blessing.
EZEKIEL 34:26 (NIV)

As a teenager, I can distinctly remember feeling "green with envy" when after my best friend got a brand-new Honda Prelude, I received an old, dented, rusted-out brown Honda Civic. How unfair was that! Sadly, even twenty-three years later, these emotions still invade my life.

Like me, why do many women struggle with envy and jealousy? As a matter of fact, one group surveyed more than fifty thousand women and found that almost half acknowledge having "significant" feelings of jealousy (www.selfesteem4women.com). The main reason is that we tend to notice what we don't have or what is missing. Because of our human nature, we become so envious over what other's have or their opportunities that we miss what God has given us and discontentment takes root. It is here that the Evil One has the perfect opening to cultivate seeds of bitterness and ungratefulness. Jealousy truly has the capacity to break up relationships, strain friendships, devastate families, and destroy careers. Worst of all, it disconnects us from the true source of life—our heavenly Father.

How can we deal with jealousy? First and foremost, ask God to remove any feelings of ungratefulness, envy, or jealousy that have taken root in your heart. Next, reflect on your blessings by writing down what God has provided. Thank Him for each and every blessing He has bestowed upon you, including the special gifts and talents He is calling you to use. Battle the temptation to become resentful over what you don't have or who you weren't created to be. You'll see the blessings are all around you. Even an old, rusted-out brown Honda Civic!

Linda Clare

The Lord will command his lovingkindness in the daytime; and His song shall be with me in the night, a prayer to the God of my life. PSALM 42:8 (NASB)

On the worst days, it's easy to decide that faith is a crock. You lose your job, your kid becomes the village addict, your mother, favorite uncle, or grandson has cancer. There's heartache and joint pain and no matter how many Roach Motels you set out, the bugs still find a way to roam the kitchen. So you think, Bah, no Creator, no Savior, no resurrection. No afterlife, you sniff, and then you duck in case a thunderbolt zaps your ungrateful little heart.

But then, if you're listening, God steps onto the stage and sings. The song goes deep and straight to the truth and you wonder how you ever doubted.

Why does He bother with me or anybody else, slow beings that we are? In one way or another, we're all bent, broken, twisted. Damaged goods. A lot of the time I'm too crippled to see how much God loves but I'm strong enough to doubt the minute life starts to smell funny. Lucky for me, God doesn't give up. Instead of throwing His hands up in frustration, He sings, *Don't be afraid, I love you.* These days, I try to be a little more grateful.

On my crazy, overpopulated faith road, I can be way too stubborn. I ask way too many questions. Sometimes I refuse to see what's right in front of me as I elbow my way through the crowd. Yet, I'm tasting, smelling, touching, groping and yes, listening my way to God, and it's a mystery but it's working. I may never know why I hear God as a song. Shh, listen.

When you feel afraid for any reason, try singing to God. Then listen closely for God "singing" back to you in the form of a beautiful day, an unexpected hug or while you read your Bible.

Tammy Maltby

It happens so regularly that it's predictable. The moment I decide to do good, sin is there to trip me up. I truly delight in God's commands, but it's pretty obvious that not all of me joins in that delight. Parts of me covertly rebel, and just when I least expect it, they take charge. ROMANS 7:21–23 (MSG)

I've always loved before-and-after stories of lives changed by the ever-gracious Savior. Often it's implied that once a person accepts the Lord, sinning stops and brokenness is laid aside. And that's just not true—or it's reality for just a fraction of Christians I know.

"We must keep God looking good." "We must cover up the ugly stuff," we say in self-protection. How do I handle pain? Can God really handle who I am, what I've done?

When we do that, we send the message to those who are hurting, broken, truly weary, and burdened that they are not welcome in our churches and our lives—including those who are already Christians!

When we send that message—even to ourselves—we're actually working against the God who can work miracles, making short work of sin and guilt. Pride, dishonesty, and self-deception slow down His rescue efforts.

The Lord knows what we're like, what we're capable of, what we've actually done, and He can handle it. There's nothing we can throw at Him that He cannot help us with—but *letting Him* is a choice we all have to make.

We can keep our "good Christian girl" image and hide our brokenness, or choose to open up our lives, depending absolutely on the love and forgiveness of One who gave up His own life so we could live free of condemnation. Trust Him with your sin and brokenness.

Anita Lustrea

And we, who with unveiled faces all reflect the Lord's glory, are being transformed into his likeness with ever-increasing glory, which comes from the Lord, who is the Spirit.

2 CORINTHIANS 3:18 (NIV)

My mother hates beards. My husband has a beard. My fifteen-year-old son can't wait to grow a beard.

When the *Chicago Tribune* ran a story titled, "Beards are Back," my husband immediately picked up the phone to alert my mother. Thankfully my mom enjoys his good-hearted ribbing.

The truth is, my mom's dislike of beards isn't a big deal. But it is a big deal to discover what Bill Hybels calls our "Holy Discontent," what we truly can't stand. It's that one thing, that passion, that God has put inside us. That "something" that wrecks us, or breaks our hearts. That "Holy Discontent" that God puts inside us might be the very thing that He wants us to partner with Him on to make a real difference here on earth.

For me it centers on women. I can't stand to see women oppressed and abused. I feel a deep call and commitment to communicate freedom to women. I live out that passion by helping women live into the fullness of who God created them to be.

What is your "Holy Discontent," your passion that God has placed squarely on your heart? I have an exercise that might help you discover it. Frederick Buechner once said, "The place God calls you to is the place where your deep gladness and the world's deep hunger meet." Take a piece of paper and make two columns. Label column one, "My Deep Gladness." Label column two, "World's Deep Hunger." Now start listing those items that fit in each category. Once you've done that, start drawing lines from column one to column two when you see a "gladness" that fits a "world need" you've written down. Then, begin exploring ways you might live out the intersection of those two. I wonder what God might have in store.

Leslie Parrott

Therefore, I urge you, brothers, in view of God's mercy, to offer your bodies as living sacrifices, holy and pleasing to God—this is your spiritual act of worship. ROMANS 12:1 (NIV)

What's your biggest fear? I'll never forget the answer Michelle Akers, world-champion women's soccer star, gave to this question. Before I tell you what it was, let me tell you about Michelle's journey.

Suffering from Chronic Fatigue and Immune Dysfunction Syndrome, Michelle looked like anything but a world champion. Her four-year marriage was ending, her body was racked with debilitating pain, and her spiritual life was practically nonexistent. Then she met conditioning coach Steve Slain, who invited her to church.

She agreed to go, more out of courtesy than genuine desire. Months later, Michelle decided to grieve her broken marriage and get right with God by taking a personal retreat outside Seattle. It was there that she made a renewed and deeply felt commitment to letting God redirect her life.

In 1995, soon after she returned to Florida for training, the American team came in a disappointing third at the Women's World Cup. Michelle had been knocked unconscious within the first minutes of the game. She was devastated but steadfast in her spiritual commitment—and in her determination not to give up. A year later, Michelle was standing on top of the gold-medal podium at the Atlanta Olympics.

Since that time, Michelle has received numerous awards, including U.S. Soccer Federation Female Player of the Year three times. But more and more, you'll find Michelle speaking on a platform for such ministries as Campus Crusade for Christ, Fellowship of Christian Athletes, and the Billy Graham Association.

So what's Michelle Akers's biggest fear? "Not making my life and work count in God's eyes." Michelle is determined to make a positive difference. Her motto, for soccer and for life, is the same: "Go hard or go home." Every woman who makes a difference can identify with Michelle's unyielding determination to make her life matter. She is resolute on giving it her all and making sure she gives her all to what matters most.

Sharon Hanby-Robie

And my people shall dwell in a peaceable habitation, and in sure dwellings, and in quiet resting places. ISAIAH 32:18 (KJV)

As an interior designer, I have come to realize that the most inspiring rooms start simply by decluttering. When I first visit a new client it's easy for me to see the cluttered tabletops and counters, or the stack of magazines that have accumulated with the good intention of reading because I have a fresh perspective. I have learned that a simple photo easily gives clarity to the situation—so I take a camera along with me to each new appointment. Most clients, after seeing the photo, are receptive and take on the challenge of decluttering with ease.

But occasionally I find someone who could be better defined as a hoarder. The struggle for these folks comes down to a heart issue and not simply a matter of owning too much stuff. Excessive clutter and disorganization can be symptoms of emotional trauma, depression, grief, or even chronic pain. Often it is simply a fear that the memories attached to these items are the last or the most joyful memories they will have.

We must understand, as composer Richard Wagner expressed, "Joy is not in things, it is in us." It's okay to keep reminders of good times for awhile but learn to let go so you can look forward to the new joys of tomorrow. Give yourself the freedom from things so that you can enjoy all the blessings of life more abundantly. Let your home and your heart be filled with the fullness of God's presence and His glory.

Consider thoughtfully the things that you keep. Are you surrounded with clutter? Create one clean and uncluttered place in your home as a beginning to the decluttering of your life.

Tracy Groot

Those who go down to the sea in ships, who do business on great waters; they have seen the works of the Lord, and His wonders in the deep. Psalms 107:23–34 (NASB)

Sometimes a particular area in our life needs realignment; we call upon tried and true techniques, and we pull it off again. Other times, our tried and true measures seem to betray us. What worked before is not working this time, and we end up frustrated and not a little discouraged.

It takes more effort to expel a bully than a pest. You know the Red Phone, the one only used during times of global calamity? Time to use that phone. Time to do business, and not the ordinary kind.

It isn't easy to face a bully, especially the bullies of our own making. But everyone knows if you knock him down and show him you will not be pushed around anymore, he won't come around again anytime soon. Here's the trick: hit the bully right on the nose. This technique causes an impressive amount of bleeding and subsequent black eyes: shock and awe results; word gets out you are not to be messed with.

Today may be your day of reckoning.

Who will see the works of the Lord, and His wonders in the deep? They that do business.

Do business today. Doesn't matter so much what it is—just do business. Try something different to knock down that bully this time. Get creative. If it's fasting, then fast, a meal or a day. If it's prayer, get on your knees and pray until you have peace; you don't need an answer right away, answers will come; peace will do for now.

You want to see the works of the Lord in your life? Get down to that sea and do business. Decisive measures may produce surprising results—and you might be amazed at how short a time it takes to get yourself out of troubled waters.

What's the first thing you do to bloody the nose of a bully?

Make a fist.

Victoria Saunders Johnson

"If any one of you is without sin, let him be the first to throw a stone at her." JOHN 8:7 (NIV)

As a boys' group home social worker, part of my job entailed interviewing young juvenile offenders. Usually I'd meet with them in jail and I usually had to wait. I often prayed during that time. I had read their files and the majority of them mentioned sexually inappropriate behavior—usually to a child.

I now had to fight the temptation to prejudge. My motherly protection cried, "Keep him permanently off the streets. Throw the book at him. Make his life hurt like he hurt others." Like the accuser of the woman caught in adultery, my stone was already firmly in hand. But I'd pray, "Lord, help me to see this young man with *your* eyes."

Somewhere in the middle of my routine questions I'd look up and really see *the young man's* eyes. Instead of a hardened criminal staring at me, I'd see a crying little boy, pleading for protection and love. I felt little arms reaching out to me.

Every now and then I'd push my questions aside and really listen to a heartbreaking story. Mamma had a baby before she left babyhood herself. A stepdad who hit way too hard. A grandmother who died too soon. The streets become home. The inappropriate touch to another's body, learned from inappropriate touches upon his own. As I listen the rock in my hand slides down, slowly dropping to the floor.

Ask the Lord to help you today to take time to look into the hearts of people with His eyes. Ask for help to avoid accusations, pointing fingers, feeling superior, or withholding compassion. We need His wisdom to understand. May God give us strength to go and sin no more.

Leigh McLeroy

For I am convinced that neither death, nor life, nor angels, nor principalities, nor things present, nor things to come, nor powers, nor height, nor depth, nor any other created thing, shall be able to separate us from the love of God, which is in Christ Jesus our Lord. ROMANS 8:38–39 (NASB)

At the car wash, a perky, on-screen video-girl chirps a greeting, and tells me to select my wash and "insert cash or a credit card." Then the only human in sight points me toward a rolling belt that will capture my tires. Once I'm properly aligned, he motions for me to put the car in neutral.

And then the fun begins.

I'm on a track I can't see, moving at a rate of speed I can't control. I can't back up. I can only go forward. Moving arms and swirling brushes assault the car, flinging foamy soap every which way and slapping the windows with surprising force. Once the brushes descend completely, my vision is obscured. I could be around the corner from home or in the Ukraine, for all I can tell. I hear threatening thumps just inches away, and the car rocks slightly as it eases forward. I can't see where I started, or where the end might be. I don't know what spray or gel or finish will come at me next.

The car wash is a lot like life. I can't manipulate the mess and motion around me, or halt the things that threaten me. But no matter what assails me, or for how long, I will be released at the appointed time—bright, shiny and clean—and surely better for the ride.

Imagine: Four dollars worth of spiritual tutoring not three blocks from home. Now *there's* a bargain.

Anita Lustrea

Likewise, two people lying close together can keep each other warm. But how can one be warm alone? A person standing alone can be attacked and defeated, but two can stand back-to-back and conquer. Three are even better, for a triple-braided cord is not easily broken. ECCLESIASTES 4:11–13 (NLT)

One thing I'm convinced of, we need good traveling companions on our life's journey. Scripture agrees. We've got to be traveling toward the right destination, that goes without saying. We also need to be drawing nearer to Christ. But if we don't have those close companions that we can be authentic with and accountable to, we're in trouble.

Our deepest desire is for someone to know us. Our biggest fear is that someone will find out who we really are. It's that age-old fear of rejection. We can't imagine that someone would really love us as we are.

There is a significant small group movement in many of our churches today, which has done much toward the development of community. Ultimately, though, it's up to us. We decide if we are going to open up to God and to others and let them in to our lives, give them access to the more secret places within us. The rewards are worth it.

About ten years ago now my life came crashing down around me and I, out of desperation, went barging into my neighbor's life. Thankfully when I literally knocked on her door, Faith let me in and listened to me. She walked with me through some hard stuff. Since that soul-bearing time in my life, we've had opportunity to say some hard things to each other because we had developed community.

Who are you in community with? Who can you bare your soul to?

Leslie Ludy

"I am the vine, you are the branches; he who abides in Me and I in him, he bears much fruit, for apart from Me you can do nothing." JOHN 15:5 (NASB)

Leading a busy ministry, my greatest weakness has been letting urgent tasks crowd out the things that are truly important. For the past two years, God has challenged me to guard my time with Him as the most precious part of my day. Even if it means I have to get less sleep, give up my "veg-out" at night, or get less done during the day than I had hoped, I have made it my goal to steal away for ample time with Him every day,. With two young children and endless ministry responsibilities, this can seem like a difficult commitment to keep. But surprisingly, I've found that everything in my life flows far more smoothly whenever I make Him the highest priority of my day.

It reminds me of the disciples fishing all night long and catching nothing—and then when Christ came and stood in their midst they simply let down their nets once and brought in more fish than their boats could contain. With Christ, they were able to accomplish in minutes what their own human strength could not achieve after an entire night's work. This is His pattern. Whenever I build my life around Jesus Christ, rather than fitting Him into random corners of my day, life has purpose, clarity, focus, and fruitfulness. Whenever I rush ahead and obey the "urgent" ahead of the "important," life becomes cloudy, chaotic, and futile.

Today, take inventory of the seemingly *urgent* things in your life, and then contrast them to the things that are truly *important* in God's eyes. As we realign our life with heaven's priorities, we will be marked by unwavering peace and joy that cannot be taken away by the constant pressures of the world.

Carol Ruhter

Out of the depths I cry to you, O Lord;
O Lord, hear my voice.
Let your ears be attentive to my cry for mercy.
If you, O Lord, kept a record of sins,
O Lord, who could stand?
But with you there is forgiveness . . .
PSALM 130:1–4 (NIV)

When my mom was a kid, she wanted to check out the depth of her local swimming hole. So she jumped in holding a large rock. As she descended deeper into the darkening gravel pit, her joy quickly turned to panic and she forgot why she was sinking.

How many times do we hold on to things that bring us down? We hold on to grudges, guilt, childhood issues, low self-worth. Like my mom, we're seldom aware of *why* we're sinking. Often, we subconsciously fear that forgiving others or ourselves might expose us to being wounded—or wounding others—again. So, we hold on to those feelings of unforgiveness, keeping a close eye on the shortcomings in ourselves and those around us, to ensure the "guilty" have learned their lesson.

God sees the rock you're clutching. It's safe to drop it now. Shoot to the water's surface and breathe life-sustaining air. Trust that God will gently wipe the water from your face, and comfort and protect you. In His perfect wisdom, He'll deal with those who have hurt you and with those you've hurt.

I'm here today because Mom dropped the rock. Will you drop yours?

What will you no longer allow to drag you down? Try this: On a rock, write a few words that represent the "weight" you're letting go, and then throw that rock into a lake, an ocean, or a stream.

Anita Lustrea

But the Holy Spirit produces this kind of fruit in our lives: love, joy, peace, patience, kindness, goodness, faithfulness, gentleness, and self-control. There is no law against these things!
GALATIANS 5:22–23 (NLT)

"Be patient, be patient, don't be in such a hurry." Remember the words of Herbert the Snail in the old Agapeland Music Machine recording for kids? I can still sing it. Unfortunately I still need to sing it. Despite the fact that patience is a fruit of the Spirit, it is still a fruit that I'm struggling with.

Those who belong to Christ Jesus have nailed the passions and desires of their sinful nature to his cross and crucified them there. Since we are living by the Spirit, let us follow the Spirit's leading in every part of our lives. I'm doing okay with just enough fruits of the Spirit to start becoming smug; then the need for patience rears its ugly head in my life once again and I get knocked down to size. Maybe it's just a battle of waiting in the checkout line at the grocery store, maybe it's something a whole lot more serious like waiting for God to answer my prayers for healing a friend suffering with cancer. Getting impatient at checkout lines is a bit ridiculous, but don't I deserve to be impatient when the prayer is for something of a serious nature, like healing a sick friend?

Waiting invites us to live our lives in small pieces, slowly. Sometimes, as Psalm 25 (NASB) says, we're waiting on God. "Make me know Your ways, O Lord; Teach me Your paths. Lead me in Your truth and teach me, For You are the God of my salvation; For You I wait all the day." It's hard to wait when the object of our waiting is a baby at the end of a long adoption, or an acceptance letter to our first choice of schools. But we learn patience in the waiting. God's agenda always supersedes our own.

What are you currently waiting on God for? Are you in a season of your life learning more about patience than you'd like to? Patience reminds us that there are no quick fixes, and that we have to trust the fullness of God's timing. We see that message echoed throughout Scripture from creation to the incarnation. Make a list of all you're waiting on God for and ask for the fruit of the Spirit to be evident today in your life!

Janice Elsheimer

Lord, you have assigned me my portion and my cup; you have made my lot secure. The boundary lines have fallen for me in pleasant places; surely I have a delightful inheritance. PSALM 16:5–6 (NIV)

My husband likes to wake up to National Public Radio every morning, but I prefer the sound of birdsong, wind in trees, rain on roof, or silence. I don't need stories of war, famine, and mayhem first thing. Let me ease into the day without words

In the silence of the morning, I ponder my "delightful inheritance" from God. Let me stroll through my gardens, listening to the quiet before I allow the rest of the world in. Let me experience what living within the boundary lines God has laid out for me feels like. Let me have this time to think about my portion and my cup, the pleasant places in my life, before jumping into the have-to's of the rest of my day.

Throughout the darkest days of my life, I've asked, "How could I believe God gives me just what I needed for my journey, my portion, and my cup, that my life is circumscribed by pleasant boundary lines?"

The answer is that I chose to believe. Whatever I felt about the precariousness of my position, I chose to believe God set out my boundaries in pleasant places. From that seed of faith, from choosing to believe even when every day was a struggle, grew an oak tree of conviction that continues to support me through both times of growth and times of dormancy. I still begin each day meditating on God's good promises.

Memorize Psalm 16:5–6 and choose to believe that your security is not in this world or your own efforts, but in the "delightful inheritance" God promises you.

Janet Thompson

So we keep on praying for you, asking our God to enable you to live a life worthy of his call. 2 THESSALONIANS 1:11 (NLT)

I want her back more than you do! I heard those words from the Lord while crying out to Him for the salvation and return of my prodigal daughter. I had been praying daily for her, but still she moved deeper into her chosen lifestyle. Then one morning as I desperately cried to the Lord that it just didn't seem like my prayers were working and I feared for my daughter's eternal future, God graciously sent me reassurance.

Whew . . . that took a burden off my shoulders. God was rooting for her even more than I was! From that day forward, I prayed daily with conviction, perseverance, and expectancy. I prayed God's Word back to Him on my daughter's behalf, and I prayed as if she already was the woman I wanted her to become. Five years later, she started the journey back to me and to the Lord.

Sometimes we think that God isn't listening when we don't get quick results. We live in a world of instant oatmeal, drive-through fast food, instant computer messages, and instant replay to name just a few. Is it any wonder that we expect God to be an instant provider? But He seldom works that way. God's not a vending machine where we put in our prayer request and out pops our desired result.

I know there is nothing more painful than watching a child self-destruct, but don't give up on him or her, and don't give up on God. He hears you. He's listening. He's doing His part, and He wants to know we're doing our part. And what is a parent's part? Praying God's will for our child. One way to accomplish that is to pray Scripture. Practice by personalizing the opening Scripture as a prayer for your son or daughter.

Ellen Vaughn

Take your everyday, ordinary life—your sleeping, eating, going-to-work, and walking-around life—and place it before God as an offering. Embracing what God does for you is the best thing you can do for him. Don't become so well-adjusted to your culture that you fit into it without even thinking. Instead, fix your attention on God. You'll be changed from the inside out. ROMANS 12:1–2 (MSG)

What comes into your mind when you think about God? The great preacher A. W. Tozer wrote that "we tend, by a secret law of the soul, to move toward our mental image of God." So it's crucial that our idea of God correspond as nearly as is possible to the true being of God.

Certainly, in our limited human condition, we cannot think of God as He really is. But if we are drawing our image of God from the wrong sources, then He'll be too small.

Today, since "spirituality" is so big in our culture, celebrities and people of influence often talk about their relationship with God . . . but for many, God seems to be a vague deity they've made up, a personalized edition of a spiritual force who exists to make people feel good about themselves.

We need to take care not to be squeezed into the mind-set of the culture around us. In every situation of each day, we have a choice. We can fix our attention on ourselves, and recast God in our own image. Or we can fix our attention on God, as the Scriptures really reveal Him to be.

Today, in every wild, weird, frustrating, busy moment that comes your way, practice fixing your attention on God. He will begin to change you, as Romans says, from the inside out!

Nancy Kane

Like apples of gold in settings of silver is a word spoken in right circumstances. PROVERBS 25:11 (NASB)

We have all experienced the agony of a broken heart and the wounds of rejection.

Science is now discovering that these expressions are truer than we ever knew. The emerging field of social neuroscience, or rather the science of biology and the brain reveals that we are "wired to connect."

While this is no surprise, researchers Naomi Eisenberger and Matthew Liberman at the University of California, Los Angeles, have documented that our brains physically register social rejection. The same part of the brain that becomes activated when someone feels physical pain also becomes activated when a person feels social pain. So when we feel rejected or misunderstood, our brains register those pains of rejection as if we experienced a physical assault on our body.

What the science of the brain has also discovered is that positive connections and loving interactions actually reduce the flow of stress hormones, which wear on our systems so powerfully. Words of kindness spoken from others actually calm our hearts as well as our bodies.

When Jesus commanded us, as His followers, to love one another, His instruction had more implications for our lives than what we sometimes realize. God knew that learning how to interact in loving ways with each other would not only heal the soul but the body as well. The book of Proverbs tells us that the lips of the righteous bring forth wisdom and blessing. But, when we speak unkindly we replace the opportunity of being a blessing with words that literally impact others' emotional, spiritual and physical well-being. The choice is ours.

Our words and actions matter more than we know. The benefits of self-control outweigh the costs. How can we measure peace of mind and body, furthering the kingdom through love and forgiveness, and being known as people who are menders of broken hearts? It matters physically, emotionally, and spiritually. We must love each other, for truly our very lives depend on it.

Joanna Weaver

"Come, follow me," Jesus said, "and I will make you fishers of men." At once they left their nets and followed him.

MATTHEW 4:19–20 (NIV)

One thing in the Bible is clear. When Jesus walked the earth, it was nearly impossible to be in His presence and not be changed. You walked away either loving Him or hating Him. Staying indifferent about who He was and what He said was difficult at best.

For when Jesus came on the scene, occupations changed. Fishermen became fishers of men. Tax collectors became philanthropists and wrote Gospels. At His word, addresses changed. Demons became pig dwellers. Lepers got to go home. Reality was drastically altered. Dead children came back to life. The lame walked. The blind saw. The deaf heard and water was turned into wine.

All because of the presence of Jesus. But in every encounter, there came a choice. To heed and follow or resist and walk away. The rich young ruler came seeking validation but went away sad. Challenged—but unchanged. Though Judas walked with Jesus for three years, his heart followed his own agenda. For sadly, we can appear to worship yet never give in to worship's demands.

We can claim Christianity, but until we allow Christianity to make a claim on us we may be stirred, but we will never be changed.

What has God been saying to you lately? Or has it been a while since you've really sensed His presence or heard His voice? May I encourage you to go back to the last thing He said to you—to the "last point of obedience" as one wise writer puts it. For until you obey God there, you will never know the joy of moving forward into everything He has for you.

Heed and follow. That's all Jesus asks. He'll lead the way.

Lori Neff

Give thanks to the Lord, for he is good.
His love endures forever. PSALM 136:1 (NIV)

The fact that God loves me unconditionally has always been a hard concept for me to grasp. What really blows me away is that He loves me no matter what. I don't have to do anything to earn it—He just loves me. I've heard people say that God's love for us is like our love for our own children. I don't have children, but I do have cats and I love them just for living. I love being around them and when they snuggle up to me. They make me smile when they do nothing but sleep and eat. If I feel such imperfect love and tenderness toward a cat, how much more does God, in His perfection, love me!

A smart and confident friend once commented to me that she gets frustrated that she feels like she needs continued affirmation. I've been thinking about that because I feel like I need affirmation a lot—from my hubby ("Do you love me?"), from my friends ("Do you like me?"), from my boss ("Am I doing a good job?"), and from God ("Do You really love and value me the way You created me?"). I wish I could live in that place of security—knowing that I'm loved. Sara Groves' song "Maybe There's a Loving God" touches my heart by talking about the amazing love of God.

I wonder if there will ever be a point in my life where I'll just realize I'm loved and be forever confident in that. . . . But, then again, it sure is a nice feeling to be reminded that people care about me. Who doesn't love to hear that they're loved?! How about telling someone today that you care about them?

Kathy Peel

Even the very hairs of your head are all numbered.

MATTHEW 10:30 (NIV)

Do you believe that God cares about the details of your life? That He wants to get personally involved in helping you manage your schedule, get your home in order, rebuild your marriage, parent your children, make wise decisions, face pain with courage, experience personal peace, and become your best self? According to the Bible, He does.

I love Matthew 10:30 because it tells me, a woman who loses enough hair daily to stuff a pillow, that God continually has to recount. If He cares about the hair caught in my hairbrush, He cares about backed-up toilets, computer crashes, strong-willed children, empty pantries, gas tanks, and bank accounts, and every other problem we encounter. Actually, the Bible says that He cares about us more than we can imagine, loves us more than we can comprehend, and invites us to tell Him when we feel frustrated and need help.

But God not only tells us to pray, He tells us to obey. There are things that only God can do for us and times when only His direct intervention will solve a problem. But God has also given us resources that He wants us to use faithfully as we call on Him for help. Among these resources are our minds, our abilities, and our relationships. He has also given us wisdom about life in His Word that He wants us to know and obey.

Waiting for God to act on the things we can't do when He has given us some things we *can* do is a little like asking Him to lower our cholesterol while eating potato chips every day for lunch. He expects us to live wisely and change the things we can while at the same time pray about the things we can't.

Is there a frustrating part of your job as mom and family manager in which you could use some help and support from God? What step can you take today to change things while you wait for Him to change something you cannot?

Mary Grace Birkhead

Forget the former things; do not dwell on the past. See, I am doing a new thing! Now it springs up; do you not perceive it?
ISAIAH 43:18–19A (NIV)

Much of the time when God begins to bring change in my life the feelings I have are not those of happy anticipation. I long for "the same" because it gives me confidence and assurance. God is calling me to something new and to trust Him more.

I expect things to be a certain way and when they are not my natural response is sadness, anger, and fear. Yet God, in His mercy, is calling me to something better. He's calling me to Himself. He is calling me to reject the notion that my soul can be satisfied with what this world has to offer. I'm looking for a quick "pick-me-up" and He's calling me to eternity. He calls to me, "Let Me remind you of your worth. Let Me satisfy your craving for attention. Let Me fill you with contentment and rest. Let Me bring order to your mind." Will I take the time to hear Him?

This is not a one-time event. This "new thing" happens daily, weekly, monthly, yearly. God is always trying to pry my hands off of what I think gives me life and identity and worth. He wants me to cling to Him and the identity He gives to me. In my frustration will I go to Him or will I try to return to the familiar?

What changes is the Lord bringing into your life? What is stirring in you? Ask the Lord, "Give me Your perspective. Give me Your grace to walk through this. Give me Your peace to sit in the unknown!"

Begin, by faith, to thank God for all the new things. Let the unknowns drive you to Him and into His presence. He never changes. Take great delight and receive peace from the fact that He is going out before you and surrounds you on all sides. He longs for you to place your faith in Him and not the familiar.

Jane Rubietta

Let us fix our eyes on Jesus, the author and perfecter of our faith . . . HEBREWS 12:2 (NIV)

He stands on pencil legs
Watching
Patient
Focused
Keen-eyed
Seeing beneath the surface to the movement below.
I want to be like the Great Blue Heron.

So often, my life, my schedule, my worries distract me. I don't pay attention well. Not to God, nor to the people in front of me, nor to my own soul and its often-twisted workings. Oh, to see below the surface of my own heart, where lack of trust troubles the waters and the potential for peace. To listen past the words from an upset teenager to the message of his heart. To hear underneath another's anger to the deep, ever-present longing to be safe, to be loved.

This watching, this wakefulness, comes when we fix our eyes on Jesus. Brother Lawrence wrote about this in *Practicing the Presence of God.* He kept up a running dialogue with God, running thoughts, worries, requests past Him. We can do this, too: exhaling our stress and inhaling God's peace. Take the five-minute challenge: sit still, without words, and let God love you, and love Him back. Write the morning's verse on a 3 x 5 card, and carry it with you through the day. Refer to it, asking God to help you apply those words to your life. Pray for the couple in the car behind you, the teen passing your house after school, the child crying in the grocery store. When you feel pain, use it to remind yourself of brothers and sisters around the world, in pain because of their faith, or their poverty.

How will you, like the great blue heron, watch, today? How will you fix your eyes on Jesus? And then, just watch Him perfect your faith!

Adele Calhoun

"What do you want me to do for you?" MARK 10:51 (NIV)

Desires are windows to the soul. What we desire, or want, shapes us and our choices.

We make time for what we want, spend time with people we want, change when we want—not simply because we ought to. Desire springs from a different well than "shoulds" and "oughts." That's why Jesus repeatedly asks people what they want.

- "What do you want?" (John 1:38 NIV)
- "What is it you want?" (Matthew 20:21 NIV)
- "What do you want me to do for you?" (Luke 10:51; Mark 10:36 NIV)
- "Do you want to get well?" (John 5:6 NIV)

What do *you*—not your mother, spouse, or kids—want?

Jesus knew that desire was fuel for growth. Desire can be an ache in God's direction. "I want healing." "I want to slow down." "I want rest." "I want sanity." "I want a baby." "I want a job."

Desire can make us feel vulnerable and out of control. Sitting with God and our desire can put us in a risky space between wanting and demanding. But if we will wait and let desire draw us deeply into conversation with Jesus we will find, over time, that our impatient, entitled hearts soften. We stop treating Jesus like a genie in a bottle. We settle into and learn the way of trust, whether desires are met or unmet.

Read Mark 10:46–52. Imagine that you, like Bartimaeus, are calling out your desire to Jesus. What do you "cry out"? Jesus turns His full attention to you and asks "What do you want me to do for you?" Rest with this question. Do you know the deep desire of your heart? It is fuel for conversation with Jesus.

Linda Clare

So we do not lose heart. Though our outer nature is wasting away, our inner nature is being renewed day by day.
2 CORINTHIANS 4:16 (RSV)

I don't know about you, but when I'm happy, people say I look younger. On my fifty-fourth birthday, my friend Bonnie took me to lunch. The crowded restaurant teemed with young professionals. I felt really old. Bonnie said, "I should have given you a Botox gift certificate instead."

I frowned, but then remembered not to antagonize my worry lines. "You're only as old as you feel, right?"

Our twentysomething hostess led us to a table. "Let me tell you about our special."

I scanned the menu. "I don't see the fountain of youth anywhere on here."

The hostess looked bored. I'd hit middle age. I wished I could reinvent myself, or at least have a little work done.

We ordered a chef's salad to split and two plates. While we waited I thought about how decrepit I felt in body, but how young I felt in spirit. Paul, in his epistle to the Corinthians, points out how our bodies are temporary and fallible. Boy, can I relate to that! But he also reminds us that our inner natures are being renewed every single day. We've become new creatures in Christ, Paul says. Knowing Jesus changes everything. What if He sat across from me instead of my friend? I sucked in my gut and put on a smile.

The waitress returned with our salad—dressing on the side, mind you. We divided it and started to dig in, but not before our server returned to ask if everything was all right. "More than all right," I said. "Everything's terrific."

This week, renew yourself by making a list of five things you could do to improve both your inner and outer natures, such as reading your Bible, taking a walk, or smiling at a stranger.

Melinda Schmidt

Be still before the Lord and wait patiently for him.
PSALM 37:7A (NIV)

Dr. Richard Swenson, author of *A Minute of Margin: Restoring Balance to Busy Lives*, and other books on what he calls "the overload syndrome," talks about the overloaded life we often settle for characterized by fatigue, hurry, anxiety. Tolerating that stressful, numbed-out lifestyle, we forgo energy, calm, and a settled spirit.

Overwork and the feeling of being "overcooked" can often come from these attitudes:

- A lack of trust in what God can do
- A need to feel important by "rescuing" people or causes
- A prideful spirit, "I'll take care of this God, my way."
- Spiritual apathy

"Self-care" can be a way of saying, "God I leave it all up to you. There's nothing more I can do. I trust you. I will rest, waiting to see what You will do here." Then our list may include more of this:

- Having more mind space available for productive thinking
- Going for that walk you never have time for
- Writing thoughts in a journal that you never have time to think or process
- Spending some play time with your youngster outdoors , making cookies, or playing carpet ball
- Relaxing before a fire and staying in after supper

A.W. Tozer said, "The simplicity which is in Christ is rarely found among us. In its stead are programs, methods, organizations and a world of nervous activities which occupy time and attention but can never satisfy the longing of the heart."

What will you choose to put aside and what will you do instead, modeling trust in God for yourself and for others? Ask God to help you do today what will truly satisfy the longing of your heart.

Arloa Sutter

"I have loved you with an everlasting love."

JEREMIAH 31:3 (NIV)

I was sitting by a pond in a park on an absolutely beautiful day. The sky was a deep blue with no clouds. A gentle breeze made it a perfect sunny day. The flowers and trees were in full bloom, ducks and geese swam placidly on the water. I was in awe of the majesty of God's creation and filled with a sense of God's shalom and blessing. I watched as a young mother pushed a stroller with a young child toward me, another image of the blessing of children and motherhood. God seemed so good and lovely and in control of the world.

Then I saw the face of the child in the stroller. It was horribly disfigured. I caught my breath with shock. It was so startling, so ugly, so revolting. In the midst of what had been joyous communion with God, I screamed at Him in my head. "God, how could you?! How could you create all of this beauty in nature and then mess up with this young child's face?!" I protested angrily.

Immediately I heard the gentle voice of God respond in my thoughts. "What makes you think I messed up? Don't you know this child is beautiful to me and I love her dearly just the way she is? Who are you to say she is revolting?"

Oh, the love of God, love that reaches out to us just as we are, embracing us in our brokenness, when our faces and our lives are twisted and marred. How dare I ever despise the weak, the disfigured, the vulnerable, the lost, and the lonely? Jesus gave His life in excruciating pain for them, for me. May God help me today to see people through your eyes of love.

Dee Brestin

The bride belongs to the bridegroom. The friend who attends the bridegroom waits and listens for him, and is full of joy when he hears the bridegroom's voice. That joy is mine, and it is now complete. JOHN 3:29 (NIV)

Sometimes I think single women are better equipped to understand the portrait of Jesus as our Bridgroom. I certainly learned a great deal from my coauthor, Kathy Troccoli, when we wrote a trilogy on the Bridegroom. I remember the first night we went out to dinner together.

"Dee, let's have a romantic evening."

"I don't understand."

"Oh Dee—your definition of romance is so limited! Romance is so much bigger than a guy and a girl. Romance has to do with making things lovely because of love. Candles, food served elegantly, and meaningful conversation."

Kathy has helped me see what a romantic God we serve. He set the stars in place, He writes to us in poetry, and He gives us love stories in the Old Testament—parables to help us understand *His* love for us. In each of them, there is a bride who feels unworthy—but then there is a Bridegroom who loves her just the way she is—but too much, as Max Lucado puts it, "to let her stay that way."

Ruth, the Shulamite maiden, and Gomer all felt unworthy. Yet each one was deeply loved and taken higher by her Bridegroom. Boaz "covered" Ruth with his garment, as Jesus covers us with His righteousness. Hosea bought Gomer when she was naked on the auction block, as Jesus bought us. Though the Shulamite pleaded for Solomon not to look at her, he told her she was "a lily among thorns," and pleaded with her, "Come away, my love."

Will you believe that you are loved by your heavenly Bridegroom? Will you trust that His righteousness covers you? Will you abandon yourself to Him and allow Him to take you higher?

Nancy Sebastian Meyer

I saw heaven standing open and there before me was a white horse, whose rider is called Faithful and True.

REVELATION 19:11 (NIV)

What do Cinderella, Rapunzel, and Sleeping Beauty share in common? Their problems magically disappear. Foes are vanquished. Each tattered dress becomes a breathtaking ball gown. Best of all, they are swept into *ever after* by a perfect man who will love them forever. *Deep sigh.*

You feel it, too, don't you? Somewhere in your innermost heart exists a yearning for perfect love that brings complete fulfillment. No matter how handsome, powerful, generous, or compassionate your man, no one is perfect. Indeed, most of us struggle with shattered dreams and devastating disappointments resulting from overrated expectations of a Prince Charming.

We try to give up fairy-tale dreams. We know we should put away childish reasoning (1 Corinthians 13:11). We fill our minds with the Word of God so we can be transformed by the renewing of our minds (Romans 12:2). But have you looked at Revelation 19:11?

When I read about a white horse whose rider is "Faithful and True," my heart resonates once again with hope. This hope, however, comes from a different perspective than the world offers. Married to a pastor-turned-agnostic, I have learned to look to God alone as my Prince of Peace (Isaiah 9:6). He solves my problems, vanquishes my foes, and clothes me with love, joy, peace, and so much more. This Prince changed *me*, when I thought my husband had all the problems. He returned my love for Rich and gives me daily joy, despite unchanged circumstances.

Someday my prince will come, riding on a white horse, to carry me close to His heart into His eternal Kingdom to reign with Him happily ever after. This is not "The End," but the beginning!

How can the hope of your eternal Prince carry you through today?

Christine Wyrtzen

Who can understand the spreading of the clouds and the thunder that rolls from heaven? Job 36:29 (NLT)

God has always been faithful to lead His children. He spoke to them as children, and just as children need a specific language to understand a parent's direction, God's children need to hear in ways that accommodate their limited understanding. How the kingdom works is so diametrically opposed to the world they live in that God must continually be instructive.

Am I brave enough to seek God's heart and try to discern His voice above all the other noise clamoring for my attention? God will still direct by unorthodox means. He is still so creative as to use a "cloud by day and a pillar of fire by night." If I but ask for direction and listen with ears that have no preconceived bent, He will speak. It may not always be the answer I like but it is the one that brings me life eternal. He is even gracious enough to give multiple confirmations of His leading.

Is following His lead worth it? I can tell you that it always has been. Today, he may tell me to walk in a way that means sacrifice. Perhaps it even involves a movement that takes me way out of my comfort zone. I say to you, by faith, I follow Him to such places. And I say to you, by faith, that it has to be the way of eternal life for God does not lead His children anywhere else. Though sometimes I follow with tears on my cheeks, I really wouldn't have it any other way. The feel of my hand in God's is unmatched by the touch of any other. I follow His lead, even to the clouds over my head.

Anita Lustrea

For God so loved the world that he gave his one and only Son, that whoever believes in him shall not perish but have eternal life. JOHN 3:16 (NIV)

February 14, 2008, was a horrible day. Normally we hear that date and we immediately think "love." After all, it is Valentine's Day. In 2008 it was the day that five students lost their lives in a tragic shooting on the campus of Northern Illinois University and more than a dozen others were injured.

I was out of town on a business trip, but glued to the TV listening for details since it took place so close to home. Then I got the call from my husband. A friend of ours had lost his son in the shooting. This tragedy was no longer at a distance—it was up close and personal. My husband, Mike, officiated at the funeral and I attended. I was reminded of many things that day.

1. It is a deeper sadness when someone dies too young.
2. A parent was not meant to have to bury a child.
3. The grief of death stirs up other deeply buried griefs in us.

It was moving as I listened to the voices of fellow classmates and fraternity brothers talk about their friend who had been taken too soon. You could see the resolve in their eyes and hear in their speeches that their lives were going to count. They would live boldly and purposefully for their fallen friend. And then my husband began to speak. He talked about the hope that we have in Christ, and how Dan, the slain student, had confirmed his faith right there on the very platform my husband was speaking from. And how he was with Jesus at that very moment.

Do you have that same hope? The hope of living in eternity with Christ? John 3:16 (NIV) is probably the most well-known Scripture verse of all time. "For God so loved the world that he gave his one and only Son, that whoever believes in him shall not perish but have eternal life." Believe and choose life today.

Virelle Kidder

Then he looked at those seated in a circle around him and said, "Here are my mother and my brothers! Whoever does God's will is my brother and sister and mother." MARK 3:34–35 (NIV)

Jesus had problems with His earthly family, too. In Mark 3:21, 31–32 (NIV) we read about their reaction to His early ministry: "When his family heard about this, they went to take charge of him, for they said, 'He is out of His mind.' . . . Then Jesus' mother and brothers arrived. Standing outside, they sent someone in to call him. A crowd was sitting around him, and they told him, 'Your mother and brothers are outside looking for you.'"

Jesus looked at the circle of followers pressing close and said, "'Here are my mother and my brothers! Whoever does God's will is my brother and sister and mother'" (vv. 34–35).

How that comforts me! As a new believer nearly forty years ago, everyone in my family thought I'd parked my brains and become a religious fanatic. My mother and brother, even my husband, rebuked me for my new faith. Who did I think I was claiming to know God? It was two long years before my husband came to faith. At night, I often cried myself to sleep with deep loneliness. Then I found this passage in Mark 3 and realized Jesus understood. His family had treated Him as a fool, too.

But wait! When He said, "whoever does God's will is my brother, and sister, and mother," that meant me! We were family! It had to mean all believers are members of God's family. Such happy news!

If you have members of your earthly family who don't share your faith, trust God to change their heart. My mother came to Christ when she was eighty-six. In the meantime, consider writing a thank-you note to those loving and loyal members of God's family who prayed you into the kingdom of God. It'll make their day.

Sharon Hanby-Robie

So that Christ may dwell in your hearts through faith.

EPHESIANS 3:17 (NIV)

My friend Cathy is single, her grown children living in various places throughout the country. Ready for a change, she sold her home and stored all her furnishings, leaving her virtually "homeless." Her plan is to travel about visiting children and friends while focusing on her physical and spiritual health. With no self-imposed time frame or particular destination, she expects this to be a wonderful journey. However, as the time grew near for her departure, she began to feel anxious. The reality of being out on her own, far from friends that she has known for decades created a sense of fear and loneliness.

Recently, having learned to weave rugs, I mentioned Cathy's story to my weaving teacher/friend. She suggested I ask each of Cathy's friends to supply a yard of fabric from which I could weave a rug. We chose fabrics specifically to remind Cathy of our individuality and our timeless affection. I finished the rug by attaching a label which read, "Life is a tapestry of friends. Wherever your travels take you this rug will be your firm foundation of friends to stand on." The rug is the perfect size to roll up and take along on her travels.

Cathy cried when she received it exclaiming that it would be her magic carpet to fly on through this great adventure. She expressed her gratitude and said that whenever she felt lonely or homeless, she would sit on the rug, pull her knees to her chest, and contemplate the good friends and love that she knows will always be there for her. Cathy also knows that Christ took residency in her heart, laying a firm foundation on the rock of love.

When you feel shut out or isolated, remember that you can never lose God's love. It reaches every corner of your experience and continues the whole length of your life.

Anita Lustrea

And may you have the power to understand, as all God's people should, how wide, how long, how high, and how deep his love is. EPHESIANS 3:18 (NLT)

I remember a few years ago going through a really difficult time. God met me in the middle of it and didn't let me go. He walked with me every step of the way and even sent others to be in the trenches with me. That difficult spot in my road passed and you know what happened? A little while later another struggle came along. The truth is I had already forgotten what God had done for me in my past. I'm so thankful for Scripture that reminds us through the lives of others to remember. One of the continual messages to the children of Israel was "remember." Let's look at what God says to the Israelites in Deuteronomy 15:15 (NLT): "Remember that you were slaves in the land of Egypt and the Lord your God redeemed you!" I am so absentminded when it comes to what God has done in my life. Sometimes I don't even see the miracle of the parting of my own Red Seas.

What about you? Do you have those times of spiritual amnesia where you forget about the grace of God that has intersected your life many times over? I think that if for no other reason than to remember what God did in the past, journaling is an important exercise. Sometimes we are people of little faith and we need to remember what God has done. Take a look at this past week and write down some of the ways God met you in your need. Why not make that practice a habit?

Kay Yerkovich

My heart is not proud, oh Lord, my eyes are not haughty; I do not concern myself with great matters or things too wonderful for me. But I have stilled and quieted my soul; like a weaned child with its mother, like a weaned child is my soul within me. PSALM 131:1–2 (NIV)

Perhaps you have weaned a baby that was not happy about your choice to withdraw the breast. Were you prepared for the protest and the fight that followed? Let's think of the process from the baby's (or toddler's) perspective. Perhaps if the baby could articulate their thoughts it might sound something like this:

"Hey, what's going on? Mom, you have always laid me in your arms and given me nice milk and cozy snuggles. Why won't you let me nurse now? I want to nurse! I'm confused. It makes no sense and I just don't understand."

It takes time and quite a battle before the child can lie in its mother's arms and not fight for the breast. Gradually, the child accepts the change without ever understanding the reason.

David is describing this same process spiritually. God works in various ways in our life in different seasons. Like a baby, we begin to think we can predict Him and count on Him for certain things. Sooner or later we are mystified, disenchanted, and confused. David has walked with God long enough to stop calculating how He will work. Over time, God wants to teach us to be like David and learn as he did to come close and rest on God's chest without fighting or questioning when our Father's ways don't make sense to us. Can you come close and rest in God's arms when He has frustrated or disappointed you?

Jan Silvious

Teach us how short our lives really are so that we may be wise.
Psalm 90:12 (NCV)

Last week, I met three of my longtime friends for lunch. The laughter was easy, the joy of acceptance was sweet, but reality hovered close by as we talked about our friend who wasn't there. She died two years ago after a long, tough battle with cancer.

In the last year before she left us, we met for lunch many times because we all knew her days were limited. We spoke of sweet memories as well as of death and dying. There were things she wanted to say and questions she wanted to talk over with us. When she died, we knew she left secure in the love and welcome of God. Her last year had not been about arriving at her final destination—that was settled. It was about being wise, taking care of the words that needed to be spoken, and giving the gifts she wanted to give while she was still alive. It was about making a transition from here to there that would be done well because she chose wisdom.

I wonder if you have any sense of the brevity of life. Are there words you need to say? Are there gifts gathering dust that you need to go ahead and give? Are there questions you need to answer for someone you love? Are there questions you need to ask?

Wisdom teaches us to live our lives always aware that our times are brief.

Lisa McKay

Six days you shall labor and do all your work, but the seventh day is a Sabbath to the Lord your God. On it, you shall not do any work . . . Exodus 20:9 (NIV)

One of the great blessings (as well as the great curses) of working as a stress management trainer is the constant hypocrisy check it provides—if you want to have integrity in your work it forces you to be intentional in how you choose to care for yourself in body, mind, and spirit. While I would never claim anything approaching mastery in any of those domains, I also can't stand up in front of a group with a straight face and speak about anything I haven't, to some degree, explored myself.

This is perhaps why alarm bells went off recently when a friend asked me casually how I was, and I replied, "Busy."

This was accurate, that wasn't the problem with my statement. The *problem* was that "busy" or "tired" had over the last several months become my default answers to that common question.

As I've thought this over I've returned to this fourth commandment. In the midst of lots of travel lately I've been reasonably responsible about exercising, eating right, sleeping enough—many of the basics. But I'm now wondering whether I haven't been rather too careless with another basic—observing the rhythm God established of once a week setting out a significant chunk of time to "switch the channel" away from work. Why do we feel so entitled to treat this commandment rather more casually than the other nine?

Today, think about what the "work" is that God has entrusted you with at this stage of your life. It's challenging, but have you set aside a day a week when you stop that work and do something different? What that "different" is will vary for every person. What would it look like for you? Would you commit today to trying this for the next four weeks?

Sabrina O'Malone

But he said to me, "My grace is sufficient for you, for my power is made perfect in weakness." Therefore I will boast all the more gladly about my weaknesses, so that Christ's power may rest on me. 2 CORINTHIANS 12:9 (NIV)

My oldest son asked me if there was anything cool about having brown skin (and platitudes about God's paintbrush wouldn't satisfy him this time.) He continued, "People with dark skin sometimes get treated worse because of it. Is there anything good about it?" Hmm.

The first response that came to my mind was about the value of overcoming adversity, but I suspected that would be over his head . . . so I blurted out the very next thing that popped into my head.

"People with dark skin don't get sunburned as easily. . . ."

Sadly, I actually said that—and no, I'm not kidding.

I choked.

I panicked.

I didn't have a ready response.

And you'd think I would've been able to come up with something; I've had nearly forty years of practice having brown skin! Admittedly, my first response was weak. But the Lord's strength is made perfect in weakness. Eventually I remembered the Word of God. The Apostle Paul helped untangle a prickly situation where believers were questioning the benefits of being a Greek Christian, or Jewish Christian: "In Christ's family there can be no division into Jew and non-Jew, slave and free, male and female. Among us you are all equal. That is, we are all in a common relationship with Jesus Christ. Also, since you are Christ's family, then you are Abraham's famous 'descendant,' heirs according to the covenant promises" (Galatians 3:28–29 MSG).

So here's my final answer: "Who you are in Christ gives you far more blessings and benefits than any skin color."

Margaret Feinberg

"Let us fix our eyes on Jesus, the author and perfecter of our faith." HEBREWS 12:2 (NIV)

On the edge of the village was a spot where a boy would go to sit, relax, and look at a rock formation in the distance. The rocks strangely resembled an old man—complete with oversized nostrils and deep wrinkles around the eyes and lips. Even as a young man, and with family responsibilities mounting, he still found moments to sneak away to this place of solitude and rest.

With his own children now tending their own families, he found more time to recline on the knoll, gazing at the resemblance of the old man carved into the mountain.

One day a tourist stopped the man and asked him, "Did anyone ever tell you that you look like the face on the side of the mountain?"

As Fil Anderson, author of *Running On Empty*, observes, whatever we love the most will eventually shape our lives. Simply put, we become what we focus on.

If my primary concern is money, the almighty dollar will eventually begin to shape me. If my focus is accomplishment or power, the desired successes will affect my work ethic, decisions, and lifestyle. If I focus on myself, selfishness and self-absorption are natural effects. Eventually, like the rock formation on the outskirts of the village, I will take on the likeness of the object of my desire.

If we find a grassy knoll in our daily lives in which to escape the bustle, noise and demands of this life, and simply learn to gaze on Him and meditate on His word, then we cannot help but begin to reflect His image in our own. Make some time to center your thoughts on Jesus today.

Melinda Schmidt

He makes me lie down in green pastures,
He leads me beside quiet waters,
He restores my soul. PSALM 23:2–3A (NIV)

When I have been snuggled in bed with some infection or even surgery recuperation, I have seen the irony in the physical position of my body—on my back, looking up, heavenward. Still and weak, yet open to an active and powerful heaven-voice that in periods of good health, I often have not made time for. That occasional horizontal position has become a posture of openness to my heavenly Father's voice. As a captive audience, I have begun to whisper, "What do You have for me during this time of illness, Lord? I am all ears. What do You want to say to me?" Gutting out each miserable day took on more purpose than just "more fluids and take one pill, twice a day."

Common illnesses that take a week or two out of our lives can be a time to hear God's voice anew. Is there a spiritual book you can pick up and read? Scripture on which to meditate? Authentic prayers to voice? Journaling the concerns of your soul? Discipline yourself to put aside the latest tabloid magazine or tempting TV show and devote some time to hearing God.

The next time you find yourself sick and on your back with whatever happens to be going around, let God know you are open to His words of truth and ask Him to make them plain and His message clear. Commit the duration of your recovery to Him and write down what He speaks to you. Today, if you know of another who is sick in bed, ask God to make the most of that time of recovery and pray for a time of spiritual renewal for that person.

Bethany Pierce

Do not conform any longer to the pattern of this world, but be transformed by the renewing of your mind. ROMANS 12: 2 (NIV)

When I was a little girl, my dad told me I would turn into a TV head if I watched television too long. My head would pop into a square, my face would become a screen, my nose a channel dial. Worriedly, I would touch my nose and feel the sides of my face, checking.

Of course my dad was teasing, but there was some truth to his admonishment. Our minds absorb the information spoon-fed to us by television programs, sitcoms, and (most dangerously) commercials. These programs change the way we think about our needs, our bodies, and our rights. Companies pay millions to shape the way we perceive the world. In essence, we are in danger of becoming TV heads.

Our imaginations need exercise. Our minds need training. Though I struggle with Scripture reading as much as the next Christian, it makes sense that if overexposure to the media can shape my worldview, God's Word can counter the pollution and even transform my thinking until my interior world, focused on God, is content, joyful, and at peace—all the things commercials promise but fail to produce.

Paul writes that God can do "immeasurably more than all we ask or imagine" (Ephesians 3:20 NIV). Do we imagine enough? What if we were to take the desires, fears, and hopes the media preys upon and submit them to God? What if we reined in our worries and translated them to prayers infused with hope and a grand dose of imagination?

Anita Lustrea

Then Jesus said to his disciples, "If any of you wants to be my follower, you must turn from your selfish ways, take up your cross, and follow me." MATTHEW 16:24 (NLT)

It's February. Unpredictable weather, at least in the north. But it always tempts us with a few warm sunny days and the promise of spring. It's a gateway month. We get to hear from Punxsutawney Phil, the world's most famous weather-predicting groundhog. We find out how many more weeks of winter we have to endure. We are ready to embrace spring; in fact we run towards it.

February is also a spiritual gateway time this year. Lent begins and we commence our walk toward Holy Week.

When I was a child we were requested to 'give something up' during Lent. The reasons were varied but as I recall it had something to do with helping us to identify with the sufferings of Christ. That was a tall order for a seven-year-old and so, in all honesty, "giving up" was a painful process of denial for what I thought was no really good reason. But I did it. I gave up candy usually and waited impatiently for Easter, the great feast day of sweets denied children everywhere.

Now I'm older. Lent is no longer viewed through childish eyes. There is something compelling about focusing daily on what forces me to remember who I am in light of the story of creation and salvation. So I'm going to "give up" some things this year. My prayer is that the minor sacrifices I make will help me grow closer to Jesus and that I will have greater clarity about who I am in light of the story of hope and promise that Easter crystallizes.

How about you? How are you going to do Lent this year? And how might it draw you closer to the crucified Christ?

Kathy Koch

Many, O Lord my God, are the wonders you have done. The things you planned for us no one can recount to you; were I to speak and tell of them, they would be too many to declare.

Psalm 40:5 (niv)

There was an audible gasp. The eye contact that followed was purposeful, seeming to beg me to repeat my statement. I was happy to.

"Raise the children God gave you, not the children you wanted to have."

Parents nodded knowingly, picked up their pen or pencil, and concentrated on writing what I said. All of this was accompanied by a nervous silence.

I continued. "Some of you wanted an astronaut. You didn't get one. Get over it. You wanted a ballerina. You didn't get one. Get over that, too." People relaxed. Laughter followed.

Far too many children say things to me like, "Dr. Kathy, my mom said she knows I'll have a good year in math. What does she think happened in the summer so this year would be a good year? Can't she get it? I'm not good at math!"

It's damaging to children's souls to be unaccepted for who they are. It's damaging to your soul to not accept yourself. We should work to improve what can be changed, but we must choose to accept what can't be. Changing our attitude toward these things is a mature and wise choice.

God made us the way He wanted us to be. He gave us the children He wanted us to have.

Where do you stand on these scales? How could any necessary changes occur?

I don't accept myself.	I do accept myself.
I don't accept my children for who they are.	I do accept my children for who they are.
I wish God had consulted me when He created me/my children.	I can trust God's decision to make us as He did.

Dannah Gresh

He who spares the rod hates his son, he who loves him is careful to discipline him. Proverbs 13:24 (NIV)

Rob, my seventeen-year-old, was late. He'd spent the night at a friend's house. He had my car for the night, promising to be home by ten o'clock so I could go grocery shopping on this Saturday morning.

It was ten thirty and no one was answering the phone at the house where he'd stayed.

Then it became eleven o'clock. Then, eleven thirty. Then, noon.

That's when my mother's heart panicked.

Rob had overslept and no one in the home had awakened him. He showed up apologetic. It really wasn't his fault. I just hate disciplining my kids. I'd rather have a root canal. And I don't even like to have my teeth cleaned! But, he was *two hours late*!

I prayed.

"God, what do I do?"

Eureka!

"Robby, this happens," I said. "I forgive you and it's not a big deal, but there are consequences. I'm behind in my schedule. So, you're going to fix the problem. Here is my grocery list!"

For the next two and a half hours, I took phone calls from my patient son.

"Mom, what's bleach?"

"Mom, do you know how many kinds of white bread exist?"

"Mom, where can I find peanut butter?"

It was as painful for me as it was for him, but the creative consequence of sending him to find peanut butter enabled me to live out Proverbs 13:24.

It seems to me that many of today's contemporary moms and dads find discipline archaic. God doesn't. If you love them, discipline them!

Have you been disciplining your kids? If so, have you been using logical consequences so it trains them? On a scale of one to ten, how are you doing?

Adele Calhoun

My soul waits for the Lord more than watchmen wait for the morning, more than watchmen wait for the morning. O Israel, put your hope in the Lord, for with the Lord is unfailing love and with him is full redemption. PSALM 130:6–7 (NIV)

How we wait reveals (tests) what is in our hearts. In waiting, our attachment to our own agenda rather than God's shows up. In waiting, our need to control shows up. Waiting presents us with choices to let go and wait with Jesus. Just as Jesus waited for a public ministry, for people to respond, for God to answer, so we too wait. We don't jump in and just do something—we wait.

I have been told that when an autistic child reacts in a hysterical manner the most important thing for the teacher to do is to wait. By not jumping in, doing something, taking control, but instead, waiting and contemplating, the child's teacher becomes aware of what precipitated the crisis. Waiting is the way forward both for teacher and child.

And God also waits. He waits—patiently—for us to respond, to obey, to grow up, to follow.

Do you consider yourself a control freak? How might choosing to stand in the longest line or drive in the slowest lane lead you into the spiritual discipline of waiting with Jesus? What does the way you are waiting reveal about your heart's motives? Where is God waiting—patiently—for you to act, to obey, to respond, to follow Him?

Sara Groves

The Lord is my light and my salvation—whom shall I fear? The Lord is the stronghold of my life—of whom shall I be afraid? PSALM 27:1 (NIV)

A couple of years ago I had the profound privilege of hearing Elizabeth's* testimony in Washington, DC. Elizabeth was the oldest of seven children from a Christian home in Southeast Asia. Her dream was to go to Bible college and work in ministry, so on her summer break between her sophomore and junior year in high school, she took a job in a neighboring community to save money for tuition. She never could have dreamt that her traveling companion, a trusted woman in the community, would betray her. Just miles from her home, the woman turned on her and began to abuse her. She sold her to a trafficker, who sold her to a brothel owner. At fifteen years old, Elizabeth found herself in a foreign country, subjected to horrible abuse.

She prayed every night that God would save her, even as the other girls in the brothel mocked her and said that God could not hear her in such a place. After eight months of captivity, an International Justice Mission (IJM)—a human rights agency—operative found Elizabeth and rescued her from the brothel. When IJM staff went into her small room to collect her belongings, they saw these words written on the wall above the mattress, "The Lord is my light and my salvation, whom shall I fear? The Lord is the stronghold of my life, of whom shall I be afraid?"

Her testimony has changed and challenged me deeply, her story has put my fears in perspective, and it has reminded me that God often answers prayers through the actions of His people.

Elizabeth was sent to an aftercare home to receive help and healing, and eventually graduated from Bible college. She now works in ministry as a translator, and shares her story to bring about freedom for more girls like herself.

**To conceal the identities of victims and safeguard ongoing IJM casework, pseudonyms have been used though the accounts are real.*

Christine Wyrtzen

Look straight ahead, and fix your eyes on what lies before you.
PROVERBS 4:25 (NLT)

I have to be careful not to see a verse like this and think it is an excuse to ignore my past. I can choose to keep my eyes on the road ahead without having any regard for the ways my life has shaped me. Everything I am today is due to the choices and influences of long ago. It took decades for me to acquire my beliefs about myself, about God, about matters of faith, and about how life works. My biases were born in the past. Many of my deepest wounds were born there. To ignore them is folly.

I often hear others tell me, "Whatever has happened to me is over. I can't change it. It's painful to me to think about it. So, I'm just looking ahead to my future." Sounds good, but the future I create will only be as good as my mental and spiritual health. If I have been tenacious in allowing God to show me my past through His eyes in order that I might gain wisdom, chances are that I will carve out a future worth living. If I learn nothing from my past, and choose only to close my eyes to it, the past will most likely repeat itself. Some encounter troubles, move out of town to start fresh, only to experience similar scenarios over and over again. They didn't leave their history, they took it with them.

The only way to leave the crooked ways of the past is to acknowledge the truth of them, ask God for healing, and allow Him to rewrite my life's script.

Anita Lustrea

They refused to obey and did not remember the miracles you had done for them. Instead, they became stubborn and appointed a leader to take them ***back*** *to their slavery in* ***Egypt****! But you are a God of forgiveness, gracious and merciful, slow to become angry, and rich in unfailing love. You did not abandon them.* NEHEMIAH 9:17 (NLT), emphasis added

A long time ago the Jewish people were slaves, and Pharaoh had a one-word agenda for their lives: WORK. To make sure they did their work he appointed taskmasters who kept the workers in line. To emphasize their authority, taskmasters were given whips that they used both frequently and joyfully.

When God delivered the Jewish people from their slavery you might think that the joy of freedom changed their hearts. It didn't. The new adventure of freedom was too much for too many. Some yearned to go back to Egypt. It wasn't good there but it was predictable, known.

That's the story of life, I think. We're set free from something that enslaves us but get scared off and begin to slink back to what we hated. A woman breaks free from an abusive husband. She can't handle being set free. She starts to date what she knows best. It's another abusive man. Back to Egypt.

A man breaks a pattern of sexual impurity but now finds himself late at night chatting on the Internet, weaving lies about who he is. Back to Egypt.

Don't you want to be free? I do.

I slink back toward my own Egypt sometimes. Why I'd want to trade freedom for slavery is beyond me but it's a tendency I sometimes have. How about you? Are you free or are you enslaved? Ever find yourself slinking back to Egypt? What stops you? What are the habits and relationships keeping you from freedom?

Dee Brestin

When you're given a box of candy, don't gulp it all down; eat too much chocolate and you'll make yourself sick; And when you find a friend, don't outwear your welcome; show up at all hours and he'll soon get fed up. PROVERBS 25:16–17 (MSG)

How thankful I am for women friends and for chocolate and homemade bread! But I also know I can take a beautiful gift from God and turn it rancid by allowing it to become a "god" in my life. When I am stressed or depressed and turn first to His gifts instead of to Him, I am on the slippery slope to idolatry.

In my book, *The Friendships of Women,* I tell Christy's story. Christy had an unhealthy pattern in friendships, clinging too tightly to her friends, not giving them room to breathe. She would become anxious, even to the point of feeling ill, if they were not immediately available to her or if they were with another friend. Fortunately, other friends encouraged her to get counseling and she had the humility to go. The light came on for Christy through this conversation with a godly counselor:

"Christy, do you think you need a Savior?"

"Of course I do. I'm a Christian. Jesus *is* my Savior."

"You have let Him save you from the wrath of God—but will you let Him save you from this?"

"From what?"

"From relational idolatry."

The term *relational idolatry* turned the light on for Christy. When we continually cling to God's gifts instead of to Him, the chains of addiction are slipped over our wrists. Instead of being free in Christ, we are in bondage.

Think about this: Is Jesus still your first love? Where do you run first? Pray through Revelation 2:4–5 for yourself.

Glynnis Whitwer

On the walls all around the temple, in both the inner and outer rooms, he carved cherubim, palm trees and open flowers. He also covered the floors of both the inner and outer rooms of the temple with gold. 1 Kings 6:29–30 (niv)

I once worked for a developer of retirement communities. The CEO was a woman with a passion for building beautiful living communities for seniors. One of her pet peeves was cluttered administrative offices. Consequently, we never taped anything to windows or walls, drank our sodas out of glasses and didn't eat at our desks. Pretty organization was required.

I learned a lot from my boss. She was always teaching us her philosophy on caring for the aging and creating a beautiful home for them. One day my approach to organization changed forever because of her guidance on keeping our workspaces attractive and clutter free.

It was the day she warned us to stay away from "The-cereal-box-on-top-of-the-refrigerator syndrome." I wondered if someone told her about my house. The top of the refrigerator was exactly where my cereal boxes were, and had been for years.

While there's nothing wrong with that, her point was to try and make things beautiful and functional. Needless to say, the cereal boxes came down, I scrubbed off layers of grime, and replaced the cardboard boxes with an attractive potted plant.

Keeping things in beautiful order is a practice we find in the Bible. In the book of 1 Kings, we find records of the temple Solomon built to the Lord. Not only are we given construction details, but we get a hint of its beauty, complete with floors of gold, engraved cherubim, and tops of pillars in the shape of lilies.

While our offices aren't temples, they can be a place where God is worshiped and honored. Perhaps if we looked at desks or workspaces with a fresh perspective, there might be ways to increase both beauty and order. It may just take a few changes to create a place of organized inspiration.

Look at your workspace with new eyes. What hits you first as being the most cluttered element? Make a plan to tackle that project first.

Kathy Peel

"Never, Lord!" he said. "This shall never happen to you!"

MATTHEW 16:22 (NIV)

Sometimes everything in life seems hard. If your spouse announces that he got a pay cut, or if a friend spews critical words at you, or a teacher calls to schedule a meeting about your child's behavior, it's easy to adopt a victim mentality: "If only we had more money, if only my friend would treat me with respect, if only my children didn't misbehave and my life was as easy and (seemingly) seamless as everyone else's, then I could be happy." When we begin to feel sorry for ourselves, what we're really saying is, "I deserve better than this."

This frame of mind can cause our disposition to deteriorate faster than we can say, "Poor me." It steals our joy and the joy of those around us. Jesus identifies the source of this kind of attitude in Matthew 16:21–23.

After Jesus told his disciples that he would have to suffer and die, Peter took him aside and rebuked him, saying that this should never happen to him! But note how Jesus responded to Peter: "Get behind me, Satan! You are a stumbling block to me; you do not have in mind the things of God, but the things of men" (Matthew 16:23 NIV).

What if Jesus had answered, "You're right, Peter. I don't deserve to suffer and die. After all, I'm a good person. As a matter of fact, I've lived a perfect life. I deserve better than this!" I know that I would have been tempted to answer like that.

But not Jesus. He didn't allow Himself to think like a victim and feel sorry for Himself. Instead He singled out the source of this kind of thinking: Satan.

When we start wallowing in self-pity, we have a choice. We can choose to think like a victim or we can take responsibility for our reaction, confess it to God, and ask Him to renew our mind with His perspective.

What about you? Have you been thinking like a victim?

Ellie Kay

You do not have, because you do not ask God. JAMES 4:2 (NIV)

"Is this your best price?"

I was stunned as I watched my high school girlfriend Tammy ask the sales clerk at Casual Corner this question. I'd never heard someone ask an employee at a retail store for a discount.

Tammy continued, "Because there's makeup on the collar and I don't want to pay full price for damaged goods." The clerk went to find the store manager and within minutes she came back with startling news, "Sure, my manager said we can take 30 percent off the price because these are going on sale in a few days anyway!"

As a financial author for the last decade, my research and experience has discovered that consumers miss out on savings in the thousands of dollars for goods and services each year because they do not ask for discounts, rebates and cash back incentives. It's oftentimes ours for the asking—if we'll ask.

We can be that way in our spiritual life as well if we fail to pray for those things we need—even little things like a parking space, lost keys or a wise response to a difficult neighbor. We need to ask God for specifics in order to experience the joy of having Him answer in specific ways. It is in His answer that we feel His love and know that He is working through us to help others.

Today when you pray, be specific in what you ask of God. Ask for those things you need in order to serve Him better, including __________________ and __________________.

Lynne Hybels

Speak up for those who cannot speak for themselves, for the rights of all who are destitute. Speak up and judge fairly; defend the rights of the poor and needy. PROVERBS 31:8–9 (NIV)

Like most women who grew up in conservative evangelical churches I was often challenged to be "a woman of noble character," as described in Proverbs 31:10–31. In recent years, however, God's specific call on my life has found shape in the two verses preceding that passage. As a woman blessed with economic stability, social freedoms, and relational and spiritual support, I feel called to lift my voice on behalf of women throughout the world who "cannot speak for themselves . . . are destitute . . . are poor and needy" (Proverbs 31:8–9 NIV).

I believe that we women in the resourced world have been blessed by God so that we can be a blessing to our sisters in need. Unfortunately, it's possible to be so consumed with the details of our own lives that we remain unaware of the desperate needs of others. In order to speak up for our sisters in need, we must become intentional about knowing their needs. I frequently peruse the Web sites of Christian organizations that serve women globally.

Sisters in Service (sistersinservice.org) strengthens grassroots global initiatives related to health, education, and economic and spiritual development. International Justice Mission (ijm.org) is a human rights agency that secures justice for victims of slavery, sexual exploitation and other forms of violent oppression. Opportunity International (opportunity.org) helps the poor through providing small business loans so women can earn a steady income in order to feed and educate their families. Bright Hope International (brighthope.org) gives help and hope to people earning less than one dollar per day.

I give every woman who reads these words the same challenge I give myself: to join the sisterhood of women by opening our minds and our hearts to their needs, lifting our voices on their behalf, and giving prayerfully and financially as God enables us.

Leigh McLeroy

. . . what man is there among you, when his son shall ask him for a loaf, will give him a stone? Or if he shall ask for a fish, he will not give him a snake, will he? If you then, being evil, know how to give good gifts to your children, how much more shall your Father in heaven give what is good to those who ask Him! MATTHEW 7:8–11 (NASB)

Funny thing about the word *no*. It never gets any easier to hear. I wasn't fond of it when I was seven, or eleven, or twenty-one. And I don't like it one bit better today. I learned as a child to order my request to the one who was most able (and likely) to grant it. I said "May I please," and I said it to the parent I hoped might answer "yes." I walked the fine line between persistence and annoyance like a tightrope.

I've been hearing "no" a lot lately. I don't believe my requests have been unreasonable, or even selfish. I've asked respectfully, and as often as I dare. I've offered up to God what Charles Spurgeon called "order and argument" in prayer, and I've prayed believing. I still believe.

And I'm still hearing "no." Or at least, "not now."

When my requests were denied or deferred as a child, I eventually relented. I moved on. But there are some desires that simply cannot be abandoned, even when holding on to them hurts more than ditching them might. And whether God's answer is yes or it's no, He is the One I want to hear from. So in case you're wondering, I'm still asking. And unless or until you hear otherwise from Him, I think you should be, too.

Are you waiting to hear from God on a matter, or have you heard his distinct "no"? If the jury is still out—will you be brave enough to ask again?

Beverly Hubble Tauke

It is not by sword or spear that the Lord saves; for the battle is the Lord's. 1 SAMUEL 17:47 (NIV)

Odd, isn't it? The very people who should have known David best didn't know him at all. He was the invisible kid to his dad, Jesse, who showcased seven other sons for national leadership but ignored David (I Samuel 16:9-13). He was the annoying runt to his elder brothers, who ridiculed junior's intrusion into their military mission (I Samuel 17:28).

When it came to their youngest, this family had no clue. Fortunately for them, David was *not* clueless about his calling, thanks to:

• **Clarity:** David's vision came through spiritual, not physical sight. His eyes measured mammoth Goliath. His spirit measured his all-powerful God—envisioning awesome opportunity where others saw sure calamity.

• **Competence:** In the boondocks with his sheep, David's bull's-eye slingshot skill annihilated wild predators. His proven expertise prepared him for a mission that was both military and spiritual.

• **Conscience:** Powering David's judgment were such internal factors as conscience, knowledge, values, and God-based spirituality. He was not externally controlled by the groupthink of his family or the power and prestige of his king. Superior maturity of mind and spirit gave David wisdom, courage, and radar that made him the giant of his family and culture, and ultimately, in his match with Goliath.

The very survival of others depended on David's capacity to tolerate their disdain as he followed God's lead. What about you? Do you wound your conscience to please your family or friends? Do they wound their consciences to please you? As David knew, that is one risk not worth taking for anyone.

Connie Neal

"Leave her alone," said Jesus. "Why are you bothering her? She has done a beautiful thing to me." MARK 14:6 (NIV)

The guys just didn't get it. Jesus determined to return to Jerusalem. While the disciples argued about who would hold which important position in the kingdom, Jesus repeatedly told them that he would soon be rejected, arrested, and crucified. Somehow the guys managed to take that metaphorically. Only one person seemed to understand and believe what Jesus had been telling them.

Mary accepted what Jesus said and did what little she could for Jesus. She knew that crucified criminals were denied a decent burial. So her only recourse was to prepare His body for burial before his arrest. This came at great cost. The ointment of pure nard was worth a fortune. Still, she broke the alabaster jar, pouring the perfume on Jesus, doing what she could to dignify his burial. Not one of the disciples understood. They all spoke against her. Only Jesus came to her defense.

"*Leave her alone*," said Jesus. "Why are you bothering her? She has done a beautiful thing to me. The poor you will always have with you, and you can help them any time you want. But you will not always have me. *She did what she could.* She poured perfume on my body beforehand to prepare for my burial. I tell you the truth, wherever the gospel is preached throughout the world, what she has done will also be told, in memory of her" (Mark 14:6–9 NIV, emphasis added).

"Leave her alone; she did what she could." I'd like that framed or done in cross-stitch to hang on my wall. All Jesus asks of us is to do what *we* can, responding to His word. When we do that, Jesus will defend us against all assailants. What can you do? Maybe you can create an artistic display of those words for your own reminder.

Melinda Schmidt

How great is God—beyond our understanding! Job 36:26 (NIV)

The patient was wrestling daily with negative thoughts causing depression, stress, and anxiety to be a way of life. Her days had become miserable. I listened as a psychiatric doctor counseled her to think positive thoughts upon awakening each morning.

How would you characterize the thoughts that enter your mind each day as you awaken? I started thinking about "Wonderful Words" to start my day:

God is the Master of the universe (Job 38–41). When was the last time *you* tried to keep the planets behaving overnight? Feed all the animals from Mongolia to Memphis? Load clouds with moisture and decide if rain or snow—and how much—should fall?

God cares for the world 24/7. While you were asleep, He was watching over you and the needs of everyone else on the other side of the planet as well. And as you dreamt, He was thinking about you and working in your life (Psalm 139).

God is your Savior (Psalm 91:2). As you begin today, God is at your side, battling the circumstances that seem like encroaching enemies. He will be not be foiled.

What will be your Wonderful Words as you start each day? Could you

- focus on God's character and linger there
- think of five good things in your life today
- commit to writing a list of ten blessings by day's end
- pray for the needs of three other people
- ask God to help you think more hopefully about what is troubling you today
- make a list of your own daily Wonderful Words

If psychiatric caregivers know the value of positive thoughts as we start the day, how much more our Creator who said, "I made today—be glad about it!" (see Psalm 118:24).

Ellie Lofaro

Whatever you have learned or received or heard from me, or seen in me—put it into practice. And the God of peace will be with you. Philippians 4:9 (NIV)

I strongly reject the notion that believers should not involve themselves in public forums. I am puzzled by pastors who will not allow current events and local issues to be discussed and brought to light from their pulpits. Of course, the prayer room is where our efforts must begin and end but there are an awful lot of battles to be won. David, Joshua, and Gideon didn't just pray about their enemies. They faced them and with God's help, they defeated them. In each case, righteousness prevailed and the course of history was altered. I am saddened by the passivity of congregations that have the potential to radically change the course of events and the fabric of their communities as well as far off places. Many of our towns are looking a lot more like "Pottersville" from *It's a Wonderful Life* with each passing year. We must not let that happen! God is able but whom will He send?

I'm so grateful there were fervent Christians in the room when the Constitution was signed. I'm indebted to the artists who lovingly recreated biblical accounts on canvas and the actors who participated in passion plays of old. The world would be a duller place without the gifts of Handel, Bach, or Mozart. Imagine our loss if Pascal, Newton, and Pasteur didn't think Christians should pioneer new territory. How tragic it would be if William Wilberforce decided that faith and politics didn't mix.

So why do we get so excited when a public figure or someone with resources professes faith in Jesus? Isn't it because, like children, we want the biggest and best guys on our side? We all love a winning team but so few are willing to take the field. Christians need to be salt and light in *all* facets of our societal structure. The Army tells us to "Be all you can be." So does God.

Nancy Sebastian Meyer

From one man He made every nation of men, that they should inhabit the whole earth; and He determined the times set for them and the exact places where they should live. God did this so that men would seek him and perhaps reach out for Him and find Him . . . ACTS 17:26–27 (NIV)

Do you wonder if God is as personal as some people say? Does the Maker of the universe really concern Himself with our everyday lives? These verses prove God knows even the mundane details of our past, present, and future—and cares.

How many places have you lived in your lifetime? I had lived in my parents' home, college dorms, an apartment, and two houses before my husband and I settled into our present home nineteen years ago. I recently filled out a form asking for the addresses of my last three residences. I could no longer remember some of those details—but God knows!

These verses in Acts clearly indicate that God knows "the exact places" where everyone lives. He remembers every one of my addresses and, more incredibly, the exact places I will live in the future.

This understanding of God gives great consolation to people in the process of moving, who wonder if they will ever find a new place to call home. Even greater is the realization that if God knows our addresses, how much more must He care about the overwhelmingly large issues in our lives!

Why does God want us to know that He knows? His desire is for us to respond to His loving attention and reach out to connect with Him. Amazingly, He longs for a personal relationship with you and me.

Think back to the places you've called home and thank God for His gracious provision then, now, and in the future.

Anita Lustrea

I want to know Christ and experience the mighty power that raised him from the dead. I want to suffer with him, sharing in his death, so that one way or another I will experience the resurrection from the dead! PHILIPPIANS 3:10–11 (NLT)

Did you run track in high school or college, or were you a cross-country runner? At the beginning of the race you feel pretty good, but then you come to a point where pain enters the picture and you have to start focusing in on the fact that you trained for this. You have to have faith in the work that you've put in. It's like that for the Christ follower, except we don't have to have faith in the work we've done, but in the work Christ has done for us. But we can stake our lives on His work and then press on with our race.

Philippians 3:10–14 (NLT) says it well: "I want to know Christ and experience the mighty power that raised him from the dead. I want to suffer with him, sharing in his death, so that one way or another I will experience the resurrection from the dead! I don't mean to say that I have already achieved these things or that I have already reached perfection. But I press on to possess that perfection for which Christ Jesus first possessed me. No, dear brothers and sisters, I have not achieved it, but I focus on this one thing: Forgetting the past and looking forward to what lies ahead, I press on to reach the end of the race and receive the heavenly prize for which God, through Christ Jesus, is calling us."

That's an important message that we need to hear regularly. We need to keep doing the work that Christ has entrusted to us and keep pressing on.

Take a moment to think about some of the roadblocks that pop up on the racecourse. How do you respond? How have you responded in the past? How might you move past roadblocks in the future?

Tiffany Taylor

How we praise God, the Father of our Lord Jesus Christ, who has blessed us with every spiritual blessing in the heavenly realms because we belong to Christ. Long ago, even before he made the world, God loved us and chose us in Christ to be holy and without fault in his eyes. His unchanging plan has always been to adopt us into his own family by bringing us to himself through Jesus Christ. And this gave him great pleasure.

EPHESIANS 1:3–5 (NLT)

One of the highlights of working in orphan ministry has been traveling to Russia. In 2006 I returned to Orphanage #47 in St Petersburg, Russia, where I visited many children I already knew. One of the orphans was a five-year-old boy named Sasha. When I walked in his room, Sasha was so excited he ran to my arms and hugged me fiercely around the neck. I started telling him (through a translator) how excited I was to see him. He showed me his room and his locker where he kept his prized possession, his Spiderman cap. Sasha loved everything Spiderman! I was so excited to spend time with this darling boy that it was hard to tear myself away and go downstairs to organize the shoes we were distributing to Sasha and all his friends.

As I cut open the first box, I was shocked to see a pair of boys Spiderman shoes. Is it possible that these shoes are Sasha's size? They were. I was reminded that God knows our size and He loves His children and provides for them each day in a personal way that only He can orchestrate.

Maybe you feel alone and forgotten. It is important to remember that He has loved us even before He made the world and that He has not left us alone, but has adopted us all into his family. He provides for the smallest things that bring joy to an orphan in Russia and for the things that are a burden to your heart today. Be open to seeing His plans in your life.

Kristen Johnson Ingram

For I have set you an example, that you also should do just as I have done to you. JOHN 13:15 (ESV)

I had never seen a footwashing when I was six or seven, but my grandmother's little neighbor girl led me to the hedge behind an old-style church. "My mom calls 'em dunkards, or drunkards or something," the girl told me. "Watch when they come outside." Eventually, the plainly dressed folk filed out of the gray church building and lined up by what I had thought was a small rectangular fishpond. One by one, the women knelt and washed the other women's feet, and then the men did the same for one another. It was the oddest practice I had ever seen, and I could scarcely contain my giggles, hiding in the hedge.

Suddenly a hand grasped my shoulder. It was my father, who, as he led me away, lectured me sternly on the privacy and sacredness of others' religious rites. But I was still smothering my laughter, so when we were back at my grandmother's, he read the story from the Bible about Jesus, washing the disciples' feet, and he repeated twice the part about doing as Jesus did.

"Why don't we do that?" I asked, worried that maybe all the Christians I knew were doomed to hell for their failure to wash feet.

"We do," my father said. "But not enough. Life should be a footwashing."

It took me many years to understand what he meant about life being a footwashing. And I'm still wondering: does that mean being a servant at all times, or does it mean having the boldness and humility to say, like Peter, "Will you wash me, Lord?"

Have you ever washed another woman's feet, or had your own feet bathed? Invite a few friends over and have a footwashing. And allow someone to wash *your* feet.

Ask God for the spirit of servitude, as well as the grace to be served.

Lori Neff

God is our refuge and strength, an ever-present help in trouble. Therefore we will not fear, though the earth give way and the mountains fall into the heart of the sea, though its waters roar and foam and the mountains quake with their surging. PALMS 46:1–3 (NIV)

I've struggled with fear for most of my life. For years, I've asked for God's help in difficult situations, but then would still try to fight my way through. My prayer was, "God, get me out of this!" I would often feel discouraged and disappointed because He didn't take the trial away. So, I fearfully bumbled through, feeling a bit angry and confused at God's apparent lack of response. Lately, I've truly come to the end of myself (again!) as I've gone through some trials. My plea has changed to "God, would You help me get through this?" That has been the cry of my heart—to not just be rescued from a situation, but to be helped through it. I am finding that He is so much bigger than I ever imagined and He is willing to help me when I rely on Him. I think I'm beginning to understand how His strength is shown in my weakness. It seems that He delights in helping me through the trial instead of removing it. I can relax and not fear—I know that God will give me strength, wisdom and direction to take me through the trial. Isn't it good to know that God can use these difficult times to refine us and draw us closer to Him?

Kendra Smiley . . . .

Do nothing out of selfish ambition or vain conceit, but in humility consider others better than yourselves.
PHILIPPIANS 2:3 (NIV)

I don't know when I first heard someone use the suffix "-ish," but it quickly became one of my favorites. I would attach it to arrival times and used it to blur departure times. I even affixed it to my estimations of project completion times.

"I should be there by ten thirty-ish," I would say knowing I was giving myself a little pad in the arrival time. "The project will be done by May 1-ish." "I'll have dinner ready-ish when you get home." Sounds pretty silly, doesn't it?

Beyond a shadow of a doubt, the suffix "-ish" became my preference. It seemed to release me from some degree of responsibility . . . at least that was my perception. And then one day I was doing some writing and I chose to hyphenate a word. That word? "Self-ish." Ouch! Could my suffix of choice actually be attached to a behavior that was to be avoided? Maybe the truth was that "-ish" made the timing of various things "all about me."

When I put an "-ish" after a time or a date or a promise, I was in essence declaring that I would try to be true to my word, but I didn't have to be. Maybe -ish isn't the best suffix. Maybe I should look for another one to choose as my favorite. I think –ly might be a good choice—as in godly or heavenly or joyfully. Yes, that is definitely an improvement.

Maybe you need to take a look at your vocabulary or even more importantly at your actions. What do your actions and decisions say? Beware! Don't let the -ish take over in your life. Avoid the temptation is be self-ish. That's the Next Right Choice!

Anita Lustrea

But you, O Lord, are a God of compassion and mercy, slow to get angry and filled with unfailing love and faithfulness.
PSALM 86:15 (NLT)

When was the last time you got good and angry, blistering the wallpaper off with your anger?

When was the last time you got so angry that you decided to hide, refusing to come out of your hole for a week, two weeks, a month, or more?

When was the last time you got so angry that you took the coward's way out and carried out a "whisper" campaign to get even?

When was the last time you got so angry that you killed someone with your sarcasm, a smile never leaving your face?

So when was it?

To be honest, I've tried most of them. I've watched friends earn a Ph.D. in Avoidance and Withdrawal. I've listened in on "whisper" campaigns and cringed at the venom. There are probably 101 ways to ineffectively deal with anger and most of them just don't work.

Do you have an anger problem? Most people struggle with it. The Bible tells us that it's a big issue. But God over and over in Scripture is described as being "slow to anger" (Exodus 34:6, Numbers 14:18, Nehemiah 9:17, Psalm 86:15, and more, all NIV). Instead, we find that He is abounding in love, compassionate, and faithful. God doesn't avoid or withdraw. He doesn't lash out just because He's hurt.

When we see ourselves clearly and look clearly at our anger issues, then we can invite Christ to join us in the "fixing" process. We start to become more and more like the person God wants us to be, and in the process we become a deeper, more trustworthy woman of God.

In your journal, write down some of your trigger points for anger. Make a list and keep it handy and start regularly praying about a new and better way to respond, with compassion and grace, abounding in love and faithfulness. Pray that God would mold you more closely into the image of His Son.

Mindy Caliguire

"Whoever welcomes a little child like this in my name welcomes me." MATTHEW 18:5 (NIV)

Lately, we've had fishing line strung from the upstairs loft to the corner cabinet in the kitchen. Why? It's a zip-line for Lego stunt vehicles! Welcome to my world of boys.

Once, our family formulated a few house rules. Alongside the expected *No Hitting* and *Obey Mom and Dad* came an entry borne of past chaos and scoldings: *No Wearing Underwear on Your Head.* Stifling my laughter, I dutifully wrote it down (please do keep that in mind if you visit).

In the relentless daily drama, I can get prickly and miss the point of love. Especially if I've neglected the well-being of my own soul, I have trouble instilling worth and value into my kiddos. It's about the underwear.

I'm learning that mothering is the lifelong process of *welcoming* our children. Our English word *welcome* originated from a combination of two words, *willa* and *cuma*, literally meaning "one whose coming is in accord with another's will."

Children have clearly been given to us "in accord with Another's will." When we welcome them, unconditionally during all seasons, we do so in surrender and acknowledgement of Another's will and desire.

In the midst of underwear on the head, zip-lines, late-for-school arguments, and unfinished chores, parents are the primary welcomers of life into this world. Through our words, tones of voice, attitudes, eyebrows, and hands, we hold unique God-given power to convey "you are wanted." Or not.

How might you convey a sincere "welcome" to family members or friends daily, even hourly? Is there a child in your life whom you can welcome? A neighbor? A grandchild? Niece or nephew? You welcome far more than just that child, for, ". . . whoever welcomes one of these little children in my name welcomes me" (Mark 9:37 NIV).

Paula Rinehart

Therefore having been justified by faith, we have peace with God through our Lord Jesus Christ, through whom also we have obtained our introduction by faith into this grace in which we stand; and we exult in hope of the glory of God. And not only this, but we also exult in our tribulations, knowing that tribulation brings about perseverance; and perseverance, proven character; and proven character, hope; and hope does not disappoint, because the love of God has been poured out within our hearts through the Holy spirit who was given to us. ROMANS 5:1–5 (NASB)

Oh wow! If you stand back and think about the path you've been walking with Christ, isn't this the story of your life? Faith, which is itself the gift of God, has brought you into a secure place called "grace" where you anticipate sharing the actual glory of God.

In this rooted place, though, you encounter your own share of hard times. "Tribulations," the Bible calls them. But now, those hard times actually lead somewhere—to a small string of life-changing experiences that shape your life for good. The ability to hang in there, a life that's as deep and true as it appears, and finally, a hope that does not disappoint—this is the golden stuff we long for.

So much of life ends in disappointment. But the hope God gives is different. This hope finds its source in His love. So no matter what happens to us, this passage claims that experience, sifted through God's hands, can only lead us to a deeper taste of his love. Only the redemptive power of Christ is strong enough to take the worst life can throw your way and use it as a channel of his love to others.

Perhaps the sheer wonder of it all is the reason this small paragraph is one of the longest sentences of the New Testament. Paul was too excited to find a period!

How does the thought that God is working in you "a hope that does not disappoint" motivate or encourage you?

Marcia Ramsland

She sets about her work vigorously; her arms are strong for her tasks. PROVERBS 31:17 (NIV)

Is it time for spring cleaning at your house? "Spring Cleaning" conjures up a mental picture of a warm, sunny day spent airing out bedrooms, washing windows, and thoroughly vacuuming carpets. It signals the passing of winter gray outside and the freshness of a spring transformation inside your home.

The Proverbs 31 woman set about her work vigorously—and so can we as God's women today. Put on those gym shoes, turn up the praise music, pull out the vacuum, and away you go!

Target the rooms that are most used and need the most help. If you start in the family room, clear the clutter off the coffee table(s), dust and rearrange what you put back before tackling one book or media shelf at a time. Run a dust rag over everything in the room before you vacuum and put things back.

In the garage, begin in the center and move items to the perimeter putting gardening tools, toys, sports equipment, recycle bins, and storage boxes by sections. Sweep the floor and deliver extra items to charity for new space and freshness.

While you're at it, picture yourself as the Proverbs 31 woman in action today, putting her faith in action with strength and vigor as she sets about her tasks. This woman wasn't halfhearted about anything. She put herself into each task and God commends her for it.

Whether you decide to spring clean on a weekday or a weekend, don't wait for a sunny day. Any day can be "Spring Cleaning Day" with a vigorous attitude.

Anita Lustrea

Thank you for making me so wonderfully complex!
Your workmanship is marvelous—how well I know it.
PSALM 139:14 (NLT)

My husband thinks I'm pretty intense.

My response is always, "No way, I'm just focused."

The truth is that I am intense. I like to dig in and dig deep. I want to get to the "good stuff" fast. I want to see where God is at work in whatever I'm reading, talking about, or observing.

Sometimes, my focus serves me well. Other times, not. Those are the times I know I need to find another speed, another emotional level.

Sometimes I wonder what causes my intensity. Is it just the way I'm wired? Is it how I'm wired coupled with some pain or anxiety? Is it genetics + pain + circumstances all wrapped up together?

Whatever it is, it's who I am. I can fight it but it's how I'm created. My job is to make sure I don't use my genetics or my pain or my circumstances as an excuse to justify any behavior that would stop me from looking at Jesus and conforming to Jesus.

The Scriptures tell us that we are wonderfully made, that despite our circumstances or our built-in wiring we can rise above it all, focusing on the One who made us. Psalm 139:14–16 (NLT) reads, "Thank you for making me so wonderfully complex! Your workmanship is marvelous—how well I know it. You watched me as I was being formed in utter seclusion, as I was woven together in the dark of the womb. You saw me before I was born. Every day of my life was recorded in your book. Every moment was laid out before a single day had passed."

When you're tempted to complain about some of your traits today, remember that God's workmanship is marvelous and that he did make you wonderfully complex. Take some time to write down some of those personality traits you struggle with and purpose to thank God for how you are wired, not excusing behavior, but thanking him that you are an unrepeatable miracle of God. Be attentive today to how God might use those very things for his Glory.

Leslie Ludy

Charm is deceptive, and beauty is fleeting; but a woman who fears the Lord is to be praised. PROVERBS 31:30 (NIV)

Only 1 percent of women think they are beautiful, according to a recent survey by Dove. The plastic surgery business is booming. Beauty products are boundless. We are surrounded by a plethora of books, magazines, and TV shows that provide us with all the techniques we need in order to become attractive. Yet in an ironic twist, most of us still feel ugly and insecure.

A graphic designer for a major clothing label once told me, "In real life, no model really looks as perfect as what you see in clothing ads or on catalog covers. We digitally alter nearly everything about her." The world lifts up a standard for beauty that is literally impossible to achieve in real life.

Instead of allowing movie-makers, the fashion industry, and advertising executives to define who we become as young women, it's time we look to the Author of all true beauty. When we allow God to remake us from the inside out, we will glow with a beauty that cannot be matched by the most elaborate Hollywood makeover.

Ezekiel 16:9–13 (NKJV) describes how God adorns us with His beauty: *"Then I washed you in water; yes, I thoroughly washed off your blood, and I anointed you with oil. . . . . . I clothed you with fine linen and covered you with silk. You were exceedingly beautiful, and succeeded to royalty."*

I don't know about you, but I would much rather be attractive to the King of all kings than to our finicky pop culture. I'd much rather receive a makeover from the true Creator of beauty than from the best plastic surgeon in the world.

Today, make a conscious effort to tune out the endless messages from society that make you feel ugly or insecure. Instead of pursuing magazine cover-beauty, pursue the loveliness of Christ by allowing Him to mold you into His image. When *His* beauty shines through you, you'll glow with a radiance that no makeup in the world could ever achieve.

Ellie Kay

Well done, good and faithful servant; you were faithful over a few things, I will make you ruler over many things.
MATTHEW 25:21 (NKJV)

Have you ever gotten a phone call that changed your life? I have. I still remember when I got the call from the doctor's office, telling me I was going to be a mom. "Oh boy!" I thought, "I'll be able to eat anything I want and not worry about gaining weight!" In that instant, I knew that life would never be the same and the prospect of being responsible for another human being was powerful. Some major life changes are good and some are not so good.

Most of us will not face a major life-changing event today but almost all of us will have to handle a series of small things that can threaten to change life's outlook for that particular day. Dozens of these little events happen from morning to night: a coworker doesn't do her job, a friend talks about you behind your back, the checker at the store had an a-ti-tude, the kids argue all the way home from school. After each incident, we have a choice. We can choose to act with a positive purpose, or we can just react to the situation. I know that when I react to the little things throughout the day, the final result is not very pretty. By the end of the day, I'm stressed and snarky or I'm scarfing chocolate and coffee. On the other hand, when I give these little incidences to the Lord as they happen, then the end of my day is far more pleasant and I'm a lot better company to my family as well.

It's the small stuff that matters most.

Anita Lustrea

In spite of all this, they kept on sinning; in spite of his wonders, they did not believe. So he ended their days in futility and their years in terror. Whenever God slew them, they would seek him; they eagerly turned to him again. They remembered that God Most High was their Rock and their Redeemer. But then they would flatter him with their mouths, lying to him with their tongues. . . . Yet he was merciful; he forgave their iniquities and did not destroy them. PSALM 78:32–38 (NIV)

On *Midday Connection*, the radio program that I cohost, we regularly have programs focusing on parenting. As I talk with some of the best parenting experts around, I'm continually brought face-to-face with my parenting shortfalls. The only consolation I have is that we're all in the same boat. No one is the perfect parent except God. How many times have you wanted to really let your son or daughter have it? How many times have they provoked you or worried you or saddened you or directly disobeyed you? How many more times have we done the same thing to God, our Father? And yet, as Psalm 78:38 (NIV) reads, "He was merciful; he forgave their iniquities and did not destroy them." Oh Lord, may we have mercy on our own wayward children.

I have a friend who recently made a small collage on an 8½ x 11 piece of construction paper. She cut out from magazines all the words that she thought described me. It had an amazing effect on me. I still regularly look at that collage. It sits framed in my office. Now maybe you're not the creative type that my friend is, but I'd really like you to try this exercise. You can either cut out words from magazines and paste them with a glue stick to the construction paper, or just write words in different color markers or crayons that describe the great characteristics your son or daughter possesses. You can't even imagine how their countenance will brighten when they realize you spent that much time thinking about them.

Carol Kent

Therefore, as God's chosen people, holy and dearly loved, clothe yourselves with compassion, kindness, humility, gentleness and patience. COLOSSIANS 3:12 (NIV)

A middle-of-the-night phone call turned my life upside down. Our son, a graduate of the U.S. Naval Academy, had been arrested for the murder of his wife's first husband. For hours I alternated between sobs and denial. My mind swirled with questions. Several hours later our worst fears were confirmed. Our son had pulled a trigger in a public parking lot and a man died.

After two and a half years and seven postponements of our son's trial, he was convicted and sentenced to life in prison, without the possibility of parole. We were definitely living in a new kind of normal—long waits to get through security lines to visit our son at a maximum security prison, unwanted publicity, fear for his safety, and an agonizing sadness for the family of the deceased and for all of our lost hopes and dreams.

It has been eight and a half years since that phone call, and God has changed my heart. I used to pass signs on the highway that said "Prison Area, Do Not Pick Up Hitchhikers" and I would lock my doors and drive fast, trying to get out of the danger zone quickly. Now I slow down and look for buildings where I know inmates are housed. I pray for them and for their spouses—that they will find creative ways for keeping their marriages strong. I pray for their children who don't know how to answer the question, "And what does your Daddy (Mommy) do?"

Corrie ten Boom once said: "What did you do today that only a Christian would have done?" Genuine compassion reaches a hand toward the person in need and does something tangible to help. My husband and I launched the nonprofit organization, Speak Up for Hope, and we minister to the needs of inmates and their families.

God changes our hearts and our actions as we apply Colossians 3:12 (NIV). What one thing will you do today for someone who needs help worse than you do?

Sharon Hanby-Robie

For God is not a God of disorder but of peace . . . But everything should be done in a fitting and orderly way. 1 CORINTHIANS 14:33,40 (NIV)

Peace—when you hear that word what do you think of? For me it's a word of comfort that coincides with relaxing, safe, and well organized. Does that description fit your home? It should. Our homes, after all, should be reflective of what we are striving for in our daily walks as Christians. This verse tells me that in order to have peace—we must have order. Without order, we have chaos and that usually brings about stress.

I believe that homemaking is one of the sacred tasks of life. Creating a nurturing environment for our children and visitors is important. Finding a balance between the spiritual and the physical needs within the home is critical to creating an atmosphere of love. Proverbs 14:1 (NIV) says, "The wise woman builds her house, but with her own hands the foolish one tears hers down." I am awed at how much influence women have within their homes. We set the tone and the atmosphere—not our decorating scheme—but us! And that impacts the lives of all who enter. What a responsibility. What an opportunity! As Christians we have such an advantage to be good home builders. The Lord is the giver of wisdom. By following his example we can be sure that we are building homes that will comfort and nourish both body and soul.

Occasionally, we need to take a few minutes and simply listen to the noises in our homes. Are they generally happy sounds? Are your words and tone gentle? Are you fostering an attitude of joy in togetherness? Listen to the sounds of your home with your heart. It will guide you to a beautiful home.

Mary Whelchel

Then he (Jesus) said to them, "Give to Caesar what is Caesar's, and to God what is God's." MATTHEW 22:21B (NIV)

The Pharisees were trying to trap Jesus by asking him if it was right to pay taxes to Caesar or not. In responding, Jesus gave them a principle which holds true for us today.

We can think of "Caesar" as anyone in our lives to whom we owe some degree of allegiance or loyalty. Therefore, our employer is one of the "Caesars" in our lives, and we must know what we owe our employer and what we don't. What are the things you should be giving to your employer—the things that are rightfully his or hers?

1. **Hard work.** Christians should never take advantage of their employers by cheating them out of time and work that is due to them.

2. **Protection of the employer's assets.** Whether it's pencils and paper clips or expense accounts, we always use our employer's resources for business purposes, not personal ones.

3. **Loyalty.** We owe those in authority over us respect, not malicious office gossip.

What do you not owe to your employer?

1. **Dishonesty of any sort.** An employer has no right to ask an employee to lie or deceive in any way.

2. **Participation in any activity that is dishonorable.**

This is Jesus' principle, and we need to apply it daily in our lives.

Think about it. Have you been failing to render to your employer what is his or her rightful due? Or have you been giving them things that belong to God?

Anita Lustrea

. . . The Lord, who scattered his people, will gather them and watch over them as a shepherd does his flock.
JEREMIAH 31:10 (NLT)

The Word of God is full of good news. Take a look at these words from Jeremiah 31:10–12 (NLT): ". . . The Lord, who scattered his people, will gather them together and watch over them as a shepherd does his flock. For the Lord has redeemed Israel from those too strong for them. They will come home and sing songs of joy on the heights of Jerusalem. They will be radiant because of the many gifts the Lord has given them—the good crops of wheat, wine, and oil, and the healthy flocks and herds. Their life will be like a watered garden, and all their sorrows will be gone."

And now from Isaiah 61:1, 3 (NLT), "The Spirit of the Sovereign Lord is upon me, because the Lord has appointed me to bring good news to the poor. He has sent me to comfort the brokenhearted and to announce that captives will be released and prisoners will be freed . . . To all who mourn in Israel, he will give beauty for ashes, joy instead of mourning, praise instead of despair. For the Lord has planted them like strong and graceful oaks for his own glory."

What situation is hanging over you like a cloud? Is it is a failing marriage, do you have a prodigal child that is breaking your heart? Do you really believe God can give beauty for ashes? Taking God at his word is sometimes the hardest thing we have to do. That old trust issue is a tough one especially when you're talking about situations you've been praying over for years.

Take a look at your heart. How have you changed since you've been trusting God for a situation that hasn't changed? We don't know when the "beauty for ashes" will occur, but be confident there will be praise instead of despair. Today, find those things in your life that you can offer praise to God for.

Kay Yerkovich

The Lord your God is in your midst,
A victorious warrior.
He will exult over you with joy,
He will be quiet in His love,
He will rejoice over you with shouts of joy.
ZEPHANIAH 3:17 (NASB)

This verse brings me wonderful visual images of my loving God. I'll give you my own visual picture and then ask you to take a few minutes and write your own.

I am lying in my hammock in my sunny, California backyard. I meditate on the truth of this verse. The Lord himself is near, as close as my breath. I have no fear for He is a victorious warrior. He is strong to save and protect and I allow myself to completely relax in His presence. He stands beside the hammock looking down at me. His eyes light up as I meet His gaze and His expression is full of pure delight. He begins to thank God the Father for me, recounting the ways I am unique, the gifts He has bestowed on me, and the ways I have served him. His eyes never leave me and He finds great happiness in speaking to the Father about me.

Then He is quiet but his eyes still speak of love. He pulls up a chair and whispers, "Rest." He gently rocks the hammock and I close my eyes and enjoy the gentle swaying. I listen for His quiet breath as it mixes with the sound of the breeze in the trees overhead. I rest in the quiet of His love.

Suddenly He is vivacious and His words are full of excitement and anticipation as he looks ahead to all He has prepared for me in heaven. He is rejoicing and singing exuberantly about His victory through the cross and the joys ahead.

Now take a moment to imagine and write out your own scene of God loving and rejoicing over you.

Lois Evans

Be strong in the grace that is in Christ Jesus. 2 Timothy 2:1 (NASB)

Did you know that the strength you need every day to live the Christian life is found in God's grace? First we are saved by God's grace (see Ephesians 2:8), and grace is what also keeps us. That lesson usually comes in the midst of hardship.

Paul learned the lesson of sustaining grace through an affliction that dogged him all his life. He wrote about it in 2 Corinthians 12, where he says he asked God three times to remove this affliction; but God's answer was grace: "He has said to me, 'My grace is sufficient for you, for power is perfected in weakness'" (v. 9 NASB).

God was saying to Paul that His grace is so comprehensive, it's sufficient to deal with the problems that don't go away. Paul's physical problem didn't go away, but grace covered its presence.

We all need that kind of powerful grace, because we all have to deal with things that won't budge, with problems that won't go away.

The frustration we often feel is why this is happening to us. The answer could be that your next lesson in grace is wrapped up in that hard circumstance or immovable problem. One thing God wants to teach us is that even when we are out of answers and out of strength, grace always has a fresh supply.

No wonder Peter referred to God as "the God of all grace" (1 Peter 5:10 NASB). He has all the grace we will ever need, and His grace is totally comprehensive. It touches every area of our personal lives, our marriages, and our families.

If you have not yet discovered how great God's supply of grace truly is, you have a wonderful surprise coming! God's goodness is staggering, and He's waiting to give it away to you!

Think about this: all you have to do is ask God for the grace you need. It's already there.

Kim Hill . . . .

You keep him in perfect peace whose mind is stayed on you, because he trusts in you. ISAIAH 26:3 (ESV)

My great-grandmother lived to be 103 and while much of her life was unimaginably difficult—she picked cotton in the Georgia heat and raised ten children, mostly as a single parent—she wasn't bitter or resentful. I think Granny Hornsby hung on to her joy (and her sanity!) because she understood what I'm still learning; that this world isn't our home and we'll never get all our expectations met here. Instead of grumbling she chose to appreciate God's simple gifts like having enough food to eat, a roof that didn't leak and maybe enough spare change for her kids to buy a Coke. Although "luxuries" like restaurants and indoor plumbing were beyond her reach, peace and contentment were firmly within her grasp.

When I grow up, I want to be more like Granny Hornsby. I want to really *get* the fact that I'm raising my beautiful boys on a broken planet where life doesn't often turn out the way we want it to. I want to teach them to find their hope in Christ instead of trying to manage their disappointment with retail therapy. And I want to do more than just *survive* my circumstances; I want to thrive in light of God's promises.

Of course my goal is lofty. There will surely still be seasons when my sons are tempted to complain, "Our mom sings Christian music on the road but she sure is stressed out at home!" I know I'll fall flat on my face again if I give in to my own anxious heart instead of trusting in our heavenly Father to take care of us. But I believe God is bigger than my fickle faith. He promises to be a strong tower and safe refuge in times of trouble, and I'm going to take Him at His Word!

Who's the most content Christian in your life? Invite them out for coffee or dinner and then dialogue about how they maintain a quiet spirit and peaceful heart.

Carolyn Custis James

The Lord God said, "It is not good for the man to be alone. I will make a helper [ezer] suitable for him." GENESIS 2:18 (NIV)

The creation of the woman was a showstopper. God disrupts his steady rhythm of creating, then declaring "It is good!" to draw attention to the woman and underscore man's need for her.

Obviously, *ezer* has a lot to do with the woman as wife and mother. I always thought that summed up what an *ezer* was meant to be, until I hit a ten-year stretch of singleness and wondered if I was missing God's calling for me. Then bigger questions surfaced.

Is God's blueprint for women too small? Too small to include the wife who never brings a baby to term or the ninety-year-old missionary who never married, but has poured herself into Christian ministry? Too small for any of us when we are young or for wives who end up on their own through death or divorce?

If *ezer* only means wife and mother then a lot of women (all of us at times) are, like Cinderella's stepsisters, trying to squeeze into a glass slipper that is hopelessly too small.

Ezer is a powerful Hebrew word used most often in the Old Testament for God Himself as the strong helper, the warrior who comes to the aid of His people. At creation God was launching the most ambitious enterprise ever: for His image bearers to speak and act for Him and to run things here His way. He calls us—male and female—to do this together in every sphere of life. No woman is excluded. Nor is any man. According to God's assessment, men and women need each other.

In the world, male/female relationships are often described as the battle of the sexes. But God calls us to something better—to deeply value each other, to bear each other's burdens, to build one another up in the body of Christ.

We have kingdom work to do. A world to reclaim for Jesus and His gospel. Our brothers need us, and we need them.

Linda Clare

The earth is the Lord's and the fullest thereof, the world and those who dwell therein. PSALM 24:1 (RSV)

Recently, I was out for a walk in my neighborhood and I accidentally dropped a gum wrapper on the street. A woman who must have noticed followed me for three blocks. When I arrived back at my own driveway, she handed me the wrapper as if I'd just clear-cut a stand of old growth timber. I apologized, but she sniffed, "I'll bet you don't even compost."

How did she know? I hung my head and rushed into the house.

I live in one of America's greenest cities—and not only from the substantial rainfall per year. Eugene, Oregon is a haven for those back-to-the-land folks from the '60s and '70s, complete with rainbow colored busses and tie-dyed T-shirts. Eugeneans take "green" very seriously.

Though I try my best to be eco-minded, I've got a long way to go.

God saw all of this coming, naturally. Throughout the Old Testament, God warns people to take care of Earth. And throughout history, we've messed up *terra firma* time and again.

Yet after the Great Flood, instead of punishment, God gave us a promise, a new covenant. Thinking about God's promise never to destroy the Earth again, I look around at the green place where I live. I thank God for it, but I know I must also act to help keep Oregon and everywhere else as beautiful as God made it.

Muppet Kermit the Frog used to say, "It's not easy being green." Years later, the whole world is scrambling to reverse or at least slow down climate change and global warming. I'm prayerfully learning all I can about how to preserve the resources so abundantly given to us by our Creator. At the very least, I'll never litter my neighborhood again.

Nancy Kane

We have this treasure in jars of clay to show that this all-surpassing power is from God and not from us. We always carry around in our body the death of Jesus, so that the life of Jesus may also be revealed in our body. 2 CORINTHIANS 4:7–10 (NIV)

I have some friends that I call the "Quiet Christians," the ones who live out St. Francis' often-quoted instruction, "Share the gospel at all times and when necessary use words." They rarely use words to articulate their faith but powerfully communicate the presence of Christ through sacrifice, service, and love. One of my colleagues at Moody is known for his gentle wisdom; he rarely speaks of himself and only offers an opinion when asked (and even then he seems uneasy). Or my neighbor, a retired high school teacher, who sacrificially and lovingly cares for his adult mentally disabled son. Or a friend of mine that took up residence in one of the poorest sections of Chicago because of her deep love for the homeless. Quiet Saints faithfully evidencing glory of Christ in the world around them.

I asked my quiet, wise colleague why he never spoke about himself. The question made him visibly uncomfortable. I jumped in and said that I thought it might have something to do with wanting to follow God's mandate to "consider others better than yourself." He glanced at me, shifted his feet, looked down, and said nothing. He knew that I had discovered the secret behind his actions. I had stumbled on a jewel of great price. At that moment I was standing on holy ground. It is difficult to describe the emotion that occurs when you see the workings of God revealed in someone else. Words escape me. Motivation to live differently stirs me.

Witnessing the presence of Christ in my friend's life only highlights to me the significance of who Christ can be in each one of us. The Scripture today reminds us of this. A treasure from God, His indwelling presence, the very Son of God being manifested in us.

Arloa Sutter

If you spend yourselves in behalf of the hungry and satisfy the needs of the oppressed, then your light will rise in the darkness, and your night will become like the noonday. The Lord will guide you always; he will satisfy your needs in a sun-scorched land and will strengthen your frame. You will be like a well-watered garden, like a spring whose waters never fail.

ISAIAH 58:10–11 (NIV)

In Isaiah 58 the children of Israel have a problem. They are fasting and praying and trying to get close to God, but it seems God isn't listening. They are eager for God to come near them, but God is far away.

God's response is surprising. In short, God instructs them to share their food with the hungry and to provide the poor wanderer with shelter. "Then you will call, and the Lord will answer," God says in Isaiah 58:9 (NIV).

Certainly the lives of those without food and shelter are made safer and more comfortable by the gifts of food, clothing and shelter, but this chapter says nothing about the outcome of such generosity on the lives of the poor. The chapter is all about what happens in the lives of givers when they open their hearts and hands to the poor.

When we care for the physical needs of the poor, *our* lives are changed. God hears *our* prayers and guides and strengthens us. *Our* light shines forth like the dawn and *we* become like a well-watered garden.

Do you want to be near God? How about volunteering at a ministry that intentionally builds relationships with broken people?

Ellie Lofaro

He brought them out of darkness and the deepest gloom and broke away their chains. Psalm 107:14 (NIV)

I spent an Easter weekend in prison. Not a lily, new hat, or pair of patent leather shoes in sight. No chocolate, no marshmallow chicks, no turkey dinners. I encountered endless country roads, bunker housing, large gates, a guard tower, the dogs, barbed wire with large razor blades—all ominous and yet strangely fitting for a gray and drizzly Good Friday. I have based my entire existence on the fact that Jesus rose from the dead and that all who believe will do the same. Perhaps some prisoners would be encouraged to hear His story. The prospect of speaking with the inmates face-to-face was somewhat intimidating. I took a long, deep breath before walking through the visitor's gate.

I passed through the metal detector and was then frisked and asked to remove my shoes. We proceeded down to a small gym with one section of bleachers. I learned earlier in the day that it was a medium security facility with three hundred fifty women. About two hundred of them opted to attend the program that night and as they streamed in from their cells, I was not prepared for what seemed like a cruel surprise. They were young. They were *so* young. They were well groomed and neatly dressed and they were pretty. *Lord, how can this be? It looks like a high school pep rally. What have they done? Where are their parents? Save them, Jesus.*

The program was powerful, the salvation message tearful, the brief conversations unforgettable, the Lord ever faithful. Many surrendered their heavy burdens that night and learned of a true love they had never known. Bondage to freedom. Darkness to light. Pain to comfort. Fear to peace. Some cried loudly from a hollow place I had never heard before. Some wept quietly. Some held friends tightly in a huddle and some dropped to their knees.

The resurrection of Jesus Christ changes everything. There will be many surprises in heaven. It was by far the best Easter I've ever had.

Leigh McLeroy

Why do you seek the living One among the dead? He is not here, but He has risen. LUKE 24:5–6 (NASB)

Johann Sebastian Bach's *The St. John Passion* was first performed on Good Friday in Leipzig, Germany, some 280 years ago. I heard it for the first time in a small Lutheran church in Texas. The libretto combines the text of John's gospel, stanzas of old church hymns, and poetry.

As the words were sung in German, I followed the English translation in my lap, but I could have closed it—and my eyes—and still understood.

Loud, angry cries of *Kreuzige ihn!* needed no footnote. I got it. And the music itself told me the moment my Lord said "It is finished!" Then a soprano voice sang these words: "Dissolve in tears my heart, in floods of weeping in honor of the Most High. Tell the earth and the heavens your anguish: Your Jesus is dead!"

That's as dark as it gets.

Have you ever been in utter, total, can't-see-your-hand-in-front-of-your-face dark? The kind of dark that makes you wonder if there'll ever be light again? Maybe the dark you remember is not physical dark, but darkness of another kind. Perhaps a moment when you lost something so precious that you thought the sun couldn't possibly bring itself to rise another time. Maybe then you thought, "This is as dark as it gets."

It wasn't.

"As dark as it gets" was when the Father's only Son breathed His final breath, and it looked like death had won. "As dark as it gets" was when communication ceased between God the Father and God the Son. "As dark as it gets" was a sealed tomb, a buried promise, and the empty hours between Friday and Sunday.

"Rest well, sacred limbs," the chorus sang as the music ended. "Sleep well, and bring me too, to rest." Rest well. "As dark as it gets" happened once. And it will never be that dark again.

Remember one of the "dark hours" of your life. Does it look any different to you in light of Jesus' death and resurrection?

Anita Lustrea

Suddenly, their eyes were opened, and they recognized him. And at that moment he disappeared! LUKE 24:31 (NLT)

Day after day, through Midday Connection, the radio program I cohost, I receive countless emails of tragedy and struggle and despair. I would throw in the towel if it weren't for one important truth. HE IS RISEN! That Jesus did what He said He would do, and rose from the dead, means we have hope. And this hope, the hope firmly planted in Jesus, does NOT disappoint.

So what does this Resurrection Day mean to us? What impact does it have on our everyday lives?

Just as the resurrected Jesus walked the road to Emmaus with two of His disciples, He walks with us on our road to the hospital for chemo, on the expressway to work for that difficult meeting, and on our journey through sleepless nights as we are on our knees praying for that prodigal child. Like His encounter with the disciples, sometimes we recognize Jesus, and sometimes we don't. He sends us journeying companions that sometimes come as a surprise. We see Jesus wrapped in the embrace of a compassionate friend when we're hurting, through a warm meal brought to our house after we've had surgery, and through the consistent prayers of that friend who means it when she says she's praying for you.

Ask God to help you to not lose heart on your journey, to help you to recognize His face and voice through those He sends as ministering servants.

How can we be the "Living Hope" to those in our world? How can we "Go and tell" both with words and with actions? Who has God placed directly in your path today for you to be the living expression of "He is Risen Indeed!"?

Shauna Niequist

He who rebukes a man will in the end gain more favor than he who has a flattering tongue. PROVERBS 28:23 (NIV)

I was very pregnant, and very behind on a book deadline when I sent a dramatic, complaining email to my friend Kirsten. Kirsten and I went to college together, and now she lives with her family in Alameda, a darling beachy hippie town across the bay from San Francisco.

I was trying to learn how to write, which would have been a great thing to do before signing a book contract, and it was harder than I thought it would be. I was bored and frustrated, and Kirsten is one of my oldest, best friends, a deeply creative, empathetic, soulful person. I thought that certainly she would tell me she loves me just as I am, and that all this nonsense about writing is overrated, and I should just make myself a snack and get in bed in with a novel if I feel like it.

The email she sent me back immediately—two pages long, single spaced—affected me so profoundly that I printed it right then and hung it next to my computer, and it hasn't moved since. She told me to stop thinking and start writing, and that real artists don't hide behind phrases like "I don't feel like it." She said that if I passed up this opportunity she would hate me a little bit forever. (At the end said she'd never hate me, but she wondered how I'd feel about myself if I didn't finish the book.)

I wanted her to coddle me, sympathize, send me out shoe shopping instead of all this boring, intense work. But she told me the truth, and it was an extraordinary gift. I've known her for more than ten years, and her friendship has shaped me in thousands of ways, but possibly never more than in that moment.

Are there voices in your life that will tell you the truth even when it's difficult to hear? Are you committed to truth-telling in your friendships? How have you demonstrated that commitment recently?

Victoria Saunders Johnson

Think about it! Talk it over. Do something! JUDGES 19:30 (MSG)

Most biblical scholars teach every word in the Bible is worth examination. No person or principle should be ignored. Yet, I'm still waiting to hear a teaching on the passage in Judges 19–21. There lies a dead woman. I imagine her to be young—maybe even a teenager. Cause of death: a brutal sexual attack. Sounds like a story you'd read on the Internet in our time, but not in the Israel Daily News.

But here she is. Her story crying out for explanation/application. So many women, children and yes—even men suffer the devastating long-range effects of sexual assault. Teen pregnancy, criminal behavior, divorce, learning disabilities, depression—the list is endless of social, emotional, and spiritual ills which find their roots in sexual abuse. These precious ones are attempting to live out their lives but engulfed in shame and brokenness. Right here in America there are thirty nine million sexual assault survivors. This statistic is probably larger because so many sufferers *never* tell.

Because of the silence of our society, our churches, even our mothers—victims sometimes think God is silent too. Not true. He parades before us the sexually hurting lives of Lot, Tamar, Bathsheba, Dinah, and others. Their sexually ravished lives are in full view. God has not forgotten. He's surrounded their stories with lessons, warnings, and most of all comfort.

Perhaps you are one who looks at your sexuality and finds nothing there but a pile of shattered pieces. If so, my prayer for you is this: "Lord, give this wounded one courage to flip the pages of Your book, and find soothing salve to warm hurting places. May she find hope and healing from You."

Now, find a before healing and after healing photo or magazine picture to post in a visible place in your home.

Miriam Neff

Do not be conformed to this world, but be transformed.
ROMANS 12:2 (ASB)

Crisis has struck! Your life is changed forever. You may see it as shambles. Your home may be destroyed, or your marriage, your career, your health, or your child's future. Tragedy comes in all shapes and sizes. Sometimes we help it happen by our own missteps. Sometimes it is just the fallout of living on this earth. What happens next?

When my husband, Bob, died I wanted to hibernate in a cocoon of grief and despair. I wanted someone else to fix my problems, repair my house, and manage my finances while I clung to the past and grieved the future I'd never experience.

But God had a different plan. The One who created us is a transformation specialist. And He began to show up in my life in new ways. A sense of mission started to renew my spirit as I looked into the eyes of widows in Africa, women who had more cause to grieve than I. Hope started to lift my heart as a sailed solo on a catamaran over the incredibly blue ocean He created. (Bob would be proud!) Comfort seeped through my soul as I passed on to newer widows the encouragement He had given me in those first days and months. None of these were miraculous solutions to my problems. He was changing me from the inside out to live fully in my new life.

He was transforming my future into a life I eagerly anticipated, not in spite of my loss, but because of it. Grief and despair were giving way to a sense of adventure. Rather than being resigned to looking backward, an uncharacteristic boldness defined my steps into the unknown.

Conformity? No, thank you. Transformation? I'll take it!

You don't have to wait for widowhood to be transformed. Try something new today. Hike a new trail. Volunteer for a new cause that is close to your heart.

Susie Larson

But I have stilled and quieted myself, just as a small child is quiet with its mother. Yes, like a small child is my soul within me. Psalm 131:2 (NLT)

When my sons were babies, one of my favorite pastimes was holding them close and watching them sleep. The steady rise and fall of their chest, their little hands curled around my fingers, and the peace on their faces, told me that all was well in their world.

One of the reasons God wants us close is so He can assure us of His great love and care for us.

During times of favor it's easy to loosen our grip and rely on our own wit and wisdom. When the storm comes and the ground shakes beneath our feet, we become disoriented and wonder why peace seems so far out of reach.

The beautiful thing is that though we wander or look the other way, peace is only a prayer away.

When Peter stepped out of the boat, he walked on water. *He walked on water.*

Not only was Peace his friend, Peter got to *walk out* a miracle.

He took His eyes off of Peace because he was distracted by the storm, and what happened as a result?

He was no longer held up by Power, he was weighed down by worry.

We must not give more weight to the storms than we do the One whom the storms obey.

We all know that the storms will come, and then they'll pass.

The goal is to be so closely identified with Jesus that we are able to quiet our soul—like a still small child—and rest with Him. When the storms threaten us, we can call out to Jesus to give us peace, knowing too that He'll eventually calm the storm.

Wherever life finds you today, be still, and know that He is your God.

Memorize the following verses: Psalm 46:10, Psalm 91:1.

Melinda Schmidt

"See, I am doing a ***new thing****!"* ISAIAH 43:19 (NIV), emphasis added

Outside, a new season was trying to be birthed but winter was engaging it in a tug-of-war. Barren branches and gray skies struggled with crocus, bits of green in the lawn, and fluctuating temperatures hoping to signal spring.

I was trying to embrace hope in God's "new thing," this time in a job shift I'd be entering within the month. My heart was filled with emotion as I struggled with leaving a beloved team and its goals, yet at peace anticipating new workplace responsibilities.

A coworker had prayed that afternoon, "Help Melinda to not just miss us, but to anticipate with joy what is ahead." Oh, I needed that. Always there is the temptation to dwell in what we must leave behind as we take on the new unknown. Second-guessing ourselves, we often forget the pleasure of the beautiful prose of Isaiah 43:19 and the truth and hope of it.

And with good reason—taking on something new means leaving something else behind. Good or bad, it's still the familiar, known, safe. Often it is a relief to leave behind; we thank God for the new path that has been made for us. That prayer jolted me and I knew I had the *choice* to believe that much good lay ahead of me, much accomplishment, new people and experiences, even satisfaction and joy.

Autumn *appeared* to lurk outside, but the calendar read *April.* My own struggle had to bow to truth—the days ahead promised new life!

Read Isaiah 43:18–19. Write it in your journal, again on a sticky note, wherever you will need to be reminded that God is bringing spring—something new—to you!

Lisa McKay

May the God of hope fill you with all joy and peace as you trust in him, so that you may overflow with hope by the power of the Holy Spirit. ROMANS 15:13 (NIV)

I am the director of training for a nonprofit that provides psychological and spiritual support to humanitarian workers around the world. This means I often find myself in places like Kenya and Ghana, working with people who have some of the toughest jobs you can imagine—providing relief in Darfur, for example, or interviewing the many thousands of desperate people who are applying for refugee status and a chance to leave the camps. Humanitarian workers in these situations see and hear about more human misery in a year than many encounter in a lifetime.

My job is to facilitate workshops that help humanitarian workers think about stress, trauma, and thriving in the face of these pressures—how to best cope with the inevitable challenges to the way they see the world, themselves, and God. Assaults to their deepest sense of meaning, purpose, and hope are some of the most significant challenges humanitarian workers will face in their work.

I have thought a lot lately about this topic of hope. We often talk of faith, hope, and love in the same breath. But of these three I think hope can be the overlooked middle child. And you do not have to live and work in a refugee camp to face many challenges to your sense of hope. These questions I frequently ask humanitarian workers: What does hope mean to you? What does it look like? Where do you find it most often? These are just as relevant for those of us who don't face such extreme circumstances.

Today, think about how God is a "God of hope" to you. What about the way that we are thinking, feeling, and acting would spell "overflowing with hope"? And what else does this verse from Romans have to say about sources of hope?

Kristen Johnson Ingram

. . . we are the people of His pasture and the sheep of His hand.
PSALM 95:7 (NASB)

We owned a lamb once who was opposed to any form of physical connection with us. We fed her every day, but if while she was munching grain from the manger we reached out to caress her woolly head, she bolted. She actually preferred the company of my son's seventeen-hand thoroughbred horse, and often grazed standing under him. The first time we had her sheared, it took us nearly an hour to capture her, throw a burlap sack over her head, and lead her to the shearing shed.

My favorite childhood pictures were of Jesus as the Good Shepherd, carrying a lamb over his shoulders. The sheep of his hand. The one he stroked and touched and loved. It wasn't until we owned our crazy antisocial lamb that I realized that to be the sheep of Christ's hand means being *willing* to be loved.

I'm a woman who tries to hang her own curtains and do up her back buttons. I have my own toolbox, my own electric drill, and I've been driving a car since I was thirteen. Without much effort, I can convince myself that I'm totally self-sufficient. But I need to be carried by the Savior of the world.

Today, pray to Jesus, the Good Shepherd, that when He takes you from the world, He will let you ride home on His shoulders. Surrender to Him.

Tonight at dinner, recite the Twenty-third Psalm as a grace before eating.

Anita Lustrea

Happy is he that hath the God of Jacob for his help, whose hope is in the Lord his God. PSALM 146:5 (KJV)

I recently listened to a friend of mine speak at a Bible conference. One of the thoughts that she put forth was about humanity's unending pursuit of happiness. It doesn't take long to think of how we try to buy happiness. The entire entertainment industry is built on the assumption that people will always be looking for happiness and therefore need to be entertained, to engage in activities that "make them happy." The sports industry is a billion-plus-dollar business. We buy tickets and concessions all to watch someone else play a game. We even try to develop relationships that, we think, will be the key to our happiness. It seems we will go to almost any length to obtain happiness. It's even written into our Constitution. What does God's Word say about all this? Psalm 146:5 (KJV) reads, "Happy is he . . . whose hope is in the Lord." That seems like such a simplistic statement, at least it does compared to the ways we try to find or make happiness. What does having hope in the Lord really mean? To hope means to expect, trust, anticipate, wish, look forward to. We have a future and that future is wrapped up with salvation and freedom and new life. It is filled with mercy and grace and love beyond measure. When compared to watching a movie or a basketball game, or skydiving, it's easy to see what's real. We try to manufacture happiness, but as we seek Jesus' face and His ways, that is reality and the only place "real" happiness can be found.

Do a self-assessment. What are those things in your life that you find yourself running to for happiness, or to make you "feel" better? Then go online, or to a concordance and do a word search on *hope*. Find some key verses that speak directly to you and then revel in the hope, the lasting hope we have in the Lord.

Tiffany Taylor

O Lord my God, I called to you for help and you healed me.

PSALM 30:2 (NIV)

On one of my trips to orphanages in Guatemala I met a beautiful six-year-old girl named Isabella. She had suffered neglect and abuse from her mother. Like most six-year-old girls, Isabella loved wearing fancy dresses and the orphanage staff said she had insisted on wearing a white frilly dress that day because she wanted to look beautiful for the American visitors. Isabella formed a fast attachment to me and took me on a tour of the orphanage. We saw the kitchen, the playroom, and the room where her bed was lined up next to all the other little beds.

Her tour ended with Isabella showing me the steps where she'd fallen down that morning and bumped her knee. She then asked me if I had a Band-Aid for her scratch. I took out a small bag of Band-Aids and placed one on her knee. Immediately she started pointing out other spots she wanted a Band-Aid. I was happy to place a Band-Aid anywhere she wanted. As she began to show me all her little "boo-boos" her eyes filled with tears and she said in a small voice, "Sometimes my mommy would hurt me." Then the tears began to fall as she said, "Why did Mommy do that? Why has she left me here all alone?" It broke my heart to realize she had hurts that no Band-Aid was big enough to cover. I held this sweet girl and wiped her tears and let her know that there was one God that could heal all that hurt her. He was a Father who loved her and had not left her.

We all have hurts deep inside that we want to cover up on a temporary basis but God wants us to call to Him for help so He can heal us. Instead of covering that hurt today, try writing it down and then giving it to God to heal. He is there for Isabella and He is there for you too.

Linda Clare

Pray without ceasing. 1 THESSALONIANS 5:17 (KJV)

In the summer of 1968, I was a teenager when I heard about a revival coming to town. When I mentioned wanting to see what one was like, Dad said, "You don't want to go to one of those Holy-Rollers places. All kinds of crazy stuff happens." This only made me want to see for myself. Without my parents' knowledge or consent, I attended the tent revival.

Inside the stifling-hot tent, I sat on a folding chair, disappointed. People around me weren't doing anything crazy. Most of the audience were boring grown-ups. Women in beehive hairdos, clutching Bibles. Somber men in dark coats and ties. Not another teen as far as I could see. Nobody rolling, either.

Swept up with the rest, I sang a few gospel songs. The beehive hairdos started to bob, the men clapped. I hadn't seen people so excited since I'd gone to a Beach Boys rock concert. The preacher hushed the crowd. He wanted everybody to pray. Some lifted their hands—something I'd never seen—while others swayed with their eyes closed, tears running down their cheeks. Soon the air buzzed with invisible energy.

Nobody rolled that night. But I experienced the holy. Before I left I prayed with my whole body—not just by bowing my head and folding my hands. Although Dad called the revivalists "crazy," I came away believing God honors any way we pray.

When you pray, maybe you kneel, lift your hands or use a prayer book. At the very least you probably bow your head and say "Amen." Yet why stop there? Everything we do can be a prayer: walking, waiting, dancing, singing, and even breathing. Have you ever thought of making your very *being* a prayer?

Try praying using a different method every day for a week. Keep a journal of how you experience God in each method.

Ellie Kay

The righteous man will flourish like the palm tree. He will grow like a cedar in Lebanon. PSALM 92:12 (NASB)

When our son, Robert Philip, Jr., was going through the turbulent early teen years, we never knew who would wake up that morning: our fabulous son, Philip, or the Phantom Menace, "Robert." There were teachers at his school who actually thought "Robert" and "Philip" were look alike brothers (and one was the evil twin.) When Philip stuck around all day—it was a good day.

I think we're not all that different from Philip, in regard to the idea of measuring "good" and "bad" days. Wouldn't it be great to look back on your day and say "Today was good and productive"? I have found that if we begin our morning by seeking God's involvement in every part of our lives, then we can expect Him to bless our day.

Today's Scripture talks about a palm tree that provides nourishment through its fruit and a sheltering shade to those who lie beneath it. The cedars of Lebanon were renowned for their fragrance, and the quality of the wood. The elements of fruit, shade, fragrance and quality are all ways in which a righteous man flourishes. We trust God to develop fruit out of our lives, we allow Him to be our sheltering shade when the rays of adversity threaten to scorch us, we offer a sacrifice of praise which is a sweet smelling aroma to Him, and we seek excellence in the quality of our work. What a great analogy to take with us as we walk with God today.

Today, ask the Lord to walk with you, to let you be a blessing to those who need kind words, a smile, or a gentle touch from Him.

Lori Neff

The Lord is close to the brokenhearted and saves those who are crushed in spirit. PSALM 34:18 (NIV)

I'm coming out of six months of darkness. My husband noticed my lack of energy and interest in things I used to enjoy. He encouraged me to visit a doctor to see if I was depressed. While I've always been quick to encourage others to visit a doctor if they suspect they need help coming out of depression, I was terrified. I felt like a failure. Why had I struggled with depression most of my life? Why couldn't I shake this off? Why wasn't I living a victorious Christian life? I searched online for the symptoms of depression and I was shocked to find that I had just about every symptom listed.

A week later, I walked into the doctor's office in trepidation. Would he tell me this was nothing and I'd have to figure out how to survive in this dark hole forever? After talking with the doctor for an hour, he gently told me that I must have a high threshold for pain. He told me that I had been suffering with severe depression and he recommended medication. I cried with relief—he had put words to my pain and I could no longer deny it. As I left the doctor's office, I felt a tiny flicker of hope. I decided to try medication; I feel like I'm seeing things more clearly and have more strength to handle the difficult issues with a counselor. This experience has helped me understand why others hesitate to get help. I understand that it can be hard to believe you can't muscle your way through. I'm so thankful that God put people in my life who encouraged me to get help.

If you believe someone you love might be depressed, gently talk with them about getting help (counselor or doctor) and that you love them no matter what.

Anita Lustrea

For everyone has sinned; we all fall short of God's glorious standard. ROMANS 3:23 (NLT)

When I think of violence, nothing positive enters my mind. And yet, if I were to hear each of your stories, I'm sure that I would hear about a violent grace from many of you. Henry Blackaby says, "God knows full well the appalling destructiveness of sin. He knows what sin has done to us; how it hurts and impairs us. In the cross he made complete and total provision for every aspect of what sin has done or ever could do." God through Christ's death on the cross radically and ruthlessly, yes violently dealt with sin. It was his violent grace. Take a moment to read Romans 3:23–25a (NLT) reads, "For everyone has sinned; we all fall short of God's glorious standard. Yet God, with undeserved kindness, declares that we are righteous. He did this through Christ Jesus when he freed us from the penalty for our sins. For God presented Jesus as the sacrifice for sin. People are made right with God when they believe that Jesus sacrificed his life, shedding his blood."

I can point to several moments of violent grace in my own life. There have been times when life seemed to be completely falling apart. Yet as I look back I see the loving, grace filled hand of God using those violent moments to move me to a new place of trust and reliance on Him. That deeper place of faith would not exist in me apart from those moments of "severe mercy" as author Sheldon VanAuken calls it.

Spend some time thinking about those violent grace moments, those severe mercy moments that have come into your life. Can you see God's hand conforming you to the image of His Son? Pick one of your favorite worship choruses or hymns and sing it to the Lord in praise for what He's done in your life through those difficult moments. The quality of your voice doesn't matter . . . it's all about the heart.

Nancy Sebastian Meyer

I know whom I have believed, and am convinced that he is able to guard what I have entrusted to him for that day.
2 Timothy 1:12 (NIV)

I know. I believe. I am convinced. These powerful concepts bespeak absolute truth. Is there such a thing? The world will say no. I say yes! Without the truth in this verse, what matters? On the other hand, agreement with this verse empowers and liberates the believer.

The apostle Paul, who saw the shining light and heard the voice of God on the way to Damascus, penned these words. Can I question an eyewitness? On the contrary, when I claim this truth as my experience too, it resonates in my mind and brings a unique confidence that cannot be shaken.

Has there ever been a situation in which I didn't feel God was with me? In the midst of my earthly existence, His invisible presence can go unnoticed. But even when I cannot see Him in a situation or feel Him in my heart, I know in my mind that He is with me. My decision to believe in God gives me hope when I don't feel like God is near and peace when I can't see His answer to a problem. "I know" makes up for "I can't feel" and "I can't see." The secret is in believing truth.

Romans 12:2 tells us we become transformed by the renewing of our minds. Certainly as we learn more about God from His Word and His world, our experience begins to affirm this knowledge that *God is!*

Choose to believe God today and watch for evidence of His presence in answered prayer and in the world around you. Remember to watch for Him with a mind that believes, not with a thought that God must prove Himself to you.

Pam Farrel

You did not choose Me but I chose you, and appointed you that you would go and bear fruit, and that your fruit would remain, so that whatever you ask of the Father in My name He may give to you. JOHN 15:16 (NASB)

As a director of women's ministry for more than fifteen years, I have noticed how much stress women in midlife and beyond were carrying:

- Dealing with tweens and teens, or launching kids into college, or careers.
- Bonus babies after forty (hot flashes and toddlers!).
- Husbands in midlife (which at times lead to unexpected divorce).
- Health issues (their own, a husband's, or caring for their aging parents).
- Career or volunteer success so everyone wants a piece of their time.
- Money flying out to pay for graduations, proms, college, cars, or weddings.
- Multiplied relationships: new sons- or daughters-in-law, and in-laws that come with them, and the delight of grandchildren.

These midlife and beyond women were holding up the world! One morning God asked me, "Pam, who's holding them up?" I couldn't think of one ministry at the time dedicated to reaching and ministering to the more than forty-three million Boomer women (*Time* magazine 5/16/05).

I had started a group called Seasoned Sisters for myself and my friends because we were dealing with all these issues, but now God was asking me to make it available around the world. I felt my plate was already full, but God kept replaying the verse above that I memorized years ago as a student.

I felt God impress upon me, "I want a ministry that helps women have a *Fantastic After 40* life. They just need a little TLC. Are you willing?"

If *anyone* else would have asked, I would have said, "I'm too busy." But I simply could not be too busy for the Savoir who is never too busy for me.

What do you want etched in your epitaph. What legacy will you leave behind? We live out our legacy each day, who and what are you investing in that will last beyond you?

Lisa Harper

And I will give you a new heart, and a new spirit I will put within you. And I will remove the heart of stone from your flesh and give you a heart of flesh. EZEKIEL 36:26 (ESV)

I considered using luggage as a weapon recently. Not to inflict mass destruction but to shush a man on the airport shuttle bus! He was one of those rude cell phone users who didn't care how his midnight bellowing impacted anyone else. The passenger sitting beside him even had his fingers jammed in his ears but Mr. Loudmouth just kept jabbering. And that's when I thought about whacking him in the shin with my Samsonite!

You've probably been in a similar situation. Maybe with a shrill woman who complains constantly in your Bible study small group or a bossy relative with whom you have to hang out on a regular basis. Perhaps you've considered poking them! Frankly I think Christians who *never* experience negative feelings are the people who might have a problem.

Let me explain.

Not too long ago I had dinner with a good friend and her family. She and her husband were unfailingly polite; dinner conversation was pleasant and they didn't raise their voices when their kids spilled food. But when we were alone the walls of "appropriate" behavior came crashing down and she wept over the lack of emotion in her marriage. She said their "peace" was actually whitewashed indifference. She longed for a *real* relationship, warts and all.

What about you? Do you feel like you're just going through the motions? Has the low-grade fever of apathy begun to weaken your heart for God and others?

If so, maybe it's time to schedule divine surgery.

Take a long walk in the park. Watch a movie that makes you laugh so hard you cry. Indulge in a few pieces of dark chocolate. And ask the Holy Spirit to help you cultivate a healthy, authentic heart.

Adele Calhoun

Although he was a son, he learned obedience through what he suffered. And being made perfect, he became the source of eternal salvation to all who obey him. HEBREWS 5:8–9 (ESV)

Embracing the path Jesus walked is not simply a matter of praying a prayer and then skipping to the empty cross and resurrection. Following Jesus means planting ourselves in Jesus' earthly life with the reality of temptation, learning obedience and being made perfect through suffering. Most of us would rather "follow our bliss" than be "made perfect" through suffering. But if Jesus had to be made perfect through suffering how can we possibly believe that our growth lies outside trials, ridicule, loss, loneliness, hardship, and pain?

But there is always a choice. Adam and Eve chose to believe the serpent's suggestion that God was withholding good. Neither Adam nor Eve denied themselves. Eve didn't choose to face the ridicule of the serpent, forgo the fruit, and defend God's honor. Adam didn't choose to face Eve's ridicule and side with God. Neither one was willing to suffer for love of God. Neither one chose to love God above what they couldn't understand.

But what Adam and Eve lost in one garden by failing to suffer for one tree, Jesus regains by suffering on another tree. In suffering we live into solidarity with Jesus. If Jesus could be humble, trusting, patient, and good in his hardships, we too can day by day be more and more transformed and perfected into the likeness of Jesus.

How does living in solidarity with Jesus help us learn to forgive or love our enemies? What in you needs to unite to Jesus' own path of suffering? How would seeing your life in the life of Jesus give you a new sense of meaning and purpose?

Melinda Schmidt

But the fruit of the Spirit is love, joy, peace, patience, kindness, goodness, faithfulness, gentleness and self-control. Against such things there is no law. . . Since we live by the Spirit, let us keep in step with the Spirit. GALATIANS 5:22–23, 25 (NIV)

Chuck Swindoll once said, "Being totally committed to Christ's increase . . . means letting our lives act as a frame that shows up the masterpiece—Jesus Christ. And a worthy frame isn't tarnished or dull, plain or cheap; yet neither is it so elaborate that it overpowers its picture. Instead, with subtle loveliness, it draws the observer's eyes to the beautiful work of art it displays."

Frames enclose priceless treasures. Frames contain the canvas of the masterpieces of great museums. Your Bible's cover enfolds and frames the very words of God. Beautiful wrapping paper surrounds a treasure of love handpicked for you.

If you are looking for a sense of purpose today, consider being a frame for Jesus Christ, whose character shines out of it for all who stand before it. When you do that, the characteristics of Christ—including humility, love, unselfishness, complete trust in God and His capabilities, and a serving attitude—will be seen by others and you will have been as the finest framing materials of the ages, enclosing the greatest Love the world has ever been given.

Today, you don't have to be the art, you just need to *frame* the art. As the Lord's character increases within your soul, you will exhibit God Himself. What is one thing you could show a waiting world today?

Nicole Bromley

People were bringing little children to Jesus to have him touch them, but the disciples rebuked them. When Jesus saw this, he was indignant. He said to them, "Let the little children come to me, and do not hinder them, for the kingdom of God belongs to such as these. I tell you the truth, anyone who will not receive the kingdom of God like a little child will never enter it." And he took the children in his arms, put his hands on them and blessed them. MARK 10:13–16 (NIV)

Children today are starving for that pure, tender touch of God's love. Abuse and neglect are a major epidemic affecting our children, and like Jesus, we should be indignant about it. Unfortunately we often sweep these issues under the rug, causing little kids to grow up into big kids with pain from the past shaping their lives. Jesus was outraged when children were held back from receiving His love. We should be too.

Jesus doesn't simply get angry at those who keep children from Him; He is compassionate to the children, welcoming them into His arms. No matter our age, we all long to be taken up in His safe embrace. As we heal from the pain of our past, we need a genuine encounter with the love of Jesus Christ.

The child who you once were is still there, buried under layers of adult anxieties, responsibilities, and hardness that comes through disappointment. Deep inside we hunger for Jesus to take us up in His arms and speak a word of blessing on us, telling us we are precious and that He delights to call us His child.

Run into His outstretched arms. He is calling you by name. He longs to bless you.

Spend time relaxing in His safe and loving embrace. Allow yourself to be a child again. Using crayons or paint, create a picture or journal a prayer to the Lord.

Melinda Schmidt

Do not let your hearts be troubled. Trust in God; trust also in me. In my Father's house are many rooms; if it were not so, I would have told you. I am going there to prepare a place for you. And if I go and prepare a place for you, I will come back and take you to be with me that you also may be where I am.
JOHN 14:1–3 (NIV)

I have a friend who has no regard for fiction with happy endings, the kind where everything comes together in the end and everyone lives happily ever after. She particularly finds it offensive in Christian fiction.

Personally, I find a feel-good story a welcome break from a hard day. Sure, a steady diet can be a negative coping skill. Great joys and feelings of accomplishment come in doing the harder work of reading classic literature. You'll pull out the yellow highlighter and mark up many a page of a classic book more than you might a current piece of fiction.

A desire for happy endings is God-given, as we long for eternity with Him in satisfying relationship, praising Him, knowing Him fully, intimately, indeed happily ever after.

In your desire for happy endings this side of heaven, ask yourself: Am I jealous that it isn't this way for me? Do I need to confess my envious spirit to the Lord? Journal those real thoughts and ask the Holy Spirit to bring truth to you about your desires. What changes might you make to your character that would bring the happiness you desire to your world and community? Do a word study on the word *hope* in the Bible.

Ask God to help you to be aware of the books, music, and movies you take in and why and to regularly do the soul work that makes you live truthfully before both yourself and God.

Shaunti Feldhahn

Do nothing out of selfish ambition or vain conceit, but in humility consider others better than yourselves. Each of you should look not only to your own interests, but also to the interests of others. PHILIPPIANS 2:3–4 (NIV)

Most of us know that we may have some selfish tendencies, but when it comes to the man in our life—our husband, or perhaps a special man we're dating—most of us try not to be selfish. We try to show him just how much we care, by saying "I love you" and trying to help and serve him. We are usually good at showing love.

The problem is, we often don't realize that men have a very different primary need than we do—and we never realize we *aren't* really looking out for their true interests.

God has put into men a deep need to feel respected even more than loved. Ephesians 5:33 tells them to *love* us, but commands us to *respect* them. Just as you would be crushed if your husband stopped saying I love you and showing his love for you, in the same way, our man needs us to avoid the temptation to be critical, to tell him what to do, to question his decisions. In other words, our man needs us to choose to unconditionally demonstrate respect. That's right—respect without strings attached . . . the way we expect to be loved!

No, he doesn't always deserve respect. Then again, we're not always lovable, are we? It takes work, because showing that kind of respect doesn't come as easily to us as showing love, but it's still important and necessary.

As you go through your day today, look out for his interests by looking for opportunities to show respect, to say "I'm proud of you," to trust him. In turn, his heart will be touched, and you will reap blessings for your efforts.

Best of all, your *marriage* will reap blessings. God made sure it was worth the effort!

Anita Lustrea

In the beginning was the Word, and the Word was with God, and the Word was God. JOHN 1:1 (NIV)

Have you ever been so busy doing things for God that you haven't had time just to be in His presence? To be with the Word and in the Word? Take a look at these Scripture passages that focus on the Word of God, beginning with John 1:1 (NIV). "In the beginning was the Word, and the Word was with God, and the Word was God"

"Every Word of God is flawless; he is a shield to those who take refuge in him" (Proverbs 30:5 NIV).

"The grass withers and the flowers fall, but the word of our God stands forever" (Isaiah 40:8 NIV).

"For the word of the Lord is right and true; he is faithful in all he does" (Psalm 33:4 NIV).

"Your word, O Lord, is eternal; it stands firm in the heavens" (Psalm 119:89 NIV).

"Your word is a lamp to my feet and a light for my path" (Psalm 119:105 NIV).

"The Word became flesh and made his dwelling among us. We have seen his glory, the glory of the one and only, who came from the Father, full of grace and truth" (John 1:14 NIV).

"For the Word of God is living and active. Sharper than any double-edged sword, it penetrates even to dividing soul and spirit, joints and marrow; it judges the thoughts and attitudes of the heart" (Hebrews 4:12 NIV).

"Let the word of Christ dwell in you richly as you teach and admonish one another with all wisdom, and as you sing psalms, hymns, and spiritual songs with gratitude in your hearts to God" (Colossians 3:16 NIV).

"He is dressed in a robe dipped in blood, and his name is the Word of God" (Revelation 19:13 NIV).

Today, be in His presence and soak in the Word! Just take one of the verses you just read and sit with it and give praise to God for the written Word and for Jesus, the living Word.

Kathy Koch

I praise you because I am fearfully and wonderfully made;
your works are wonderful, I know that full well.
Psalm 139:14 (NIV)

At the end of another day of preschool, Luka's mom asked him what he liked best about his day. He thought awhile, perhaps reviewing his day. Then he looked up into his mom's expectant eyes, smiled, and confidently responded, "Being Luka."

Isn't that great? If only every child (and adult) enjoyed being himself or herself and was able to be. Luka has clearly been raised in a positive environment where he's able to like himself and be himself. The freedom to be who he was created to be is rich. Affirming children's strengths and helping to develop them are a parent's privilege and joy. Luka's parents have done that for him.

When children believe a personal God made them the way He wanted them to be—fearfully and wonderfully, set apart for His purposes—they'll be more comfortable in their own skin. They'll more confidently live and learn in the present and approach the future.

Our Creator, God, made us the way He wanted us to be, on purpose with purpose. Believing this is essential to our choice to become who He wanted us to be when He chose in His love to make us us.

When Luka's mom asked him what he wanted to be when he grew up, after thinking just a little while, he answered, "Luka."

Why do you think God made you the way He did? Ask Him to show you more about why you are the way you are. Then spend some time thanking Him.

Joanne Heim

Finally, brothers, whatever is true, whatever is noble, whatever is right, whatever is pure, whatever is lovely, whatever is admirable—if anything is excellent or praiseworthy—think about such things. PHILIPPIANS 4:8 (NIV)

We've heard a lot about this verse around my house this year. It's the theme for the year at school, and so my children had to memorize it when school began. And in helping them learn it, I learned it too.

We've talked a lot about what each of those words mean—true, noble, right, pure—and about the connection between what we think about and what we say. If we're thinking about things that are excellent and admirable, then excellent and admirable tends to describe the words that come out of our mouths.

It's also important to think about these things, as the apostle Paul instructs, because what we think about also affects how we feel. If I'm thinking lovely and praiseworthy things about someone, then that's also going to describe how I'm feeling toward her.

Thoughts, feelings, words, actions. One leads to another. What we *think* is vitally important and has a huge effect on our lives. Of course, it can be hard to change our thoughts—old patterns of thinking get to be habit, and habits are hard to break. But part of loving God is loving him *with all our minds*—and he can change how we think when we ask.

Who are you having trouble thinking good thoughts about? Ask God to fill your mind with thoughts that are true, noble, right, pure, lovely, admirable, excellent, and praiseworthy. If a thought pops into your head that doesn't fit the list, throw it out and replace it with one that does.

Here's the way I memorized this verse. A friend told me to remember this: TNR PLA EP. Tenor play ep. Just like it sounds. Since then, I've never forgotten it and never leave one out of the list!

Anita Lustrea

I have given you authority to trample on snakes and scorpions and to overcome all the power of the enemy; nothing will harm you. However, do not rejoice that the spirits submit to you, but rejoice that your names are written in heaven.
Luke 10:19–20 (NIV)

When I speak to women about knowing and telling their story, I ask them to do a brief exercise. I ask them to remember any childhood nicknames they were given. I ask them to share those with other women sitting near them. Most often they are funny and cute. I've heard "Stinky," and "Twinkle Toes" and some other fun ones. My maiden name is Fore and my elementary school classmates thought they were so clever by calling me "Five."

The nicknames that don't get talked about are ones like "Black Sheep," "Tubby," "Clumsy." Those are the kind of names that hurt. Dan Allender has written a wonderful book titled, *To Be Told.* What he does in the book is walk you through how to write and tell your story.

He talks about the fact that most of us received names in our family of origin, and they weren't always good names. Whether it was siblings, parents, or friends who named us, only God knows our true name. And as the story of our life unfolds, so does the theme of our life. And as you discover your life theme, the message that you proclaim is that much stronger.

The theme of my life is freedom, and my main purpose in life is to communicate freedom to women.

What's your story? It might take some digging and some interior work, but it will be worth discovering your story so you can tell others the great things God has done.

Glynnis Whitwer

Now you are the body of Christ, and each one of you is a part of it. 1 CORINTHIANS 12:27 (NIV)

I grew up a freckle-faced brunette in a neighborhood of blonds—thirteen of them. To say I stood out in the crowd was an understatement. Normally it didn't matter to any of us, except when we played Big Valley.

In the late '60s, the *Big Valley* was a popular television show. As little kids we would reenact the various episodes and inevitably, there was an argument over who would get to play Audra Barkley.

Audra was the beautiful daughter, who was fussed over by her mama and pampered by her three handsome brothers. As much as I would have liked to play Audra, that wasn't an option. You see, Audra had long, *blonde* hair. I did, however, get a part. I was Nick, the dark-haired troublemaking brother.

It hurts to be left out, or relegated to a role that doesn't fit, whatever age you are. What I love about God's kingdom here on earth is that everybody gets to play! And we get to play a part specifically designed for us.

Each of us is called to serve God in a wonderfully unique way. God gives us skills and talents at birth, and then calls us into service. Once we say "yes," God fine-tunes our skills and increases them according to our faithfulness in using them. I have learned that others probably won't identify what makes me unique. Only I can discover my God-given gifts and talents and surrender them to God and His purposes.

Although my days of the *Big Valley* and playing Nick are past, I'll never forget feeling out of place, and longing to play another role. God's kingdom is big enough for each of us to fulfill the calling God has for us—and play our own brand of "Audra."

Identify one of your God-given talents (something that comes naturally to you). What holds you back from using this talent more fully?

Ellie Kay

Her children rise up and call her blessed;
Her husband, also, and he praises her.
PROVERBS 31:28 (NIV)

Ask any mother on the first day of school, after a long summer with stir-crazy kids if she's feeling "blessed" by her children. She might give a hearty response of, "Um . . . I'm blessed that they're going back to school?" Today's verse is so important because it gives a benchmark for moms that is an encouragement during the difficult seasons of mothering.

Is this Scripture saying that if your husband and children don't regularly "bless" you, then you have somehow failed to meet the mark? No, it simply describes an eternal perspective of an earthly mission. The context of this important verse is found in Proverbs 31, the "Virtuous Woman" chapter. One tired mom called it "the Virtually Impossible Woman." But if this Scripture is viewed as a goal rather than a reality, then we can see the significance of the passage—that one day, our kids and husband will see the long-lasting value in those long days and seasons of mothering.

Verbal praise isn't the only way that family members bless mom. A young child's spontaneous hug, a heartfelt "I love you, Mom," from a teenager, and a request for advice from an adult child are various forms of the "blessed" found in this verse. While this Scripture doesn't guarantee that the blessed mom will always *feel* blessed, it does give reason to keep moving forward in the joyous job of mothering—even in the middle of a long summer break!

Think of the different ways that your children and husband have called you blessed—through actions, words, and gifts. Then purpose to continue to try and be the kind of mom they can praise.

Linda Mintle

Honor your father and your mother, as the Lord your God has commanded you, so that you may live long and that it may go well with you in the land the Lord your God is giving you.
DEUTERONOMY 5:16 (NIV)

"I love my mom but . . ." You fill in the blank. We can all think of something about our moms that drive us a little crazy. That's because moms are not perfect. But hey, that doesn't stop us from expecting them to be!

Instead of focusing on the times our moms let us down, or didn't give us exactly what we thought we needed, let's look for ways to strengthen this important and powerful relationship since it impacts all our other relationships. In fact, the more we work things out with mom, the better we will be at working things out in any intimate relationship. Hopefully, this provides each of us an incentive to strengthen the mother-daughter bond, and find a way to do what God commands—honor our moms. And remember, this commandment comes with a promise.

So, here are ten suggestions that will help. I challenge you to begin today. Find a way to love, honor, and connect with your mother.

Ten ways to honor your mom:

1. Tell her one thing she did right.
2. Recall happy times and loving memories.
3. Resolve past hurts and start fresh.
4. Write a short story about you and mom and share it.
5. Send a card for no reason. Express thanks.
6. Put together pictures of you and your mom in a scrapbook.
7. Buy her dinner for no special reason.
8. Tell her you love her and the sacrifices she has made through the years.
9. Forgive her. She has made mistakes.
10. Remember important dates like her birthday and anniversary.

Mary Grace Birkhead

Learn the unforced rhythms of grace. I won't lay anything heavy or ill-fitting on you. Keep company with me and you'll learn to live freely and lightly. MATTHEW 11:29–30 (MSG)

I want people to see me and my family as all together and lacking nothing. I've been told by well-meaning people that I need to give Jesus a good name. He would want me and my family to appear practically perfect. You know, so the unsaved would want to come to church and be practically perfect Christians! If I were like a finished painting I could rest and enjoy my now perfect life.

Like an ocean, there are tides and storms in my life. There are calming waves and stinky seaweed. There are beautiful shells and gritty sand. Some days the water is smooth as glass, other days the waves are fearsome and uncontrollable. The daily contrasts can be terrifying and disappointing if I do not see my life as guided by the Creator of the seas. My spiritual growth is never finished. My goal used to be to *stop sinning, appear perfect*. Now it's *when I do sin be honest and quickly move to repentance*. It's not perfection—it's progress. The transformation of my mind, heart, emotions is an ongoing work of art.

List the places in your life where you struggle to be seen as *finished*. Is it your weight, being a great housekeeper, church attendance or service, your children's appearance and manners, your husband's job, your car, family name, political stance? . . . the list is endless. Your tight grip is taking your eyes off of Him. God wants you to let go and enjoy each day. What do you have a hold of, or really, what has its hold on you?

Anita Lustrea

Don't copy the behavior and customs of this world, but let God transform you into a new person by changing the way you think. Then you will learn to know God's will for you, which is good and pleasing and perfect. ROMANS 12:2 (NLT)

My husband and I recently attended a marriage conference. There were no new revelations about our relationship this time around but there were some great reminders about how to interact in a more productive way, especially when disagreements arise. You need to get inside your spouse's skin, to think like they do, to see things from their point of view. It reminds me of my relationship with Jesus. My deepest desire is to see things they way He does, to think like He thinks, and to react to situations the way He would.

What do I do to become more like Christ? I value my marriage enough to go to a marriage conference and connect with my spouse and talk about trouble spots in our relationship but how much do I value my relationship with the Lord? Enough to spend time with him, to connect regularly and get to know him through reading his Word? Romans 12:1–2 (NLT) reads, "And so, dear brothers and sisters, I plead with you to give your bodies to God because of all he has done for you. Let them be a living and holy sacrifice—the kind he will find acceptable. This is truly the way to worship him. Don't copy the behavior and customs of this world, but let God transform you into a new person by changing the way you think. Then you will learn to know God's will for you, which is good and pleasing and perfect."

God has the power to transform us and conform us to the image of his Son. Write a letter to Jesus. Tell him your personal desires for your relationship with Him. Tell about your anger when you feel his silence, or that you're not sure he hears your prayers. Tell him about feeling his love last week when you knew he had intervened in an important situation. The point is, be honest and open. Sometimes our marriages need a tune-up, sometimes our relationship with Christ needs a tune up too. Go repair or restart your relationship.

Leslie Parrott

Speak and act as those who are going to be judged by the law that gives freedom. JAMES 2:12 (NIV)

Proverbs 14:1 (NIV) says, "The wise woman builds her house." Maybe she builds houses for others as well. Around the United States, thirty-eight homes have been constructed solely by women who volunteered their services to Habitat for Humanity. The organization creates housing for low-income families using volunteer labor and donated money, materials, and sometimes, land. The women responsible for the thirty-eight new homes represented a broad range of professions, including stay-at-home moms, teachers, lawyers, and doctors.

And to think, the difference these women's actions have made, knowingly or not, were the result of another woman's frustration with her workaholic husband. Linda was sick and tired of Millard's money-grabbing lifestyle. She wanted Millard, not money. That's why she announced, one day, that she was going to New York to think about the future of their marriage.

"I was in agony," Millard said. "Never before had I suffered as I did during those days. Everything else—business, sales, profits, prestige, everything that seemed so important—paled into total meaninglessness."

In a tearful meeting in New York City, Millard and Linda were eventually reunited. They decided to sell their successful business, give the money to charities, and go on a mission trip to Africa, touring schools, hospitals, and refugee programs. Not long after they returned home to Georgia, they gave birth to Habitat for Humanity, a non-profit, ecumenical Christian housing ministry—now the largest non-profit housing organization in the United States.

Actions speak louder than words, as we all know. But in case you're doubting that, you can talk to any one of the hundreds of thousands who have been helped into a new home by Habitat and they'll make you a believer.

If you're like me, you can sometimes talk a good talk when it comes to faith issues. But the story of these "house-building" women challenged me to make sure I was also walking my talk. How about you?

Lori Neff

Be devoted to one another in brotherly love. Honor one another above yourselves. ROMANS 12:10 (NIV)

My old mp3 player stopped working not too long ago. I love electronic gadgets and definitely love music, but I've always had a love/hate relationship with Walkmans, Diskmans, mp3 players. I feel like they block me off from humanity . . . as if, just because I have ear buds in, it gives me liberty to completely ignore people around me and perhaps be a little rude ("Sorry. Can't hear you!"). And I don't like that I might miss something—like a warning or someone's kind comment.

The other day, my darling husband (who almost never buys me electronic doodads, though he loves to buy them for himself!), went out and got me a new mp3 player. I was *very* excited! So, I'm back to being plugged in. And somehow that dislike of being blocked off from other human beings is a distant feeling now. I've loved being isolated . . . nice and cozy in my mp3 player. But, I have to admit that I'm growing weary of the little, safe, pleasant, controlled world of my mp3 player. When it comes down to it, I really want to connect with people and to be open to them. I also find that when I am plugged in, I have a hard time concentrating and thinking things through—I miss the silence. Certainly, there's nothing wrong with listening to music to relax or inspire, but being plugged in as an escape from people is probably not such a good thing. I guess it comes down to moderation. Perhaps it's time for me to unplug for a while and spend some time in the world outside of my mp3 player. Maybe for you it's email, your cell phone, or the TV. Whatever it is, take some time to unplug.

Carolyn Castleberry

She considers a field and buys it; from her earnings she plants a vineyard. PROVERBS 31:16 (NASB)

When I first read Proverbs 31 as a young woman, I had no clue what this lady was up to, especially the part about a vineyard. Why a vineyard? Didn't she have enough on her plate taking care of her family and giving back to her community? Weren't her entrepreneurial efforts in making clothes and belts enough to keep her occupied? Why in the world would she want to add a vineyard to the mix of her multiple responsibilities?

The answer: she found it important not only to spend her time working for money, but also to make her money eventually work for her. Someday in the future, as she grew older, her hands wouldn't be able to "grasp the spindle" as she once had. As a senior citizen, she might not be able to put her hands to work creating linen garments. She needed to find a source of "passive income" for her family—that is, an investment that would provide money whether she showed up to work every day or not. The Bible is always relevant to our daily lives, and in this capable, creative woman God has given modern ladies an example to follow in every area of life—from family to finances.

Try this: instead of spending every penny you make, consider your own field of investment. What creative ideas has God given you to become a wise steward of your finances and make money work for you? The Proverbs 31 woman "smiled at her future" and you can too, even financially!

Beverly Hubble Tauke

You intended to harm me, but God intended it for good to accomplish what is now being done, the saving of many lives.
GENESIS 50:20 (NIV)

Joseph was not one to whitewash nasty family history. His grim reality was that bitter brothers human-trafficked him into enslavement and suffering. Gradually, Joseph mined remarkable gold from the rubbish of family treachery. Being jettisoned into Egypt was, in fact, God's rescue strategy for family villains and victims, alike.

Along his treacherous journey, Joseph collected life transforming treasures. Isolation from his pampering father forced him into maturity and intimacy with God that even pagan Pharaoh celebrated, catapulting Joseph into stunning power as a thirty-year-old immigrant (Genesis 41:38–40). Meanwhile, he shifted focus from what he did not have to what he did have. He lost security of family culture and roots but gained a wife and children. Egyptians valued him and even understood his spiritual power in ways his Hebrew family did not. Dark memories of family abuse were diluted as Joseph wrapped his mind around the warmth and light of God's sovereign plan for his life (Genesis 41:50–52).

Long afterwards, Moses advised a moral inventory of the family tree to secure God's blessing (Leviticus 26:40–45). Empowerment can come from reaching past mere facts to excavate greater meaning. What suffering in your own family produced stronger character? How was trauma transformed into triumph? What opportunity is God offering, even now, through family crisis or pain? How can one person break out of old family habits to help redeem a broken family—by God's grace, even the villains?

Remarkable peace, triumph and family healing are found by many who answer such questions, as Moses suggested—and as Joseph proved true.

Sabrina O'Malone

They will speak of the glorious splendor of your majesty, and I will meditate on your wonderful works. PSALM 145:5 (NIV)

Ask me who I love and that's a no-brainer. My Lord, family, friends, fellow Christians and the unsaved . . . pretty much everybody. That's an easy question to answer. But ask what kinds of things bring me joy . . . what do I love, and that's a harder question to pin down.

Have you ever considered what kinds of things you "just love?" Because you've got so much on your plate, you may wonder "What difference does it make what I 'just love'—and who cares anyway?"

For one thing, God cares. For another, you care. It's obvious you care about the things you love . . . otherwise you wouldn't love them.

Here's the big question, do you know and recognize the things in life that "just bring you joy?" What lightens your heart when you see it, hear it, touch it, or experience it? Think about it. You are somebody. Somebody fearfully and wonderfully made in the image and likeness of God. You have the right to enjoy God's creation. Just like the hymn says "This is my Father's world, I rest me in the thought, of rocks and trees of skies and seas His hands the wonders wrought" (Maltbie D. Babcock, "This is My Father's World").

So, take a moment to jot down a few things you love. Seeing a rainbow, watching a sunset, a good belly laugh, ocean breezes, blue skies, and fall foliage all made my list. After you've decided on your own favorite things, be sure to thank God whenever you encounter them. Slow down. Be grateful. Savor your simple pleasures. And remember if you move through life at the speed of light it's impossible to enjoy the scenery!

Nancy Sebastian Meyer

See to it, brothers, that none of you has a sinful, unbelieving heart that turns away from the living God. But encourage one another daily, as long as it is called Today, so that none of you may be hardened by sin's deceitfulness. HEBREWS 3:12–13 (NIV)

My husband readily admits he's a difficult person. As a youth pastor who defected to agnosticism (yet he gives me permission to tell you these things), he fits verse twelve as the man with an unbelieving heart.

Surprisingly I've come to recognize myself in verse thirteen. I easily grow frustrated with my husband—and God—when I look at all my husband's faults. Sorrow quickly morphs into anger. Soon I'm plotting ways to fix him, none of which actually work.

God's instruction seems ridiculous. Why should I encourage my husband when problems abound? How can I speak praise about one thing when he needs to be held accountable for many other things? Is it not my job to point out truth?

When frustrated, I must remind myself I can't change anyone but me. Yes, on rare occasion the Holy Spirit helps me speak out the truth when my spouse is open to hearing it. More often, however, God simply asks me, as these verses say, to *encourage* the person who is out of fellowship with God.

I look for admirable traits and specific examples of good qualities in his life. Then I find creative ways to share these things with my husband or weave them into conversations with friends or family *in his presence*. A daily dose of encouragement blesses him—and keeps *my* heart from growing hard.

Thank God for the most difficult person in your life right now. Then pray for wisdom and strength to encourage that person today.

Susie Larson

All the ways of the Lord are loving and faithful for those who keep the demands of his covenant. PSALMS 25:10 (NIV)

My middle son, Luke, practically lived in the corner. I recall on several occasions going to the corner, sitting down next to him, and striking up a conversation.

I wanted him to understand, that though there were consequences for his behavior, I'd always be in his corner; loving him, cheering for him, holding him accountable, and challenging him to grow into the man I knew he could be.

Luke recently turned twenty and is an honorable, godly young man with no traces of that feisty, strong-willed toddler I once parented.

Shortly after graduating from high school, he said this to me: "Mom, I know I was a handful when I was young, but I knew you'd never let me get away with anything. And yet, you never made me feel like a troublemaker. Quite the opposite. You challenged me to believe that my dreams were too small and that anything was possible if I chose to walk closely with God. Because of you, I feel like there are no limits to what God can do through me."

You know, the same is true for you.

Does it *feel* like your relationship with God has been reduced to one correction after another? *Listen.* God is saying so much more to you!

The Bible says that daily the heavens pour forth speech. The skies are filled with His mercy and His love is extravagant.

Yes, He will have to correct and redirect you on occasion, but always with a voice of love and concern.

He loves you, He has dreams for you, and He wants you to know that *nothing* is impossible for those who take Him at His Word.

Tell yourself today—out loud—that *you* are the object of God's affection. Remind yourself that He is cheering for you. He's in your corner and on your side.

Ellen Vaughn

. . . Since we are receiving a kingdom that cannot be shaken, let us be thankful, and so worship God acceptably with reverence and awe, for our "God is a consuming fire." HEBREWS 12:28–29 (NIV)

When space shuttle astronauts return to earth's atmosphere, reentry is tough.

Rocketing at 17,500 miles per hour, the shuttle orbiter flips upside down. Shaken and buffeted by Earth's gravitational pull, the astronauts see a huge, 3000-degree fireball outside their window.

Even if we haven't blasted off to outer space, most of us have experienced the same reality as the astronauts: coming back home isn't easy.

Maybe you've been away on a retreat, enjoying great fellowship and too much chocolate. Or maybe you've reveled in an evening out with a friend, or a peaceful walk, or a worship service that transcended everyday life and gave you a glimpse of heaven.

Even if we haven't traveled far or been gone long, reentry into life as usual can shake us up. There's often the heat of stress, conflict, demands, and tough challenges.

No surprise. Jesus said, "In this world you will have trouble" (John 16:33 NIV). Most spiritual "highs" aren't followed by a smooth transition back to normal life. We'll usually be rocked and rolled in the hot atmosphere of this broken world.

But we can take comfort. God is with us ... always. And whatever shake-ups rock our boat, they are not the end of the story. We're in this buffeting world now, but we're headed to our permanent home in a new kingdom ... one that *cannot* be shaken.

Jot down the things that are shaking you up right now. Pray about each one. Thank God that He is more powerful than any rocky challenges you're facing, that they are temporary, and that He is with you.

Dee Brestin

Someone's thoughts may be
As deep as the ocean,
But if you are smart,
You will discover them.
PROVERBS 20:5 (CEV)

My husband wanted to adopt a nine-year-old girl who was missing an arm, from an orphanage in Thailand.

I didn't.

I could give some pretty "spiritual" reasons for not wanting to do it. I had so much on my plate—four children in addition to a busy writing and speaking ministry. But I also know, as Jeremiah said, that my heart is deceitful and desperately wicked. So I talked to Sara, a godly friend and mentor.

"Dee," she asked, "do you think you are afraid because she's nine and you think it is too late to mold her?"

"I'm glad she's nine. I wish she was eighteen."

Sara laughed. "Are you afraid of the handicap? Do you think you will have to help her do everything?"

"No—they tell me she has learned how to do nearly everything by herself. They say she does some things with her teeth and her feet."

Then I felt the emotion rising in me. Suddenly I confessed to Sara:

"I don't want her to do things, especially in public, with her teeth and her feet."

Sara then did what a true friend will do. She put her arm around me and spoke softly:

"Dee—you are one of the godliest women I know. Do you think this is an area where you might grow?"

I am so thankful God used Sara to draw out my sinful heart. I am so thankful we didn't miss Beth—who is a great joy in our lives.

Are you willing to allow "smart" friends to draw out the deep waters of your soul? Are you willing to do that for them—and then, to speak the truth in love?

Mindy Caliguire

For I am convinced that neither death nor life, neither angels nor demons, neither the present nor the future, nor any powers, neither height nor depth, nor anything else in all creation, will be able to separate us from the love of God that is in Christ Jesus our Lord. ROMANS 8:38–39 (NIV)

My son had shared how distracting a fellow student had been, so I asked, "Whatever happened with your seat assignment at school?"

"Oh, the teacher gave us a new seating assignment the day after we prayed!"

"Really?!" I tried not to sound too surprised. I just love it when God answers the prayers of my children so clearly. Sensing a "teachable moment," I ventured, "Honey, doesn't that make you feel really loved by God—that He would answer your prayer?"

Immediately, he shot back, "Aren't we all?"

"Yes, but there are times when we can choose to walk away from God, and then we're less likely to ask for God's involvement and sense His answers to our prayers." It got very quiet in the backseat.

Jonathan finally offered, "Yeah, but walking away from God is like walking on a treadmill." A ten-year-old gets it.

Have you been walking away from God? Has it been days, months, since you had an honest conversation with God. Are you stuck in a compulsive behavior that mires you in shame? Or bitter and resentful—unable to let in God's goodness and love? Hope crushed yet again by the harsh realities of life? Reclaiming intimacy with God seems enormous.

Be reminded that walking away from God is like walking on a treadmill. You might have turned away, but there isn't anywhere you can go that's far from where God is. Tired of the treadmill? Just step off. Grace and irrational love await you.

Christine Wyrtzen

And Abraham said to God, "If only Ishmael might live under your blessing!" GENESIS 17:18 (NIV)

God promised Abraham a son through his wife Sarah. She was old but Abraham believed. For a while, at least. After more than a decade, he couldn't seem to sustain his faith in God's promise. He might have feared that he dreamt such a revelation. Whatever the reason, he took matters into his own hands. He slept with Haggar and produced a counterfeit blessing, Ishmael. When God appeared again and reminded him that an Isaac would be coming, Abraham pleaded with God to bless Ishmael instead. He wanted God's endorsement of what he had perpetrated in the flesh. God will never cooperate with such petitions. Not because He is an ogre, but because His dreams for us are for an "Isaac."

I want love. It is found in God, yet I have often circumvented Him and settled for Ishmaels. Too much expectation was placed on people, rather than the One who promised me all of His heart.

I want fulfillment. A ministry was promised to me long ago, yet I was inclined to generate one through my own ingenuity. My Ishmael produced scanty spiritual fruit compared to the harvest of my present day ministry. Now, I taste of God's promise. Isaac was born. The ministry Daughters of Promise bears the witness of the glory of God. It's all about Him and little about me, other than daily submission to what He unfolds.

An Ishmael will always produce a cobweb of pain and disillusionment. An Isaac brings pure joy. Today, I purpose to wait on God for His perfect gifts. No matter what. No matter how long it takes. God is a promise keeper, proven through the ages. Trust in Him.

Nancy Anderson

"Go and sin no more." JOHN 8:11 (KJV)

In 1980, my marriage was torn apart by adultery. My adultery. I knew it was wrong, yet I couldn't seem to stop.

Then, during a phone conversation with my Christian parents, they confronted me with my sin and said, "We will not support your leaving Ron, it would be out of God's will."

When I hung up the phone, I knew I was at a crossroad that would determine the path for the rest of my life and I prayed, *Lord, please show me your will for my life.* Then I remembered the simple words Jesus said to the adulterous woman: "Go and sin no more." I knew exactly what I had to do. I surrendered my will and my heart to the Lord and asked for the strength to walk away from my boyfriend, Jake, and make a full confession to my husband, Ron.

The collective pain was extraordinary. Such is the repercussion of sin. When I told my husband the whole truth and begged his forgiveness, he miraculously chose to forgive me.

I quit my job and broke off all contact with Jake. Even though my feelings for him had not yet changed, I chose to stay with my husband. It was out of obedience at first, but as I began to act lovingly to Ron, the loving feelings eventually followed. We recently celebrated our thirtieth wedding anniversary, and I am thrilled to tell you that we are deeply and tenderly in love—living proof that no marriage is beyond repair.

Perhaps you have never committed adultery, but many women have feelings of discontent regarding their marriages. Choose to focus on what is good about your husband and confess any sin of having thoughts or longings for "greener grass."

Anita Lustrea

The faithful love of the Lord never ends, His mercies never cease. LAMENTATIONS 3:22 (NLT)

I enjoy green, growing things. I especially like flowers. My absolute favorite is the pansy. My grandfather used to grow a small field of them on his farm in northern Maine. Pansies have such beautiful faces, not one of them is alike. I like the beauty and the aroma of lilacs. For different reasons I plant petunias and geraniums. But to me, one of the most interesting of all flowers is the amaryllis. Amaryllis plants grow from a bulb. Once they put a shoot above ground you can almost watch the growth occur. What we forget, though, is the time it takes for the bulb to germinate and start growing, the time that it appears nothing is happening, because we can't see anything above ground. It's a complete parallel of our spiritual lives. Our own soul's journey that takes place mostly in secret until we break through the crust of dirt into the fresh air.

I think about my life of faith that went along without much notice for years until crisis hit, and then, the greenery shot up above ground and the growth was visible to the naked eye. The green shoot isn't the most beautiful part of the amaryllis, but it is alive and growing. When the moment of flowering occurs, we are amazed at the delicate beauty. Thin fragile petals, but bold, beautiful color. Strength and grace, mirrors of the life of Christ within us. As we spend time watching the amaryllis grow and eventually blossom, it's a reminder about being attentive to the mercies that enter our lives. It reminds me of Lamentations 3:22 (NLT) that reads "The faithful love of the Lord never ends, His mercies never cease."

Growth doesn't happen without the right setting. You've got to have good soil, regular watering, and the proper light. Above all, you've got to be connected to the True Vine, Jesus himself. How's your connection with Jesus today?

Kristen Johnson Ingram

To the present hour we both hunger and thirst, and we are poorly clothed, and beaten, and homeless. 1 CORINTHIANS 4:11 (NKJV)

He was dressed in many layers of rags, with an old knit hat pulled over his long uncombed hair, his mittens cut off so his fingers were free. He sat outside the entrance to the mall, with his hands over his ears and moaning, "Shut them up, Lord, shut up them politicians."

I suspect the bureaucracy had left him with ruthless words, merciless words, smug, words that said, "Get a job" to someone who is homeless and mentally ill, or "You do not qualify for benefits" to a man who has no employment history, "No Mexicans need apply," or "Unless you have an address, we can't give you food stamps." Maybe those words hammered in his head and sent him deeper into madness than he already was.

Mercy is in short supply nowadays. The politics of compassion in our society are based first on the *cost*, and second on perceptions of whether or not a person *deserves* it. But did Jesus put anyone on probation to make sure they were worthy of his healing? And when the sixth chapter of Luke says to give money to anyone who asks, does it add "if you're sure they'll use it for food or other good things?" Giving is between you and God; how they use what you give is between them and God.

Lord, grant that homeless man peace inside his brain, I prayed. *And send someone to help him. Uh-oh. You want me to go, don't you?*

Find out what your community is doing for the homeless, and what you can do to help. Spend some time at a shelter, beg restaurants for their leftover food, help start a soup kitchen or "clothes closet" in your church.

Nancy Kane

I waited patiently for the Lord; he turned to me and heard my cry. He lifted me out of the slimy pit, out of the mud and mire; he set my feet on a rock and gave me a firm place to stand. He put a new song in my mouth, a hymn of praise to our God, many will see and fear and put their trust in the Lord.

PSALM 40:1–3 (NIV)

To be thankful for the good that happens in our lives seems easy. But, what about the things in our lives that cause us pain? How can we be thankful for the loss of a job, broken relationships, cancer, or a wayward child? How can we genuinely give thanks for these things as well?

The only way we can genuinely say "thank you" to the things that cause us anxiety and pain is to recognize God's heart of love intimately wrapped in the very fabric of our lives and to trust His purposes. The apostle Paul reminds us that God causes all things to work together for the good to those who love God to those who are called according to His purpose (Romans 8:28). And what is that good and what is that purpose? Being conformed to the very image of Himself and being uniquely changed into people that reflect the tender face of Christ to others. We are called to be a people who are transformed from self-protective grumbling folks constantly demanding our rights to people who live our lives with open arms of gratitude for all of what God has given. What can compare to being forgiven for all of our sins, eternal life, peace of mind and heart, and a hope that pervades even the darkest circumstances? How can you measure the promise of being changed to be like our Savior Himself? To be grateful in the midst of unanswered prayer, disappointments, and setbacks is to give God our deepest trust.

May we take a moment to give God thanks for all the gifts we have been given—even the ones in unseemly packaging.

Anita Lustrea

"I tell you the truth, anyone who doesn't receive the Kingdom of God like a child will never enter it." MARK 10:15 (NLT)

I was at Starbucks one morning during their weekly "storytime." There were fifteen adorable, energetic, talkative children crowded around a barista who had just transformed into the story lady. She pulled *Alexander and the Terrible, Horrible, No Good, Very Bad Day* out of her book bag and the kids were immediately transfixed. She started reading to them in a very animated way that captured their attention. What I loved was that they weren't afraid to ask questions or make comments right in the middle of the story. They'd ask to see the pictures, or why Alexander was having such a bad day. You know, the kinds of questions that we as adults have learned to keep to ourselves. I love the open, honest, inquisitive nature of children.

Jesus loved that about them too. Mark 10:13–16 (NLT) reads: "One day some parents brought their children to Jesus so he could touch and bless them. But the disciples scolded the parents for bothering him.

When Jesus saw what was happening, he was angry with his disciples. He said to them, 'Let the children come to me. Don't stop them! For the Kingdom of God belongs to those who are like these children. I tell you the truth, anyone who doesn't receive the Kingdom of God like a child will never enter it.' Then he took the children in his arms and placed his hands on their heads and blessed them."

Some of us, instead of discarding our childishness, discarded our childlikeness. I'm often guilty of that.

How can we regain what was lost? Sometimes it's a matter of purposing to play!

If today is a rainy day, go jump in a mud puddle. Remember what it is like to be like a child. Then ask Jesus to help you retain that part of who you are.

Kendra Smiley

Call to me and I will answer you and tell you great and unsearchable things you do not know. JEREMIAH 33:3 (NIV)

Have you ever noticed that your children know just who to ask for permission? Here's what I mean. When our boys were younger and they wanted to do something risky or daring or dangerous they always asked their dad. He was the one who said it was all right to ride the horse bareback or go down the double diamond ski slope. They were too smart to ask me for permission. Probably because they were pretty sure the answer would be "NO!" I'm not very enthused about taking physical risks.

But, when it came to social events . . . "May I go out for pizza after Bible study?" . . . they always asked me. Why? Because in our family, I am the closest thing we have to a social butterfly. Their dad would have wondered why they wanted to waste the time, energy and money going out for pizza.

My kids evaluated who they should call on to get a "good" answer; to get the answer they wanted. As God's kids we can always call on Him for a great answer. Jeremiah 33:3 (NIV) says, "Call to me and I will answer you and tell you great and unsearchable things you do not know."The answer that our heavenly Father gives us might not be the answer we think we want, but it will always be the loving answer that is best for us.

Are you taking the opportunity to call upon the Lord? He is waiting for your call and will "answer and tell you great and unsearchable things you do not know."

What a blessing to be able to call on the Lord. That's the blessing of prayer. And it is the Next Right Choice!

Lois Evans

If any of you lacks wisdom, he should ask God, who gives generously to all without finding fault, and it will be given to him. JAMES 1:5 (NIV)

It is precisely during the time of trials in life that you, like Job, must keenly focus on the God of all circumstances rather than complaining about the circumstances. Pray to God about His purpose for allowing those trials. The apostle James says we should ask God for wisdom during times of trials (James 1:5) and God will answer. When we focus on God, we will see how God wants to use our trials for our spiritual growth. When Jobs' trials were complete, he said to God, "I had only heard about you before, but now I have seen you with my own eyes" (Job 42:5 NLT). It's one thing to learn about God in a church service or Bible study. It's quite another thing to experience the reality of God as you go through the problems and pains of life.

The Lord is with you not only on the mountaintops but in the valley as well. He is teaching you perseverance, so, "Let us not become weary in doing good, for at the proper time we will reap a harvest if we do not give up" (Galatians 6:9 NIV).

God wants to give you a fresh experience of His reality in your life. So if times are tough, keep your eyes looking up. Just beyond the overcast skies of your trials is the shining sun of God's glory, ready to be revealed to you and take you to the next spiritual level.

Take some time to really think about the trial going on in your life. Perhaps it would be helpful to journal your thoughts. Have you been focusing on God, or on your trial? Take a breath and if you really want to know what God wants you to do, calmly ask him, believing He will gladly tell you (James 1:5).

Sharon Hersh

Wait for the Lord; be strong and take heart and wait for the Lord. PSALM 27:14 (NIV)

"I asked my mom, 'Why shouldn't I just go party with all of the other middle school kids?' She answered, 'Because you want more.' I am almost twenty-two-years old now and I still want more. I want more from/for myself. I want more from my relationships. I want more from this life."

These words from my daughter's journal tell of her journey of desire. Whether we are thirteen or sixty we know about longing for more—passion, purpose, mutually fulfilling relationships. In fact, if you were to write out right now what you long for, ache for, dream about, persistently pray for—I doubt anyone would chide you for the good things you desire.

Why doesn't God give us what we want? Why doesn't he grant our requests for husbands who are spiritual leaders, children who love and serve God, and friends who are there for us?

When our longings for legitimate, good things and God's delay or seeming refusal collide, we might determine to take care of our needs ourselves. That's how addiction grows and gains a grip on our hearts and souls. In my early twenties, I discovered alcohol. It erased the pain and eased my uptight tendencies. It made everything better until it made everything worse, but by then I was hooked.

Can you relate? People-pleasing, food, work, sex, perfectionism, gambling—allure us into chasing a feeling, a release, a sustained comfort, a sense of ease, a coming home. It's what addiction is all about.

Make a list of all the things you thought would satisfy you, only to discover they faded as your longings grew. Meditate on 2 Corinthians 4:18 (MSG): "The things we see now are here today, gone tomorrow. But the things we can't see now will last forever."

Leigh McLeroy

I'm thanking you, God, out loud in the streets, singing your praises in town and country. The deeper your love, the higher it goes; every cloud is a flag to your faithfulness.

PSALM 57:9–10 (MSG)

Some unplanned cleaning and organizing uncovered a treasure I didn't know I possessed. Some years back I purchased a mostly blank book and a set of colored markers, and filled its pages with . . . desire. Or more appropriately desires. Like a third grader gone wild, I drew, wrote, and made outrageous lists of things I'd dreamed of, but never said out loud to anyone. I spilled out in fuchsia and berry blue ink a whole trove of hopes and wishes, and then I quietly put it away.

Years later, when I found the self-made book, opened its cover, and began thumbing through its pages, I discovered that God has brought many of those forgotten dreams to pass. Most of them without any help from me at all.

I dreamed of a house with a porch swing. (Check.) A library with floor-to-ceiling books. (Check.) A horse. (Not yet.) A husband. (Not yet . . . and perhaps not in that order.) A book written in my name. (Check, check, and check.) A place to teach God's Word to women. (Check.) The chance to skydive. (Check.) See Paris. (Check.) Work barefoot. (Check.)

As I ran my fingers over line after line, I couldn't believe my eyes. God had literally given me the desires of my heart. He didn't just make my wishes come true—He placed the desires deep in my heart that He meant all along to fulfill.

Are there some longings still "outstanding"? There are. But they pale (truly!) in comparison with what He has already done. He knows me. He knows my heart. He welcomes my wanting. Designs it even, for my own good and for His great glory.

Because even when I forget, He remembers. (Check.)

If you have a list of dreams or desires, revisit it to see what God has done with your hopes so far. If you don't have one—start it today!

Dannah Gresh

. . . then birds of prey came down on the carcasses, but Abram drove them away! GENESIS 15:11 (NIV)

I was at the end of my rope.

Seven days on the road ministering to teenagers will do that to a woman! As I arrived home, I faced emails from a way-too-complicated relationship. And I sure wished God could at least keep the bank account full while I was off doing His work! What a martyr's pose I struck!

I wanted to quit.

When I feel this way, I often turn to Genesis 15 and read this holy moment in Old Testament history. It's the moment when Abram is making the covenant sacrifice to God that would seal the Israelites as God's chosen people. This was a holy, holy moment!

I can just hear angels singing! Can't you? I can see the glory of God blinding old Abram and just warming his soul. Isn't that what would happen at a holy of holy moment?

Nope!

Instead, Abram gets "birds of prey." Nasty creatures those birds of prey. They're meat eaters. And, they don't just eat their food. They pick at it.

Get this: there is nothing holy in your life that Satan is going to leave alone. He's going to send in his birds of prey.

What did Abram do? He drove them away. He didn't whine. And he didn't wait for God to do the work. He ran around like a wild man and drove those nasty things away!

That encourages me.

You'll often find me running around like a wild woman. Don't worry. I'm just learning to drive!

Do you see some birds of prey in your life right now? Ask God today what you should do to respond. Listen closely to the answer he puts in your heart. Then, do it!

Lori Neff

One thing I ask of the Lord, this is what I seek: that I may dwell in the house of the Lord all the days of my life, to gaze upon the beauty of the Lord and to seek him in his temple.
PSALM 27:4 (NIV)

Do you ever feel an ache in your heart when you see something beautiful? I've heard it said that the ache we feel is a longing for heaven. Through the earthly, incomplete beauty that we see and experience, our soul has a taste of what is to come. We somehow resonate with it and long for something more that we can't see or describe.

Isn't it delightful that God created us to enjoy and appreciate beauty? One of my favorite things to do at the end of a day at work is to stop by a small shop on my way home. As I step in, I immediately breathe in the wonderful, scented air and smile. I linger and touch the sparkly jewelry, smell the candles, read the greeting cards and feel the fabric. I rarely buy anything—I find such pleasure in just being around beautiful things. When I leave, I feel refreshed and see the world differently.

As I look at beauty in art, in nature, or in other people, I try to reflect on why I am drawn to it. What does it tell me about myself and how God created me? What do I learn about God through beauty? For example, each morning, I love to watch the sky. The colors and variety of the sky is amazing! Looking at the sky each morning, I am reminded of how I have a fresh start today and God's mercy and love is limitless. I also love to think about the incredible color and detail that God put into creation. Perhaps He put it there just for me to see today. Let's keep our eyes open for the beauty around us today.

Kendra Smiley

Get rid of all bitterness, rage and anger, brawling and slander, along with every form of malice. EPHESIANS 4:31 (NIV)

I have found that there are Bible lessons almost everywhere . . . even in a cup of tea.

A friend brought me a special treat one day. She had been to the gourmet coffee shop and, knowing I wasn't a coffee drinker, had picked up a steaming hot cup of tea for me. Within a matter of minutes she was standing before me with her gift.

As I reached for the cup, I found my friend providing me with more than just a soothing, warm drink. "The clerk gave me specific directions," she said withholding the treat until I heard all the instructions. "And I quote," she continued. "'Don't let the tea brew for too long. Pull the tea bag out after five minutes. If you don't follow my directions, your cup of tea will get bitter.'"

I listened intently to the words and to the directions and immediately my mind went to some instructions given by our heavenly Father. "Get rid of all bitterness, rage and anger, brawling and slander, along with every form of malice" (Ephesians 4:31 NIV).

God does not want any of those things to "brew too long" in our lives. If they stay in our hearts, minds, or memories for very long, we can become bitter ourselves.

Are you aware of any bitterness, rage, anger, brawling, slander, or malice in your heart, mind, or memory? If the answer is yes, toss it out. Get rid of those ugly things just like you would toss out a used tea bag.

Think of that with your next cup of tea and follow God's instruction . . . get rid of all those unpleasant things. That's the Next Right Choice!

Nancy Anderson

Break up your fallow ground, for it is time to seek the Lord, till he comes and rains righteousness on you.

HOSEA 10:12B (NKJV)

Many summers ago, I accidentally snapped off the sprinkler head that watered my flower garden. Because I didn't repair it, the flowers shriveled in the harsh sun and the dirt cracked and buckled until it looked like a concrete colored road map. The garden spot that had once been a fragrant oasis of jasmine and lavender lay in ruins: hard, unproductive—fallow.

That summer, the death of my baby, Timmy, began the Great Depression in my heart. I stopped caring—about my garden and my life. I gave in to the darkest parts of myself and wallowed, for months, in sorrow, anger, and self-pity. I was jealous of other women's babies and pulled away from the love of my family and the shelter of the Lord. I was in ruins: hard, unproductive—fallow.

Then, a friend gave me a card with Hosea 10:12 written on it, and I made a tearful and painful decision to break up the hard places in my heart (bitterness, anger, envy, and unforgiveness). I surrendered my rubble and ruin to Him, and He rained his loving righteousness on me. As I began to reconnect with my friends and family, my garden and my life began to bloom again.

Perhaps there are things in your life that have seemed unfair or you have been through heartbreaks. I know that staying in pain just brings more pain and only when we come *through* it, can we be free. Is there some fallow part of your heart that you need to break up today? Ask the Lord to bring his cooling, refreshing rain to sooth your soul. Forgive. Love. Let go. Rejoice.

Mary Grace Birkhead

Then he took the seven loaves and the fish and when he had given thanks, he broke them and gave them to his disciples, and they in turn to the people. They all ate and were satisfied.

MATTHEW 15:36–37 (NIV)

During an exceptionally difficult time in our marriage my husband and I were seeing a wonderful counselor who would occasionally say to one of us: "Well, that's their five loaves and two fish." We would look at him like he was crazy.

One day as I was driving in my car thinking about how much more I needed from my husband when the words came into my head, "Well, that's his five loaves and two fish." And it hit me—that's all he has to give right now. I want to be satisfied by the words and emotions he offers me; no wonder I'm mad at his loaves and fish! I desire to be fully comforted, fully loved, fully completed and he's coming up short in doing that for me. Only Jesus was able to take the fish and loaves and satisfy the crowd on the hillside. Only Jesus is able to take the human efforts of my husband and satisfy me.

Critical comments, sarcasm, sulking, and rage are all signs of anger. Surprisingly, so is depression, sadness, withdrawal, and isolation. Maybe your anger is with yourself. You have failed. Your anger could be toward someone else. They have failed.

Offer this failure up to God just as Jesus did with the small lunch of five loaves and two fish. It was not enough for the crowd on its own. Others will not be "enough" for you; you will not be "enough" for you!

As you sit before the Lord in prayer give Him your anger and reasons for dissatisfaction. List the events. Ask Him to be your "Enough." Ask God to lift the cloud of resentment off of you. He is Enough. By faith, if you can, thank God for the "small meal" when you expected more. He plans to do a miracle in your life because of it.

Sara Groves

For it is by grace you have been saved, through faith—and this not from yourselves, it is the gift of God—not by works, so that no one can boast. For we are God's workmanship, created in Christ Jesus to do good works, which God prepared in advance for us to do. EPHESIANS 2:8–10 (NIV)

I struggled for many years with the balance between faith and works. In a desire to please God, and the people around me, I worked extremely hard to do all of the right things. During a season of crisis in my life, the whole thing fell apart. All of the things that I was doing, supposedly for God, had brought me to exhaustion and emptiness. That difficult season brought about a grace awakening in my heart. In the days that followed I did not attempt to do anything for God—I walked with Him, and talked with Him, and that was it. I felt his great love for me in a way that I never had before, and I realized that the enormous burden of guilt I carried was not from God . . . I was saved by grace.

There is a profound difference between guilt and conviction, and I am learning to discern between the two. God is not a frowning, discontented employer. He is a Creator, and has creative plans for me. Guilt is a waste of time, but conviction comes to me as coordinates for this journey that I am on, and the works I do under this understanding have only brought the fullness and joy that God intended. Ephesians 2:8–10 sums it up for me: *I was saved by grace,* and *I am God's workmanship, and he has prepared good works in advance for me to do.*

Make a guilt list, and write down all the ways you feel like you are letting other people and God down. In prayer, give that list to God, and ask Him to help you discern between guilt and conviction. Let go of the guilt, and follow through with those convictions.

Anita Lustrea

Yet you do not know what your life will be like tomorrow. You are just a vapor that appears for a little while and then vanishes away. JAMES 4:14 (NASB)

Our church family suffered the loss of a beloved staff member last year. She was an amazing woman and the director of children's ministries for our church. Our adult Sunday school class took one Sunday morning soon after her death to process what losing this woman meant. Many of our children were touched profoundly by her. They were asking tough questions, like why didn't God answer our prayers for healing. As adults we had our own fears that surfaced. She was only forty-nine years old. That hit close to home for many of us, chipped a little hole in our invincible armor.

As many of us talked together around tables that day, we were reminded of how temporal life is and that God's ways are higher than our ways. Our understanding is so limited. And even knowing all of that and knowing our friend was so much better off in heaven where she would suffer no more, we still hurt. Our hearts were still breaking. Someone at my table talked about how they like to look at people's hands and think about the kind of work they have performed with them. That thought helped her think about the fact that there was so much more work to do, and that God wouldn't call us home before His work, through us, was accomplished.

I remember the pastor that spoke at the funeral said that we had a choice with how we respond to this loss. We can get bitter, or we can love. Isn't that the bottom line for how we respond to all of life? We can get bitter, or we can choose to overflow with the love of God to a hurting and dying world.

Do you have some situations where you've chosen the bitter path? What would it mean to reroute your journey? Ask God how you can choose forgiveness and love today.

Melinda Schmidt

"I will bless [Sarah] and will surely give you a son by her. I will bless her so that she will be the mother of nations; kings of peoples will come from her." GENESIS 17:16 (NIV)

I empathized with Abraham's initial response to God's new promise to him. It went something like this:

God: "Abraham, you are going to be a father soon, albeit an elderly one, and birth a new nation."

Abraham: (falling to the ground in fits of laughter) "Me, make a new baby? With an old wife to boot? Ho—I've got you covered—a few years back I made my son Ishmael with my wife's servant girl, Hagar, just to help you out. That's what you mean, right?"

God: "No."

I had my own potential impossibility going. My husband and I had serious doubts that both the college our daughter attended and her boyfriend there were the right fit for her. How could things change over a short Christmas break? We prayed. We trusted.

I hear you Abraham, I have done that doubting-of-the-God-of-the-universe thing too, and pretty recently. Like Abraham and Sarah, time seemed to be running out and we were feeling squeezed. But within weeks Kelly had dropped both the college and the boyfriend. Even Kelly thought it was pretty unbelievable!

How about you? Sensing God may be doing something new, but it just seems way too outrageous? Some things in life get resolved the way we want eventually, others don't. But here's an encouraging story God wanted to make sure we could read over and over: the last time I checked, that laughing, disbeliever Abraham was the father of descendents too numerous to count, occupying not only their original promised land (Genesis 17:8) but homes around the world. Because God can do *anything*!

Miriam Neff

If you falter in times of trouble, how small is your strength! for though the righteous falls seven times, he rises again.
PROVERBS 24:10,16A (NIV)

Do you have those moments during crisis times when you feel weak? You just can't stand tall like the Christian you wish to be? Join the ranks, sister. During the years of my husband's illness, I was body, soul, and spirit weary. Giving care while loving Bob intensely, and battling ALS (Lou Gehrig's disease) was one of the hardest events in my life. I both tripped and fell my way through that journey.

This proverb encouraged me greatly, especially when I learned the difference in the meanings of "falter" and "fall."

The Hebrew word "falter" means to sink down or be disheartened. It is the term used in Isaiah 5:24 (NIV), "as dry grass sinks down in the flames." It is an inside thing of letting go, giving in, succumbing to circumstances. Falling is different. This refers to external circumstances that trip us up. We can be tired, weary, and even fall, but our legs are still pumping. We're not staying down! We're on the way up because we haven't given up.

The faltering woman is in trouble. The righteous woman who falls is in a good place. Her righteousness—her right standing with her Creator—means she will rise on His strength, which is endless, not her own. She may rise because she catches a glimpse of heaven and knows something better is ahead. She may rise again, on the power of love for her lifetime companion, lover, and husband. She may rise on the encouraging words of her friends. She may rise being lifted solely by her Maker when she has no reserve or energy to press on. The reasons to rise keep showing up. Seven is a number of completeness and she will complete the journey, no matter how many times she falls.

Today, list God's resources to lift and encourage you.

Leslie Vernick

The tongue has the power of life and death.
PROVERBS 18:21 (NIV)

Growing up we all heard the nursery rhyme "sticks and stones will break our bones but words will never hurt us." It is a lie. The wounds may be invisible, but our words are powerful. They can cause deep injury and often leave permanent scars to those we hurt.

When we're angry, the Bible warns us to be very careful (Proverbs 4:4). It's at this time we feel most tempted to use our words as weapons. Don't do it. You can't delete your words once they've left your mouth and injured someone.

But let's look at what our words show us about our own heart. Jesus tells us "for out of the overflow of his heart his mouth speaks" (Luke 6:45 NIV). What comes up and out of our mouth reveals what's in our heart. When I yell at my child or my husband, for example, my words often expose my demanding, selfish, and prideful heart. I want my way. Now! And I use my words and voice tone to get it. Or, when I think I'm right and the other person is wrong, I can swiftly demean and demoralize someone with a few choice phrases.

The Bible commands us not to murder, but Jesus warns us that an angry heart with a reckless tongue can do much damage (Matthew 5:21–22 NIV). We've all experienced the wounds of an undisciplined tongue.

Decide today that you will no longer use your words as a weapon to hurt others. Instead, use the enormous power of what you say to someone to encourage, uplift, instruct and love him or her. Paul tells us that "love does no harm to its neighbor" (Romans 13:10 NIV).

Is there anyone you need to ask forgiveness for your hurtful words? Do it today.

Marcia Ramsland

Whatever you do, work at it with all your heart, as working for the Lord, not for men. Colossians 3:23 (NIV)

This favorite "work" verse takes on new meaning in our day and age. It is said that we have two hundred inputs a day with our email, regular mail, radio, and TV that we need to sift through and decide what we will act on. How are you doing?

Once I realized that God intends for me to live a well-managed work life for Him, I applied this verse to my desk work. Whew! Like me, perhaps you need to take your organization up a notch to be more wholehearted in serving Him.

The important thing when working at your desk is to accomplish your work goals by the half hour. When you ask, "What will I accomplish this half hour?" you focus on one task and get more things done in a day. With an eight-hour workday, we can accomplish sixteen items! That would be a record day if we lived each thirty minutes sending a prayer upward and asking, "What should I do this next half hour, Lord?" Often He lets us decide, and that's where we need to prioritize doing the most important item first. God is your helper and strength. He will help you do that hard report, clean out your email inbox, and find time to accomplish what your boss wants you to do.

Proverbs 14:8 (NIV) says, "The wisdom of the prudent (diligent) is to give thought to their ways." Think about your work: What could you tackle at your desk to show Him and others you are serving God wholeheartedly? Do less and accomplish more as you discern what He wants you to put yourself wholeheartedly into today.

Kay Yerkovich

Let a man regard us in this manner, as servants of Christ, and stewards of the mysteries of God. In this case moreover, it is required of stewards that one be found trustworthy.

1 Corinthians 4:1–2 (NASB)

I think back to my early days as a Christian and how enthralled I was with the Word of God and the many promises contained in Scripture. Every question has an answer, every pain had a verse to stop the suffering, every problem was due to a lack of faith, and every failure was an indication I had somehow missed God's will. All in all, I had God in a very predictable box. Black-and-white, nice and neat, cut-and-dried. In those days, I never thought of God as a "mystery."

After thirty-seven years of walking with Christ, I appreciate the mystery of God and have embraced the reality that much of God's work in my life comes through puzzling events, unanswered prayer, confusing twists and promises not yet realized or fulfilled. It is easy to trust God's love and goodness toward me when He behaves as I want or expect. But I am a steward of the mysteries of God; my trust is deepened as I rest in the truth of His character even when nothing in life makes sense.

Today, I'm far more aware of what I don't know. Sometimes, tears wash pain away better than verses. I have found failure is a blessing in disguise. Instead of asking, "Why?" I am more apt to pray, "Let me show you Lord I am a trustworthy steward as I accept your mysterious ways. I don't have to understand. I choose to trust you."

Anita Lustrea

Therefore go and make disciples of all nations, baptizing them in the name of the Father and of the Son and of the Holy Spirit. MATTHEW 28:19 (NIV)

I was twelve years old when my mom and dad made the decision to say "yes" to missions for me.

My brother David received a mailing from a youth missionary organization which he promptly threw in the trash. I pilfered through the garbage and salvaged the brochure for myself.

There were work projects and evangelistic trips to Africa, South America, Europe, and even the United States. I asked my parents if I could go to the Amazon in Brazil and be on a work team. They took two months to decide, which nearly killed this eager kid. When they said yes, you could have peeled me off the ceiling. There was one caveat. I could go (turning thirteen two weeks before liftoff made me eligible) but I had to stay in the United States. So I enlisted to be a part of the National Parks Evangelistic Team.

My parents' "yes" changed my life. I mean, literally, changed my life. I never looked back. I spent the next three summers on various teams to the Canary Islands, Guatemala, and Mexico. My heart had been broken for the needy of the world.

As parents, I think it's easy to say no. I think the "yeses" take more time and deliberation and carry more risk. We need to constantly be praying for discernment as we mold and shape those who've been entrusted to our care. I don't know what would have happened had my parents said no. Would I have the heart for missions and the disenfranchised that I have today? Thankfully, I'll never know.

Remember what Ephesians 2:10 (NLT) states. "For we are God's masterpiece. He has created us anew in Christ Jesus, so that we can do the good things he planned for us long ago." Our children are masterpieces of God's, and as we help them uncover who they truly are, God will better help them understand His purpose for their life.

Linda Mintle

"Why do you look at the speck of sawdust in your brother's eye and pay no attention to the plank in your own eye? How can you say to your brother, 'Let me take the speck out of your eye,' when all the time there is a plank in your own eye?"
MATTHEW 7:3–4 (NIV)

If you entered marriage with the idea that you can change your spouse, get ready for disappointment. We can't make other people change even though we valiantly try! That said, we can change our reaction to our spouse which does create a change in the relationship.

Think of marriage like a dance. You both have learned steps in this marital dance. Rather than trying to change his dance step, change yours. For example, if your husband spends too much time with the sports channel, and nagging him hasn't resulted in a rest for the remote, try a new dance step.

Instead of focusing on what he is doing or not doing, stop nagging and say, "I feel a bit envious of the sports channel and would love a little more of your time. How about going for a walk with me?" Your reaction involves two important changes from your old dance step of nagging: (1) You've expressed your feelings in an "I" statement and (2) you've given him an option. Both lower a person's defenses. When defenses are lower, communication is better.

Now just because you do these two things doesn't mean your spouse will jump off the couch and join you on your walk. But he might, especially if he doesn't feel you are criticizing him. So next time you are tempted to try to change your spouse, remember the dance and focus on your own step. A new step will change the marital dance!

Erin Smalley

The Lord is my rock, my fortress and my deliverer; my God is my rock, in whom I take refuge. PSALM 18:2 (NIV)

I will forever remember holding my mother as she took her last breath after a valiant battle with lung cancer.

Needless to say, it has been a difficult year for me. More than ever, I have needed to feel God's strength in the midst of my weakness and pain. Never was this more evident than when my six-year-old son ran into the house with a large flat rock held tightly in his little hand.

"Look Mommy," he shouted, "it's Jesus!"

My mind went wild trying to see what Garrison saw.

"Show me Jesus," I finally conceded.

Garrison carefully traced along the edge of the rock, outlining the perfect profile of Jesus. I gasped as I saw it. I was literally holding Jesus in my hand!

It was amazing how the Lord allowed Garrison to remind me of an amazing truth: He is my rock, my fortress, my deliverer and my refuge. He doesn't change. Though the pain of losing my mother has been great, He has been solid in my life. Much like a rock that doesn't break or sliver neither does our Lord. I know that Christ is who He says He is and even when everything around me seems uncertain, He will remain.

Life is full of loss. You may be going through the loss of a friend, a marriage, a job, an unwanted move, a tragic diagnosis, an unexpected pregnancy, or maybe the death of a loved one. In the midst of storms, take refuge.

Take time today to thank Him for being the Rock, the safe place in the midst of life's tragedies. Take the opportunity today to see His fingerprints in even the most painful times and recognize how He is growing you. Sometimes, however, we just need a child's rock to remind us.

Paula Rinehart

Praise the Lord! For it is good to sing praises to our God;
For it is pleasant and praise is becoming. PSALM 147:1 (NASB)

Do you ever walk through your living room, in one of those rarer moments when it's picked up and put in place, and just stop and savor a beautiful moment? The way colors flow together . . . that old teacup and saucer your grandmother gave you . . . the pictures of children and friends that grace the table you found at an auction. As the old expression goes, beauty soothes the spirit. Perhaps this is what drives a woman to create a room that makes others want to rest in a chair and say, "Ahhh, . . ."

The Bible says that God Himself is beautiful—so lovely, in fact, that if we could see Him, we would be blinded by His beauty. The small phrase in the verse above, "for it is pleasant" could be rendered in the Hebrew, *for He is beautiful.* The Lord of hosts who laid his glory aside to live and die as one of us and who dwells now in unapproachable light, says that one thing, in particular, befits that loveliness. *Praise is his chosen adornment.* A song of praise enhances His beauty.

As I try to wrap my mind around the beauty of God, I take note that God says it will lead me in one direction—praise. There are endless ways to decorate a room. But the beauty of God is adorned by our praise. I suspect that my physical eyes, which appreciate the way a room can be "just right," are windows to the eyes of my heart, meant to see and worship His beauty with growing awe. It is beauty we will one day share with Him.

"Praise the Lord, for the Lord is good; sing praises to His name, for it is lovely," Psalm 135:3 (NASB) says.

When are you struck by beauty around you . . . and what causes you to stand amazed at the beauty of God?

Lisa Harper

As they continued their travel, Jesus entered a village. A woman by the name of Martha welcomed him and made him feel quite at home. She had a sister, Mary, who sat before the Master, hanging on every word he said. But Martha was pulled away by all she had to do in the kitchen. Later, she stepped in, interrupting them. "Master, don't you care that my sister has abandoned the kitchen to me? Tell her to lend me a hand." LUKE 10:38–40 (MSG)

Mary and Martha remind me of another juxtaposed pair named Oscar and Felix. Remember them? They were the main characters on that '70s show *The Odd Couple*. Felix was high-strung and persnickety with perhaps a touch of OCD, while Oscar was a lovable—albeit grumpy—slob. Of course this pop culture comparison isn't a perfect theological metaphor, because although Martha does come across as fussy, Scripture doesn't say Mary was slovenly! It simply reveals that she wasn't defined by doing.

Mary was able to set aside her to-do list long enough to sit at Jesus' feet and focus on Him. But her manic sister Martha was too worried about table settings to be still and give Him her full attention. She's the type of chick you could count on for a casserole yet wouldn't choose to hang out with at Starbucks. Because you know she'd be so preoccupied scanning the room for health code violations that she'd wouldn't hear your heart. Martha had the spiritual handicap of *busyness*. Mary had the God-honoring gift of *being*.

Would your friends be more likely to describe you as "distracted" or "devoted"? Do you spend as much time alone with your Redeemer as you do worrying about what's left on your to-do list?

If you identify more with Martha than Mary, it might be a good idea to start "scheduling" blocks of time to focus solely on Jesus. I recommend first thing in the morning because communing with the Lover of your Soul is even better than a double cappuccino!

Bethany Pierce

There are different kinds of gifts, but the same Spirit . . . There are different kinds of working, but the same God works all of them in all men. I CORINTHIANS 12:4,6 (NIV)

In college I spent inordinate amounts of time writing. While other Christians led Bible studies and worked tirelessly to recruit new believers, I preferred the quiet world of my imagination. As I wrote, I was plagued with guilt: was I being a "good Christian"?

In our society we are tempted to gauge the success of an effort by its product. We think we must have outstanding church attendance or an impressive roster of friends we have brought into the Christian fold. But souls are not feathers in our cap and holy work cannot be reduced to a product.

Some are called to be teachers, some preachers, some missionaries. Some are called to be artists. The roles are different. The art a Christian makes is not a religious tract, a sermon, or an altar call. As an artist, my witness consists of the ways I interact with the people my profession throws my way: students, coworkers, curators, editors. The time I spend at my desk and in my studio is worship. With each word I type, each stroke of the brush, I am participating in the dance of imagination the first Artist began with Creation. It is a private, concentrated activity, performed in secret, like prayer.

If you are a man or woman with a passion for solitude, music, dance, art, or writing, then devote the hours spent perfecting your craft to God, knowing the work is of value to the one Audience who matters most.

Think about this: how is art making a kind of worship? Must a work of art be ostensibly mission-minded to be Christian?

Arloa Sutter

Jesus looked at them and said, "With man this is impossible, but not with God; all things are possible with God."
MARK 10:27 (NIV)

When Martha and Mary, the sisters of Lazarus knew their brother was sick and could die, they sent for Jesus. They had faith that Jesus could make him well. But, Jesus did something interesting. He waited. He waited to come until it seemed like it was too late. Lazarus was dead.

"Jesus," the sisters lamented when He finally arrived, "Where were you? If you had been here our brother would not have died. Where were you Jesus?"

Do you sometimes feel like God has not shown up in your moments of greatest need? Where were You, Jesus, when my brother died, when my child was hit by a car, when my money ran out? Where were You, Jesus?

Jesus explained, "This is for God's glory so that God's Son may be glorified through it." God was still in control even when the situation seemed hopeless. He had a plan. He had a larger glory story that they did not understand at the moment.

"Do you believe?" He asked Martha and Mary. "Do you believe that I am the resurrection and the life? That whoever believes in me will never die? Do you believe?" Do you believe, even when you don't understand? Even when your situation seems hopeless? Do you believe that God can resurrect seemingly hopeless situations in a way that will give Him even greater glory?

What might God be doing in your life today that would make your story a glory story? Can you trust Him? Will you believe in His goodness and grace? Nothing is impossible for God.

"Yes, Lord," said Martha. "I believe." And Jesus performed a miracle for all to see.

Anita Lustrea

Honor your father and mother. Then you will live a long, full life in the land the Lord your God will give you. Exodus 20:12 (NLT)

Father's Day is one of those special days that is very meaningful to many and can be quite painful for others. It's painful to some because they've lost their father. To others it is a painful time because the father-child relationship was strained, or even abusive.

Most of us, at least in part, develop our concept of God from the view we had of our earthly father. Again, for some that means a healthy view of God, for others a distorted view of God.

When I was a little girl I knew my dad as the guy who could fix anything, build anything, and make special things happen. My dad was a pastor and so I saw him model for me how to be grace-filled under pressure and how to repay criticism with kindness.

As a child it was easy to honor my father by the way I behaved. As I started thinking about how I can honor my father today, beyond the perfunctory "tie" purchase, I realized that it still might be tied to how I behave. Not in the sense of being a "good girl" or a "naughty girl," but what kind of life I'm leading. What kind of woman of God I'm becoming.

As you focus on Dad today, whether he is living or has passed on, what can you do this day to honor him? If you didn't have a good relationship with your father what is a way you can honor him without being dishonest about your past?

Christine Wyrtzen

The Lord called me from the womb. . . . He has made my mouth like a sharp sword. ISAIAH 49:1–2 (NASB)

God's original intention for each of His creations is to speak His Words. The enemy knows this. He trembles for fear that I will truly grasp this truth. He's afraid that I will see the results of such a discipline. Therefore, he's out to steal words. Make me mute. Send me to a place of wordlessness.

When I was seven, I remember making the decision to start curbing words. The older I got, the quieter I became. In my thirties, while suffering from a time of extreme depression, I lost words altogether. When those closest to me asked, "Where are you?" I replied, "In my well of wordlessness." If only I had known the antidote.

Maybe you are in a place today where you can't even cry out for help. Words of praise and exclamations of faith elude you. To even think of speaking them seems impossible. Let me assure you that "wordlessness" is an illusion of the enemy. We are never without words, just without the belief that we are destined to speak them.

If you are without praise and suffer silently, this is what I would suggest.

- Remind your Enemy that Jesus rebukes him. Through the power of the cross, command him to release your tongue to speak.
- Ask Jesus to help you get the words out. Once you start speaking Scripture, you will find it easier and easier to continue.
- Read the Psalms out loud until you feel the disbelief of your soul subside and the faith of your spirit ignite.

Our spirit, the place where words are plentiful and the faith of a mustard seed still lives, is meant to rule our lives.

Identify one place in your life today that feels absolutely hopeless, the place where you have lost all faith for change. Choose some appropriate Scriptures about God's power, put your name in the passages, and read them out loud. By faith. In trust.

Lynne Hybels

Suppose a brother or sister is without clothes and daily food. If one of you says to them, "Go, I wish you well; keep warm and well fed," but does nothing about their physical needs, what good is it? JAMES 2:15–16 (NIV)

In the mid nineties I traveled twice to Croatia and Bosnia, where the Balkan War was raging. It was a vicious war, marked by atrocious crimes against humanity: ethnic cleansing, mass murders, brutal rape. Traveling with a humanitarian organization, I visited refugee centers filled with middle-class women just like me who had lost everything: jobs, husbands, homes, their future. I visited schools where social workers tried to help kids who had watched their parents die; all day long the children sat in their classroom, silently chewing their nails, unable to escape the traumatized internal world they'd entered.

The day before I returned home I climbed to the top of a hill that overlooked the Bosnian countryside. I sat there for hours and wept and prayed for the women and children I'd seen. While I prayed an unbidden question repeated itself: *Am I my sister's keeper*? And the repeated answer was *Yes, yes, yes, you are your sister's keeper.*

And who is my sister? God, who is my sister?

They are all your sisters. Croatian Catholics. Bosnian Muslims. Serbian Orthodox. They are all part of the human family I have created.

When you open your heart to God and to the world, you end up with a huge family. And you realize that every single member of the family is as important to God as you are. You can't possibly meet the need of every family member—you can't clothe and feed each one—but you can never again dismiss their needs thoughtlessly. They're family.

This changes the way I listen to the news. It changes the way I think about war, global poverty, AIDS. Distance doesn't matter, race doesn't matter, religion doesn't matter. If there's tragedy in the world, it's touching my family.

How about you? Have you joined the family? Are you your sister's keeper?

Linda Clare

... and hope does not disappoint us ... ROMANS 5:5 (RSV)

One of my three adult sons is a meth addict. The other two smoke pot and are drinking themselves to death. My only daughter is brilliant, beautiful, and bipolar. My husband and I never saw any of this coming. We had big dreams for all of them. Sure, I'm a polio survivor and my husband spent part of his childhood in an orphanage. But, we thought, if we did all the right things we'd escape our own problems and raise successful, healthy kids. Unfortunately, doing the "right things" hasn't been enough.

Our children started out as normal as any American kids, unless you count our boy-girl twins, born five weeks early. They quickly caught up with their peers and thrived. Our older two boys attended Boy Scouts and church camp. We were among the only parents our kids knew that were still together. Yet even in elementary school our second son developed severe anxiety. He saw counselors and psychiatrists, but none could diagnose him. Meanwhile, our oldest got caught smoking pot at high school. Later one twin had school problems and the other suffered sudden breakout mental illness. I wanted to fix all of their lives for them by doing even more "right things."

But I can't fix them. As painful as it is to watch the kids suffer and wrestle their demons, I have to admit that God loves them far more than I ever could. Foremost in my prayers these days is the dream that they'll learn to trust and serve God, and that I will cling to the hope that never disappoints. Have you had dreams for your children that shattered? Do you still hold out hope?

If you are grieving over broken dreams, try writing them on pieces of paper. Stack the paper into a fire-resistant container, such as a metal incense burner or grate, and say a prayer for these dreams, offering them to God. Light them and watch them burn and know that God will give you His hope—the kind that never disappoints.

Leslie Ludy

Be anxious for nothing, but in everything by prayer and supplication, with thanksgiving, let your requests be made known to God. PHILIPPIANS 4:6 (NASB)

For quite some time now, I have been asking God to make me worry free, able to rest completely in His perfect faithfulness. Throughout each day, whenever I am tempted to be anxious over a situation, no matter how big or small, it has become my habit to put the words of Paul into practice: "Be anxious for nothing, but in everything by prayer and supplication, with thanksgiving, let your requests be made known to God" (Philippians 4:6 NASB). As I follow this prescription, I find that my fear is replaced with faith. I catch a glimpse of the peaceful state of soul God intends for me to have.

Psalm 37:8 (NIV) always makes me smile at its simple brilliance and truth: "Do not fret— it leads only to evil." When we worry, we become focused on *ourselves* rather than Jesus Christ. When we obsess over what may or may not happen, or worry about a desire we have that may or may not be fulfilled, we neglect to trust our Lord. Instead, we try to solve problems in our own human wisdom, our own feeble strength, and with our own limited vision. This pattern, the writer of Psalms says so poignantly, leads to disaster. We become filled with despair or anger when things don't go our way. We take the pen out of God's hands and try to script our own story.

True peace comes from abandoning our habit of worry, handing the pen over to the faithful Author of our life story, and letting Him have His way—whatever that may be, knowing His grace truly is sufficient in *all* circumstances. Today ask yourself what worries you've been carrying. Then make a conscious, prayerful decision to give the pen of your life back to the One who is able to lovingly script your story from start to finish.

Anita Lustrea

O God, you are my God; I earnestly search for you. My soul thirsts for you; my whole body longs for you in this parched and weary land where there is no water. PSALM 63:1 (NLT)

I remember when I was a little girl, distinctly having this feeling in the pit of my stomach. I would describe it as being hungry, but not for food. It was years later that I understood this was a deep longing within me for God. Leigh McLeroy describes this as "The Beautiful Ache." Frederick Buechner calls this "Longing for Home."

C. S. Lewis said, "If I find in myself a desire which no experience in this world can satisfy, the most probable explanation is that I was made for another world." So what do we do with that truth, with the ache and the longing?

We don't really have a choice. The longings will come, and I think the older we get they come even more frequently. When I was pregnant with my now teenage son John, I attended a college basketball game. As I was sitting in the bleachers I was overwhelmed with this longing for home. The college basketball game reminded me of a younger more innocent time in my life, and the child I carried in my womb created this overwhelming desire to protect. I wanted this child to go straight to heaven, to escape the heartaches I knew life would bring him. The longing was tangible, palpable.

What longings can you identify in your life? Use them to lead you back to the only one who can fulfill them.

Ellie Kay

If any of you lacks wisdom, let him ask of God, who gives to all generously and without reproach, and it will be given to him. JAMES 1:5 (NASB)

What if you were given a gift card that was miraculously redeemable to help you handle any problem, crisis, or life-and-death situation? Is there a time in your life when you would have redeemed it? This verse is better than such a gift card because it has God as the guarantor. That is why it is such an important Scripture to use on a regular basis.

The beautiful part of this verse is that when we know God personally and don't know what to do in a particular situation, we can go to this promise and use it—and it's redeemable any time and in any place. Everyone lacks wisdom at some time or another and this Scripture guarantees us that God is eager to "generously" give us the direction we need when we need it. It's been said that God usually isn't early, He's never late, but He's always on time.

The other encouraging aspect of this Scripture is that God won't get bothered or annoyed with us, no matter how often we ask for His wisdom. His gift is "without reproach." This gives a tremendous amount of freedom in our prayer life when we need to seek God's direction in a matter. Finally, the verse says that wisdom "will" be given. It doesn't say "maybe" or "if you say the right words" or "if I feel like it." God's promise is always there for us when we ask.

The next time you need wisdom, ask God. The problem isn't that God refuses to answer, but it's usually that we aren't asking or we're not waiting for the answer. Wisdom ***is*** guaranteed.

Kristen Johnson Ingram

Do not cast me off in the time of old age; do not forsake me when my strength is spent. PSALM 71:9 (ESV)

The day I had my old dog put to sleep, I planted peas. It was snowing, but I brushed the white flakes off the soil and furiously chopped at the hard earth with my trowel. Returning to my warm house, I wept with rage and sorrow. I was God to that little dog, but I ran out of ways to keep him alive; so finally, when he was totally blind, deaf, and close to kidney failure, I handed him over to the veterinarian.

He was my companion and went with me everywhere. When I traveled on business, he stood on tiptoe on the edge of the backseat, looking out the window and sometimes putting his head on my shoulder. When we came home, he rushed in the doorway before me to make sure the house was safe. He was overjoyed when I returned from an errand, happy when I went to bed and he could curl up by my feet, excited when I jingled my car keys, grateful when I fed and watered him. When I put him in the car for his last ride to the veterinarian, he wagged his tail.

Sometimes we're tempted not to have pets, to avoid that pain. But just as God risked his heart in the death of his son, sometimes we need to lay our love on the line, knowing we'll be hurt, yet better for that pain.

The peas I planted in anger and grief didn't come up. I had to replant a month later, when the sun was reborn and the earth was soft. We had a bumper crop.

If you have owned any pets, make a list of them (including any that are alive), and remember them for a few minutes, thanking God for their lives and yours.

Ask God to give you the strength to risk your heart, to help you love other people, animals, trees, flowers, and even weeds that occupy the wonderful world He has given us.

Ellen Vaughn . . . .

[God] is the Maker of the Bear and Orion, the Pleiades and the constellations of the south. He performs wonders that cannot be fathomed, miracles that cannot be counted.

Job 9:9–10 (NIV)

When we stare at the stars, we're linked with Old Testament Job, shivering in his robe in 2000 B.C. But Job would have been even more amazed by God's miraculous creation if he had had today's tools.

Telescopes reveal that Betelgeuse, the bright star in Orion's shoulder, is 3,000,000,000,000,000—*three quadrillion*—miles away. It is four hundred million miles wide, a red inferno with a froth of fire that streams ten million miles into space.

Or consider the constellation Andromeda. We see her not as she is "now," but as she was two and a half million years ago, because that's how long it takes the light from Andromeda—traveling at 670 million miles per hour—to reach Earth.

Creation's wonders can knock our socks off. Like Job, we shake our heads . . . if the stars are so incredibly magnificent, how much more so is the One who made them?

Take things in the opposite direction, to the wonders of the subatomic world. The dot on this *i* holds five hundred billion particles of matter called protons . . . each one imbued by its Creator with elegant complexity, proclaiming, in ways we can't yet hear, the glory of God, echoing the uncountable grains of sand in all the oceans of the world, all the stars in the galaxies of this incredible universe, all the cells in your body, singing the wonders of the One who knows every hair on your head and loves you more than you can dream.

Tonight, if it is clear enough, take a few moments to stare at the stars. Be still in the silence, and listen for what the magnificent Creator has to say to *you*.

Anita Lustrea

Jesus wept. JOHN 11:35 (NIV)

One of the books I've read this past year is *Windows of the Soul* by Ken Gire. Actually, I've read it twice. Ken talks about all kinds of windows of the soul. The windows of vocation, stories, art, wilderness, poetry, memory, dreams, writing, Scripture, humanity, tears, depression, and nature. I'm sure there are other windows that you could come up with, but many of these particular windows have spoken to me.

In the past year, the window of tears has especially spoken to me. This baffled me a bit because traditionally, I'm not a crier.

Frederick Buechner said, "Whenever you find tears in your eyes, especially unexpected tears, it is well to pay the closest attention. They are not only telling you something about the secret of who you are, but more often than not God is speaking to you through them of the mystery of where you have come from and is summoning you to where, if your soul is to be saved, you should go next."

I've cried more tears in the last six months than probably the last six years combined. They have been a gift, and they have, indeed, been a window to my soul. I've been paying attention to my tears and learning about some losses I need to grieve. I don't think very many of us pay attention to some of the quiet occurrences in our lives that are actually shouting at us. I'm learning to pay attention and God is healing me. These are ways that Jesus draws us to Himself if we will but pay attention and listen.

John 11:35 reads, "Jesus wept." We can be confident that Jesus, too, traveled the road of tears. Think back to a season of grief in your own life. Did God join you? Did He lead you anywhere unexpected? Journal about that.

Pam Farrel

Since we live by the Spirit, let us keep in step with the Spirit.
GALATIANS 5:25 (NIV)

My husband, Bill, was trying to explain Genesis 1 and gender differences to a couple in crisis. Struggling for a word picture, the Spirit prompted him to say, "Think of your wife's conversation like a plate of spaghetti, each noodle touches the other." The session went so well at the end she asked, "If I am spaghetti, what is my husband?"

Bill began to pray for a word picture that could explain how men compartmentalize. One day, our boys were making breakfast, out popped a waffle and the light went on: men are like waffles. That book, *Men are like Waffles, Women are like Spaghetti*, went on to become a bestseller affecting thousands of marriages.

Even further back, I stepped out of the shower on our honeymoon and began to criticize myself as I looked in the mirror. Bill thought, "Oh no! She is going to get depressed and it might take the rest of the honeymoon to recover." Then the Holy Spirit whispered to Bill, "You could do a better job than that mirror." So Bill lovingly whispered, "Let me be your mirror." That moment laid the strong foundation for our twenty-eight years of marriage. Our friends Boomer and Lisa Reiff wrote a song about that moment and Lifeway turned it into the *Men are like Waffles, Women are like Spaghetti* DVD series for small groups complete with a music video!

One day after I recommitted my life to Christ in junior college, two friends were talking about an upcoming leadership conference. The Spirit whispered, "Get to that conference." It was at that event I met Bill.

People often dream of what it would be like if God did great things, but what it really all comes down to is listening to the small promptings God whispers as we serve Him on the frontlines *every* moment of *every* day. *What is the Spirit whispering to you?*

Robin Chaddock

He who was seated on the throne said, "I am making everything new!" REVELATION 21:5 (NIV)

This is what I have noticed about life. Sometimes things just slip away out of disuse, disrepair, or being broken. I have things all over my house like that. Old pictures, old furniture, broken pieces of jewelry, unfinished quilts.

But this kind of disrepair or disuse doesn't have to be just about "stuff." It can be about relationships, talents, energy, a sense of humor, fitness, a sense of spiritual zestiness.

What interests me about things being made new, is that it's about "stuff" that's already there. Reclamation and restoration are about the beauties of my life that already exist, but just need some attention, dusting off, or repair of some sort. In a culture that is obsessed with new things, bigger things, more things, this might be a welcome soul sigh of relief.

The One sitting on the throne isn't quoted as saying, "I will make everything new" as if it's an event we have to wait for in the future. The one sitting on the throne is quoted as saying, "I am making everything new" in the present tense.

So what needs to be renewed, reclaimed, or restored? The One sitting on the throne wants to take what you already have and make it new. You don't need to be or have anything more than you already are or have, you just need to put it out in the open for the restoration touch.

Anita Lustrea

A glad heart makes a happy face; a broken heart crushes the spirit. PROVERBS 15:13 (NLT)

It was a crazy sight. My husband took the leadership team from the singles ministry that he pastors to Laser Quest. You should have seen this group of men and women ranging in ages from forty to eighty disrupting the birthday parties of little boys and girls. No one in the group knew what to expect. Most middle-aged folks don't hang out playing laser tag. But there they were, outside their comfort zone, wondering what in the world they were doing at a place like that.

Then they started to play. The little kid came out in everyone. Teams were formed. Strategies developed. Alliances forged. It was so much fun. They were like kids again.

When was the last time you had fun and really laughed, giggled and went home humming a song. Laughter and joy are gifts from God. Maybe one of the reasons Jesus seemed to like little kids so much is that they made Him smile. Maybe they even invited Him to play a first century version of laser Tag. In that moment, He got to relax and let himself go. Proverbs 15:13 (NLT) reads, "A glad heart makes a happy face; a broken heart crushes the spirit." My prayer for all of you is that you too can relax, let go, renew yourself and laugh a little in the process.

Here's a suggestion. Might be a little hard for some. Trust me. Get in front of a mirror, maybe even with a friend, and then start making some seriously silly faces. You'll laugh. Your heart will be glad. Just so you know . . . my mom and I did this all the time when I was growing up. I still do it today, sometimes with my mother, sometimes with my son!

It's just plain fun. Nothing wrong with that is there?

Kim Hill

Ascribe to the Lord the glory due his name; worship the Lord in the splendor of holiness. Psalm 29:2 (ESV)

Unless you've been living in a phone booth for the past several years I'm sure you've heard the theological assertion, "Worship is a lifestyle, not just something you do at church once a week." And if you're anything like me, you probably nodded in full agreement on Sunday—only to grapple with how to actually live that lifestyle later.

Frankly, when my boys dawdle while getting ready for school on Monday morning and I'm cajoling them to come downstairs then suddenly realize I've forgotten to work out the carpool schedule for the week and accidentally drop a bowl of hot oatmeal on recently mopped floors, worshipping God isn't the first thing that comes to mind! What comes to my mind is more along the lines of, "How in the world do other single moms do this without saying bad words before breakfast?"

Maybe you aren't frazzled from trying to raise two kids by yourself, but nearly every woman I've connected with at Christian conferences from Nairobi to New York have confessed to being overwhelmed. They're exhausted from staying up all night with a new baby, or from nursing a parent with Alzheimer's, or from stretching too little money over too many bills. Most of the women I spend time with are simply worn out.

That's why I think the key to a lifestyle of worship is *surrender*. Because if we don't continually acknowledge our absolute dependency on God, the harsh realities of life will definitely knock the wind—and the worship—right out of us. So carve out a few minutes from your schedule today and repeat the lines from this wonderful, old hymn before the oatmeal starts flying!

All to Jesus
I surrender
All to Him I freely give
I will ever love and trust Him
In His presence daily live
I surrender all
I surrender all
All to Thee my Blessed Savior
I surrender all

(Written by Judson W. Van DeVenter, 1896)

Joanne Heim

The wise woman builds her house, but with her own hands the foolish one tears hers down. PROVERBS 14:1 (NIV)

I am constantly amazed at the power we wield as women. More than any other member of my family, it's my attitude and actions that affect everyone else. "If mama ain't happy, ain't nobody happy" is trite, but so very true—and something that should make me think twice about a bad attitude I'm sometimes dying to have!

As women, we have the power to build our houses, or tear them down. In fact, I'd venture to say that almost every choice we make as women can be one to build our homes or tear them down. I thought about the choices I make each day and was surprised at just how many of them fall into one camp or the other—very few don't matter.

What kind of an attitude will I have when I wake my children for school? Am I excited about a new day and passing on that attitude of joyful expectation to my kids, or am I not quite awake, grumpy, and wishing I was still in bed?

Am I going to take the time to discipline something that needs my attention—carefully and prayerfully dealing with it, or am I going to blow up in anger and walk away in disgust?

What am I going to wear today? Does my appearance show modesty, or do I communicate that appearance is what matters the most?

What will I serve my family for dinner? Even what's on their plates can build them up or tear them down, either teaching them healthy eating habits or poor ones.

The choices I face in my day have lasting effect. As I approach each one—I want to be the kind of woman who wisely builds her family.

As you make choices today, think about them in terms of building up or tearing down. How does looking at choices in this way change your decisions?

Sabrina O'Malone

Therefore, there is now no condemnation for those who are in Christ Jesus. ROMANS 8:1 (NIV)

Flaming arrows of accusation seemed to come at me without warning on the job, from Christian radio and in women's retreats. My only refuge was my private prayer and Bible reading time. Can a working mother ever truly be free from guilt?

Yes—by putting on the full armor of God (Ephesians 6:10–18).

The helmet of salvation comes from accepting Jesus Christ as your Savior. Pray about being a working mom. If you still want to (or need to) be employed, yet guilty feelings continue to plague you, then it's "false guilt"—and it does not come from God.

Pick up the sword of the spirit, God's Word. The Bible describes two kinds of sorrow: "Godly sorrow brings repentance that leads to salvation and leaves no regret, but worldly sorrow brings death" (2 Corinthians 7:10 NIV). Don't let failure to live up to other people's expectations get you down. God is aware of your situation. He calls you to serve Him where you are until He gives you a new assignment. Acts 5:29 (NIV) says "We must obey God rather than men!"

The shield of faith extinguishes flaming arrows of accusation. Hebrews 11:1 (NIV) says "Faith is being sure of what we hope for and certain of what we do not see."

The belt of truth counters the lie that you aren't free to live out God's will. "So if the Son sets you free, you will be free indeed" (John 8:36 NIV).

Finally, the breastplate of righteousness and shoes of peace. Remember, your struggle is not against flesh and blood but against powers of this dark world. Continue doing what's right, and choose to live joyfully in God's perfect peace.

Lori Neff

Consider it pure joy, my brothers, whenever you face trials of many kinds, because you know that the testing of your faith develops perseverance. JAMES 1:2–3 (NIV)

My standard operating procedure for my own or someone else's pain has been to try to fix it, dull it, or make it go away—quickly! I scramble to drown out the hurt with noise, caffeine, chocolate, sleep, or work. Certainly I thought, pain should be avoided at all costs and that if I was in pain, something was terribly wrong with me. But, I was in a quandary because I couldn't reconcile my pain avoidance with the fact that this is a very painful world—pain is unavoidable and happens to godly people.

A friend of mine told me that when her son was diagnosed with cancer, she cleared the clutter from her life to make room to really be present in the pain. She *wanted* to fully feel the pain. My family went through a desperately painful time of caring for my father-in-law during his terminal illness and we tried to live a new reality after his death. I didn't want to fully be present in the pain! I planned to methodically go through the steps of grief so I could get relief. But, my plan didn't work—grieving is messy and doesn't have set rules.

Now, a few years later, my husband and I are going through a painful time where an injustice has been done to us. It's messy and painful and there's no fix for it. We just have to be in this season and go through it. I'm learning to acknowledge the pain and feel it and not instantly move to squelch it. Instead, I'm asking God more often, "What do you want to teach me here?" I'm learning to listen and be still more—and yes, fully feel the pain.

Mary Whelchel

If the Lord delights in a man's way, he makes his steps firm; though he stumble, he will not fall, for the Lord upholds him with his hand. PSALM 37:23–24 (NIV)

Failure is a part of the process of living and growing and learning. But our enemy, Satan, loves to use our failures to freeze us into inactivity by making us believe that we cannot recover.

I remember when my behavior in front of one of my peers at work was anything but Christlike. Something had irritated me, and I reacted very poorly. Now, I had been encouraging this colleague in things of the Lord, helping him to begin a serious devotional life. And after all those "spiritual" discussions, I behaved in a very unspiritual way.

God's Spirit really convicted me and my first thought was that my friend would now discount everything I had said before since I failed so badly right before his eyes. But the faithful Spirit of God showed me what I had to do. As soon as I could, I got alone with my friend and apologized. But then I went on to explain how wonderful it is that even when we fail so miserably, God's forgiveness and his healing are always available.

God used my failure to show this person, who was so afraid of failing, that failure is not the end of the road and we have a God who puts the pieces back together. He was encouraged by my experience of failure!

So, if you've been handicapped by your failure, ask God to turn those ashes into beauty. Failure is not the end of the road; it can be a beautiful beginning.

Are there some failures in your life that have held you in bondage far too long?

Kathy Peel

These commandments that I give you today are to be upon your hearts. Impress them on your children. Talk about them when you sit at home and when you walk along the road, when you lie down and when you get up.

DEUTERONOMY 6:6–7 (NIV)

When our boys were preschoolers, our family devotions left a lot to be desired—like straitjackets for the kids and smart pills for us. The painting in the bookstore had made it look so easy. The dad sat in front of the fireplace and read from the Bible. Mom, the dog, and the kids gazed at him attentively, hanging on his every word.

But we didn't have a fireplace, and our kids couldn't sit still for longer than a few seconds. So we decided to try a different approach and follow the advice from Deuteronomy—to teach our boys about God throughout the day in the normal course of life.

We started the routine of reading to them at bedtime from biblical storybooks and children's Bibles. At the same time, we realized that as important as teaching them God's truths was providing tangible examples—we needed to live out those truths.

As parents, we cannot just tell our children what's right and wrong. If we want children to adopt biblical values, we must adopt those values ourselves, living according to God's Word the best we can. Our children need to witness us spending time daily in Bible study and prayer. They need to hear Mom and Dad treat each other with respect, even when they get angry. They need to see a parent turn off a television program because it glamorizes sin. They need to watch their parents reach out to people in need.

We can't force our values upon our children any more than we can force them to sit still during family devotions. But we can influence their character and decisions by how we live day by day.

What values are your children picking up from you?

Linda Mintle

The Lord does not look at the things man looks at. Man looks at the outward appearance, but the Lord looks at the heart.
1 SAMUEL 16:7 (NIV)

The above was said to Samuel, but God could be talking to every woman in America. In today's world, image is everything. The pressure to be thin and beautiful never stops and the cultural message is that we can always improve our appearance and do more. In other words, we are never quite good enough. The Lord may be looking at our hearts, but we sure focus on the outward appearance! No wonder the normal state for most women is to dislike their bodies!

So how do we change this? First, resist cultural prescriptions for beauty and honor your individuality. God created us unique so let's stop trying to look like clones of each other and stop imitating celebrities. Second, stop comparing yourself to unrealistic media images. Remember these images are typically computer-altered, airbrushed, professionally lighted, and the subjects use the services of professional makeup and hair artists. Third, stop the inner critic from telling you how inadequate you are, that you don't measure up and will never be good enough. Silence that voice and fill your mind with what God says about you—you are wonderfully made. He delights in you! Fourth, find women who don't obsess on their bodies but value what God values. Spend time with them and turn the conversation away from body obsession.

The physician Luke was right when he told us that there is more to our lives than the clothes we wear. So let's get off the scales and on with our lives by making peace with our thighs or any other body part that causes us to hate our imperfect bodies!

Glynnis Whitwer

She makes linen garments and sells them, and supplies the merchants with sashes. PROVERBS 31:24 (NIV)

Every woman is a working woman; whether it's running a business or running a household. Today, it's easier than ever for women to do both from the comfort of home.

The idea of a home-based business isn't new. At one time, most businesses were run from homes. Proverbs 31 paints a beautiful example of a home-based entrepreneur.

In Proverbs 31:24 (NIV) we learn that the Proverbs 31 woman "makes linen garments and sells them, and supplies the merchants with sashes." Obviously she was successful in her venture or the verse might have read, "she has boxes of linen garments and sashes in her barn that she can't sell and doesn't know what to do with."

The Proverbs 31 woman *was* a successful business woman and here are just a few of the home-based business success tips we can learn from her:

Verse 27 reads, "She watches over the affairs of her household." Home-based businesses can drain your reservoirs of time and energy, because there's always more to be done. A wise businesswoman orders her priorities, allots her time, and creates a healthy balance.

Verse 17 reads, "She sets about her work vigorously; her arms are strong for her tasks." The Proverbs 31 woman worked with strength and vigor. Because our work today is often inactive, this involves a commitment to health: sufficient sleep, a balanced diet, maintaining appropriate weight and strong muscles.

Verse 16 reads, "She considers a field and buys it; out of her earnings she plants a vineyard." This woman thought ahead. A home-based entrepreneur needs a plan for the future. This might involve growth strategies, marketing plans, and identifying market trends.

A home-based business isn't for everyone, but for those whom God calls to work at home, there is honor and value in humbly serving God and our families in this manner.

Identify one way you can improve yourself professionally or grow your business this week.

Anita Lustrea

But if we walk in the light, as he is in the light, we have fellowship with one another, and the blood of Jesus, his Son, purifies us from all sin. 1 JOHN 1:7 (NIV)

Community is such a buzz word today. I confess that I'm a bit skeptical about whether or not true community can happen. It's not that I don't believe people won't try to get together in small groups, but will real life change take place? Will people really be authentic with one another?

Here are three truths I believe about community. First of all, life change happens when God's truth meets our lives. Second, I believe life change happens in community. And third, I think living in proximity to those you are in community with increases the frequency of meeting and the possibility of going deeper.

I think we've got to take a look at why this is all so difficult. Why is it so hard to build community? One thing I know for sure is that the Enemy of our souls does not want us to be in community. I believe the reason it's so hard to build solid, life-changing relationships is that we are in a spiritual battle and Satan desperately wants to keep us from building relationships that will fortify us spiritually.

John Eldredge talks about this in his book *Waking the Dead*. He uses the story of the *Lord of the Rings* to make some great points. Frodo doesn't head out alone carrying the ring. He is surrounded, not by masses of people, but by some select friends that commit to walk with him, watch his back, and fight off the enemy. That's what I'm talking about when I think of community. We are in a battle and since the Garden of Eden the Enemy has relied on one strategy, Eldredge says, to divide and conquer: get us isolated and take us out.

What does Satan use in your life, in your existing relationships, in your attitudes, in your behavior, in your thoughts, to keep you from community?

Janet Thompson

You are my hiding place; you will protect me from trouble.
PSALM 32:7 (NIV)

On a recent sunny California day, my two daughters and I each pushed strollers as we walked to our favorite neighborhood coffeehouse. The street was wide so the three of us walked side by side chatting and laughing: Shannon pushing her son Joshua beside Kim pushing her baby Katelyn, and me, Grammie, pushing Katelyn's three-year-old brother Brandon. I was basking in the warmth of the weather and the fellowship with my daughters and grandchildren, when out of the corner of my eye I saw my worst fear.

Suddenly a large dog bolted out of a garage and headed straight for us. Shannon and Joshua were the first in the dog's path. Without hesitating, Shannon rapidly positioned her body between the dog and Joshua's stroller. She firmly stood her ground—feet astride, arms outstretched—the dog would have to go through Shannon before he got to Joshua or any of us.

I was amazed at Shannon's quick selfless reaction. Just as the dog reached her, the flustered owner came running out of the house and retrieved the dog. As we continued on . . . all a bit shaken . . . I commented on Shannon's bravery, but she shrugged off my praise saying, "You always protect your child first."

Etched in my mind is the image of Shannon's arms open wide shielding her son from attack, reminiscent of Jesus who spread out his arms on the cross to protect His children from Satan's attacks. My little grandson didn't really understand the impact of his mother's sacrificial act of love, and often we don't appreciate Jesus' sacrificial love either. So the next time you avoid that near accident or giving in to a sinful temptation, take a moment to say "Thank you Jesus for standing in the gap for us."

Kristen Johnson Ingram

Thus says the Lord: The people . . . found grace in the wilderness; when Israel sought for rest, the Lord appeared to him from far away. JEREMIAH 31:2 (ESV)

After being sick in bed for a few days, I wonder what has become of my little paradise, my quiet retreat with the bedspread my grandmother crocheted, the rows of books, and the ancient rocking chair.

Disappeared under three days' worth of newspapers and decorated with some cups and plates, that's what. A fork raises its tines in an empty glass, cushions and magazines are scattered on the floor, my bedside table holds cough syrup and aspirin instead of candles and seashells; and my bed looks as if goblins have danced in it. I crawl out, wondering if I'm strong enough for a shower, knowing I still don't have the energy to clean my room.

But there's grace even in my wilderness, because while I'm standing under hot water, scrubbing and shampooing, and hoping never to cough again, my visiting daughter sneaks in and cleans up the room. She even manages to get clean sheets on the bed. When I emerge from my steamy bathroom, my hair in a towel, I look around at my bedroom oasis and realize how wonderful love is.

God offers us grace in the wilderness with the heart-shaking words, "I have loved you with an everlasting love." And if my daughter can clean up a bedroom, just imagine what God's everlasting love can do with a life.

Next time your friend is sick, try to get them into the shower or tub, then tidy up the room. A rose in a vase is always a nice touch.

Nancy Sebastian Meyer

He is like a tree planted by streams of water, which yields its fruit in season and whose leaf does not wither. Whatever he does prospers. PSALM 1:3 (NIV)

Several years ago, I arrived early at a church where I taught a weekly Bible study. After preparing the room, I still had time before the women came to pour out my heart to God and search His Word for encouragement. Teaching women to love their husbands is my passion because, after relearning to love my pastor-turned-agnostic husband, I am living proof God can keep families together. So why was I discouraged?

Earlier that week, Rich demanded that I give up full-time ministry and "get a real job." My heart crushed, I wondered how I would stand the pain of living in a spiritually divided family if I couldn't see God using my pain to help other women cope with theirs. And how would the books and message continue to encourage others without my active involvement? How could God ask me to give up the passion He Himself had instilled within me?

That day God led me to a beloved psalm about the person who walks with God. As I read, verse three captured my attention, almost as if God Himself put His finger on it. "Your leaf—your work for me," I could almost hear Him say, "will not wither and die. Whatever you have done—and will do—in my Name will prosper. Trust me, child."

Today I am still in full-time ministry with my husband's permission to share our story and my faith! But regardless of my situation—and yours, I know God will continue to use us to further His kingdom as we trust and obey.

What kind of leaves and fruit is your life producing and how can you "bloom" where you are planted today?

Marcia Ramsland

Sons are a heritage from the Lord, children a reward from him. PSALM 127:3 (NIV)

Have you ever noticed the energy with which children approach everything and everyone? Their smiles are big, their faces wide-eyed and cheery, and you're the best mom in the whole wide world—until you remind them, "Time to clean up your room."

Teaching children to deal with their rooms is like teaching them how to deal with life. After all, children's rooms are their whole world, and this should be the one place they can manage and enjoy.

Remembering that my children are a gift from the Lord, I changed my tone and expectations. Now I and the audiences I teach remember to stop ordering children to "Go clean your room" and instead give them one of five easy steps at a time. Here they are in order:

1. Make the bed so 50 percent to 70 percent of the room is clean.
2. Put everything on the floor away, from the doorway to the bed.
3. Clean the rest of the room by three categories: clothes, paper, and toys. Clothes get put away in the closet or hamper. Papers get organized into three ring notebooks and books go on bookshelves. Toys go on lower open shelves and favorite collections go on dresser tops and upper shelves.
4. Add one extra cleaning section each weekend such as the desktop, dresser top, nightstand, and closet.
5. Empty the wastebasket often.

Helping a child succeed is honoring to God as you train the "gift" He gave to you. Each day follow the first three steps with your child remembering children are a gift from the Lord, and that includes the mess they sometimes make!

Anita Lustrea

Immediately Jesus made the disciples get into the boat and go on ahead of him to the other side, while he dismissed the crowd. After he had dismissed them, he went up on a mountainside by himself to pray. When evening came, he was there alone, but the boat was already a considerable distance from land, buffeted by the waves because the wind was against it.
MATTHEW 14:22–24 (NIV)

My husband, son, and I went on a missions trip to Africa recently, where our hectic pace of life came to an abrupt end. No phone. No e-mail. No demanding timetables. It was good. The team woke early and ate breakfast together. We visited people in mud huts, visited small dirt floor churches, walked paths between villages, and visited slums the likes of which I've never seen before. We worked, we rested. It was a good, healthy rhythm.

I need to figure out a Chicago-style rhythm. Back here I drive fast, read e-mail all day and night, carry a cell phone everywhere and slowly but surely feel my blood pressure start to escalate. It's the American way.

Unfortunately, a go, go, go lifestyle isn't necessarily a "Jesus" lifestyle. For those of us who want to be like Jesus that's important to consider. Jesus took time to be alone. He cultivated a community of men and women to share life with. He considered His relationship with His Papa to be the top priority. He saw interruptions as opportunities to touch a life. He remained consistent even when life threw Him curves. He never seemed in a hurry. He knew where He was headed.

So what's the take-away from Jesus for us? We do live in a fast-paced culture. That's a given. But if we want to be a little counter-cultural start doing this: take time for solitude. Talk to the Lord and listen for His response. When the road gets curvy always remember that Jesus is with you. Do this and your life will change.

Virelle Kidder

Very early in the morning, while it was still dark, Jesus got up, left the house and went off to a solitary place, where he prayed.
MARK 1:35 (NIV)

Jesus showed His disciples what real intimacy with God looked like. It wasn't hard to observe His rhythm of prayer, work, and rest.

Even after decades as a believer, it's still easy for today's urgencies, or craving for sleep, to crowd out my alone time with God. So last night I set out my tennis shoes and clothes for an early morning prayer walk.

Stepping outside, I sniffed the sweet breeze and chuckled as lizards darted under flowering bushes on my path to the river near our home. Soon I was at my favorite spot on the dock watching mullets jump and a couple of tarpon roll in the warm Florida water. My heart hungered for God as I sensed His presence. "I love you, Lord. Thank you for this beautiful new day You have made."

He whispered back, "I made this for you." Worship flowed as naturally as the lapping waves. "I praise you, Father, for allowing me to serve You. I want to live for You today and love others as You do."

Resuming my walk, I opened my sack of troubling issues and turned each one over to Him: my daughter's upcoming move, concerns about completing new writing requests, daily sadness over my mother's advancing Alzheimer's. I wanted to walk an extra lap just to listen for His voice a little longer, but my work awaited. He'd be there with me too.

Have you enjoyed a good prayer walk lately? Why not put out your walking shoes tonight too? God is waiting to meet with you. Nothing on your list or mine matters more.

Melinda Schmidt

"If you keep quiet at a time like this, deliverance and relief for the Jews will arise from some other place, but you and your relatives will die. Who knows if perhaps you were made queen for just such a time as this?" ESTHER 4:14 (NLT)

In the film *The Lord of the Rings—The Return of the King*, Elrond says this to the Ranger, Aragorn: "The man who wields the power of this sword can summon to him an army more deadly than any that walk this earth. Sauron will not have forgotten this sword . . . Put aside the ranger. Become who you were born to be!"

As good gathers courage to face evil in the last film of the Lord of the Rings trilogy, the Elven lord Elrond sees that good's last hope is in Aragorn, and he passionately, somewhat angrily, tries to inspire Aragorn to take on the sword of leadership and save the world of men.

Often, our own sad inner voice doubtfully admits, "This is it; I've reached what I was destined to be . . . I guess." We sense God might have created us for more and we long for it. Does anyone else see something more for me as well?

It takes courage to think beyond the edges of our lives. Can I challenge you to be open to God perhaps giving new definition to your life? Perhaps He is asking you to become a new kind of leader in your home, relationships, or workplace. Perhaps He is asking you to make a new fit person out of yourself: one that is healthier inside and out—body, mind and soul. Unlike a story line in a novel or movie, consider this: perhaps God is truly calling you to put aside who you are today to rise to something else. Perhaps the passionate voice needed to call you to action—is your own! Don't wait for someone else's.

Christine Wyrtzen

"Whoever loses his life for me will save it." LUKE 9:24 (NIV)

I made a two-hour flight yesterday from Harrisburg, Pennsylvania, to Atlanta. I was cramped in a middle seat, sandwiched between two people. My books were packed away overhead and I had nothing to do except think and pray. Settling in for the long ride, I closed my eyes and whispered this prayer. "Jesus, bring some of your words to my mind and then teach me something that I've never understood before." To my amazement, a Scripture came to me. "Whoever loses his life for me will find it." Almost immediately, the following unfolded in my mind.

With my eyes closed, I saw a huge portrait of Jesus but upon closer examination, I noticed that there was one small puzzle piece of the picture missing. At that point, God reached down, picked me up, and put me into the portrait. I fit perfectly. I realized that I was the missing piece.

Right away, the edges of my being blurred and I was incorporated into the person of Jesus. I lost my life in His. To my amazement, it didn't feel like a loss. It wasn't the end of me but the beginning as I was expanded into the very life of Christ.

I realized that by losing our lives, we have access to His. Our once limited well of mercy will infinitely deepen, for the mercy of Jesus will be available to us. Our once meager storehouse of grace will be limitless, bathing those around us in divine consideration and kindness. Our once scanty supply of wisdom will expand, bringing depth and clarity to new layers of spiritual truth. Blending our lives with Jesus, we reach our highest potential.

What is your greatest need today? Where could you "blend into Jesus" and see immediate rewards? Are you willing to consider losing yourself in Him to find the resources you need "in Christ"? Allow this union to unfold in prayer and ask God to guide you.

Anita Lustrea

Joyful are people of integrity, who follow the instructions of the Lord. PSALM 119:1 (NLT)

Do you know anyone with a stubborn streak? Oh—you? I'm in the club too. But deep down my desire is to follow the Lord. Listen to these verses from Psalm 119 (NLT) on following God.

"Joyful are people of integrity, who follow the instructions of the LORD" (v. 1).

"I pondered the direction of my life, and I turned to follow your laws" (v. 59).

"Give me a helping hand, for I have chosen to follow your commandments" (v. 173).

The question is, are you ready to follow?

We grow up being told it's not good to be a follower, that we should be leaders. It's not good to succumb to peer pressure and follow the crowd. Then we open up Scripture and learn that it's good to follow the Lord. In the Gospels Jesus says to the disciples, "Come follow me." He says to you and me, "Come follow me." In fact, we get into trouble when we choose to go our own way. Time after time we have scriptural examples of those who choose to go their own way and the destruction it brings. I could give you a few of my own real life examples. We are a stubborn and pigheaded bunch, aren't we?

The more fully I know and understand the message of Christ, the easier it is to follow this Man of Sorrows. The more I see how He laid down his life for me, the more I want to run hard after Him.

What makes you want to follow Jesus?

Beverly Hubble Tauke

By wisdom is a house built; and through understanding it is established. PROVERBS 24:3 (NIV)

For sure, Sapphira was one church lady who stood by her man—right to her dramatic death (Acts 5). Lot's wife rejected such passive compliance with his exit strategy from fiery Sodom (Genesis 19). God's responses to the mindless conformer and the rudderless rebel were the same: swift, sure, and lethal.

How *does* one navigate a spiritually, emotionally, and morally treacherous marriage? An intriguing answer comes from Esther, whose mercurial, injudicious, powerful king husband agreed to genocide against her people (Esther 3:9-13). Despite reluctance to embrace her perilous mission, Esther proved a gifted crisis manager through:

1. Wise counsel (Proverbs 19:20): Noting that Esther, perhaps, had been destined to save her people from slaughter, family elder Mordecai challenged her to pursue treacherous negotiations with the king.

2. Discretion: Esther complied with Mordecai—on her own terms. Fools, noted Solomon, bumble carelessly into traps (Proverbs 22:3). Esther was no fool.

3. Mood Management—her own and others' (Proverbs 29:11): Transcending judgment-twisting fear or rage, Esther gained steely nerves for her risky challenge to crown policy. She also masterfully created an environment to win the King's favor and to entice enemy Haman into a trap of his own making.

4. Communal Power: God offers special favor to those who seek Him collectively (Mathew 18:19-20). Esther's fasting group tapped such spiritual vitality.

People of faith are not immune to injudicious responses that escalate family crisis into family calamity. But the husband, wife, parent, or child wise enough to embrace Esther's formula can, by God's grace, avert disaster and shift destiny for cherished families.

Kendra Smiley

. . . for I have learned to be content whatever the circumstances. PHILIPPIANS 4:11 (NIV)

Have you ever noticed how contented your children are when they are sleeping? (And so well behaved too!) Contentment can be a difficult thing to achieve, but it is not impossible.

In Philippians 4:11, Paul says that contentment is something he has *learned.* It was not automatic for him. Learning takes time because, simply stated, learning means a "change in behavior." Over time, Paul went from being discontent to being content. His behavior changed.

As a new bride, I learned to cook. When John and I were first married, I knew very little about it. Although my mother tried to teach me, whenever possible I opted *out* of any cooking experiences. In fact, that was one of the main problems; I had no experience. In order to learn to cook, I needed instruction and I needed experience.

Today I can say with some assurance that I have learned to cook. I finally yielded to instruction and after cooking for our family for many years, I definitely gained experience. My behavior changed from that of a woman who did not cook to one who learned to cook . . . whatever the circumstances.

Cooking can be important, but contentment is essential. In order to learn to be content, we need instruction and experience. It will not be automatic, but the Lord "who gives us strength," will instruct us and with experience we can learn.

Think about something you have learned to do. Try to remember the time and effort you gave to that process of learning. My guess is that the learning was not instantaneous but that it took instruction and experience. Let the Lord help you to learn to be content. That is a wonderful Next Right Choice!

Tammy Maltby

Neither do I condemn you; go and sin no more.

JOHN 8:11 (NKJV)

Jesus spoke these words to a woman who had been caught in the act of adultery and dragged into the public square. But did He really think she could "go and sin no more"?

No matter how hard we try, the truth is we're going to sin . . . and sin again. But that's exactly why we need to hear what Jesus was really saying—that no matter how stuck we feel, our lives can change. That He can show us how to move beyond our brokenness into a new kind of life.

It's really possible, no matter how bad things seem.

It's not just about facing our destructive behavior, though that's crucial.

It's not just about God's forgiveness, though that's real.

It's really about "What happens now?" How can we leave our shameful secrets behind and learn to live in the light of His love?

Sinful habits can be hard to break, and the agonizing consequences of our brokenness may stick with us for a long time.

We may need counseling. We definitely need support from friends, family, and others who have walked the path we're trying to take. We need time to heal, a healthy dose of forgiveness for ourselves and others.

Most of all, we need a daily walk with the only One with the right to condemn us . . . and who chooses to love us instead. Because what the woman caught in adultery learned that day is the truth that can transform your life and mine, no matter how painfully broken you may feel: who Jesus is changes everything.

He is truly the light of the world, who shines His revealing but healing ways on our darkest, most shameful secrets. Whose laser love can not only burn out our guilt and woundedness and restore us to health but also show us a whole new way to live. A whole new path to take of honesty, transparency, openness, where the inside you matches the outside you and you can freely love and be loved.

Connie Neal

. . . Though your sins are like scarlet, they shall be as white as snow; though they are red as crimson, they shall be like wool.
ISAIAH 1:18 (NIV)

It isn't easy to spill thirty-two ounces of root beer down your own back, but it can be done. I took my kids to a sporting arena and dutifully bought them a bucket of popcorn and a giant drink. While heading upstairs, my foot slipped, sending me lurching forward—desperately grasping the expensive soda and popcorn. My elbow hit an upward step sending the soda over my shoulder and down my back. Embarrassed as passersby muffled chuckles, I responded, "What? You've never seen a fallen woman?" When I returned to our seats. The kids asked, "Where's our drink?"

Without a word, I turned around, providing them great amusement.

The drink was replaced but my vest was a mess. Arriving home, I tossed it into the cleaners pile and left it. By the time I looked again it had mildewed terribly. I was sure no one could get those stains out so I delayed showing it to the lady at the cleaners. Finally I dared to ask if anything could be done. She scrunched up her face and said,

"Let me see; but next time bring it to me immediately."

Miraculously, she removed every stain (with a toothbrush and several hours of painstaking labor).

The Bible declares true religion involves keeping "oneself unstained by the world" (James 1:27 NASB). The world repeatedly stains us, through our own downfalls and others'. The trick to *keeping* ourselves unstained is to *immediately* take our stains to Jesus. His word promises: "Though your sins are like scarlet, they shall be as white as snow . . ." (Isaiah 1:18 NIV). Whenever you see a stain on your clothing ask yourself if there are any untended spiritual stains. Jesus can remove every stain, *if* we take it to him. If we hide it away it only worsens. Why do you delay taking your stains to Jesus?

Lisa McKay

And this is my prayer, that your love may abound more and more in knowledge and depth of insight so that you may be able to discern what is best, and may be pure and blameless until the day of Christ. PHILIPPIANS 1:9–10 (NIV)

A few months ago I visited Elmina castle, in Ghana. A white-washed fortress perched on the West African coast, Elmina was the Portuguese and Dutch trading post that brokered slaves until the late 1800's. As I stood on what used to be the Governor's balcony I looked down upon the barred stone cells that used to hold hundreds of female slaves awaiting the transport ships. At the Governor's pleasure the women used to be driven from these holding pens into the courtyard below to mill around until he had made his daily choice.

When I looked up I saw a church in the middle of the castle, built directly over the dungeons that used to house the male slaves. Inside that church, words from Psalm 132:14 (KJV) are inscribed above the door; "This is my resting place forever; here I will dwell, for I have desired it."

I stared, and imagined those times, and wanted to cry with rage and pain and shame. And fear. What modern blind spots or willful, apathetic, ignorance will goad future generations into similar paroxysms?

It is impossible to fully grasp or care about every single wrong that is happening in our world today. Yet this is my prayer, that we will not blithely be attending churches built over dungeons. And that each of us, in our own ways, will somehow be working to meet a need and right a wrong in a world that often feels too full of both.

Today, think about whether or how your love for God and others is abounding more and more in knowledge and depth of insight. What global or local wrongs—human trafficking, homelessness, a friend and neighbor enslaved by addiction or loneliness—is God bringing to your attention? Why?

Sharon Hersh

But he was pierced for our transgressions, he was crushed for our iniquities; the punishment that brought us peace was upon him, and by his wounds we are healed. ISAIAH 53:5 (NIV)

My young client had just returned from inpatient treatment for her heroin addiction. "Don't tell me to wait for heaven," she snapped. "I am only nineteen years old! I need something right now!" We aren't very good at waiting.

The tension between wanting more and waiting for it can be excruciating and heartbreaking. In fact, our longings can break our hearts and our spirits. Ernest Hemingway wrote, "The world breaks us all," and then he killed himself unable to bear the staggering weight of all his brokenness.

Perhaps it is a broken dream, a failed marriage, difficult relationships, financial ruin, or spiritual distress that painfully reminds you that you have wanted good things only to find yourself still wanting.

Did you know that God was broken? The New Testament tells us that He was broken for us (1 Corinthians 11). This Scripture is talking about that day when Jesus surrendered His longings, hung naked, was nailed to a cross, and said, "Father forgive them; for they know not what they do" (Luke 23:34 KJV).

I believe in this story God is saying, "I give you My Son, broken for you, *My* deepest wound to forgive and heal *your* deepest wound." Our wounds are where His wound—His love—can get in.

Consider offering all your brokenness and woundedness to God for His redemptive touch. Don't tell Him how to fix it, heal you, or reshape your brokenness. Just offer it to Him, trusting that "by His wounds, we are healed" (Isaiah 53:2-5 NIV).

Ginger Kolbaba

He said to them, "Let the little children come to me, and do not hinder them, for the kingdom of God belongs to such as these."
MARK 10:1–14 (NIV)

When my husband and I were still dating, we got into a whopper of an argument. I don't remember now what it was about—but I do remember that I was right! As I stormed from the living room of his house to make my grand exit, I made a detour to his daughter's room to tell her good-bye—and to ask her to talk some sense into her father. I wanted someone else on my side and since she was a girl and knew how stubborn her dad could be, I figured she would be the perfect choice.

Wrong! I'll never forget the look on her face as she swallowed hard and simply nodded.

Looking back now, I realize I never should have asked her to take sides—and I never should have given her a job (straightening out her father). More than twelve years later, I still cringe at the position I put his daughter in.

How tempting it can be in the heat of an argument to want to use our children or stepchildren to gather up reinforcements for our side. But the truth is that it's the worst thing we can do. My stepdaughter already has enough pressure piled on her from the pain of living in a broken family. I don't need to add to it by asking her to take sides—even in the most insignificant ways. The best thing I can do for my stepdaughter is to keep her out of it—to let her be a kid. The more I've done that, the better our relationship and the more carefree she has become.

Have you ever been tempted to bring your children or stepchildren into an argument to help you "win"? What are some ways you can protect their childhood from having undue stress or pressure?

Anita Lustrea

"But anyone who hears and doesn't obey is like a person who builds a house without a foundation. When the floods sweep down against that house, it will collapse into a heap of ruins."
LUKE 6:49 (NLT)

Did you ever use something in a way that it wasn't originally intended? I have. Once on a business trip, after I put hotel conditioner on my hair I thought, "That doesn't feel like conditioner." Sure enough, I'd just put hand and body lotion all over my hair. It didn't work too well as conditioner, let me tell you. I washed my hair a couple more times to get the lotion out, had a good laugh, and got on with my day. I thought about other things I use incorrectly, like paper clips to try to keep a chip bag closed. It doesn't work very well.

Then I started thinking about how we often treat salvation in a way that it wasn't intended. When people come to faith in Christ it is worthy of great celebration, but when salvation is treated as the end game, rather than the starting line that's not its intended purpose. Salvation is meant as the entry point, but then we've got to dig deep and lay a strong foundation for our faith. We need to be discipled, to learn to study God's Word for ourselves.

Do you have opportunities to dig deeper into God's Word? Do you have a small group Bible study that you are a part of? No matter where we are in our spiritual walk it's important to keep going deeper. Stagnation and complacency are always concerns. Talk to a trusted friend today about your journey of faith and do some self-assessment.

Adele Calhoun

When he had gone indoors, the blind men came to him, and he asked them, "Do you believe that I am able to do this?" "Yes, Lord," they replied. MATTHEW 9:28 (NIV)

Teachers know questions can take people to places instruction alone can't and the Bible is full of them. It's not just an *answer* book, it is a *question* book.

Jesus was at home in the world of questions and He loved to ask them. Studying the questions Jesus asked I found:

- seventy-seven questions in Matthew
- fifty-four in Mark
- fifty in Luke 1–12
- thirty-seven in John

Jesus asks questions He doesn't answer or He answers with a paradox or asks questions people refuse to answer. When under deep duress he even questions God, "... why have you forsaken me?" (Mark 15:34 NIV). Jesus' questions are amazing and real! His queries invite discovery, self-awareness, personal encounter. Forging connections and fostering relationship, Jesus' questions let people talk, think, converse. And in the conversation we may actually find out what we think and where we are with God.

Questions grab attention. How are biblical questions leading you into a conversation with Jesus? Jesus wants to know and hear you answer, "Do you truly love me more than these?" and, "Where is your faith?" Let Jesus' questions live in you. Wait on Him as answers take shape in your mind. Let the conversation shape how you live life.

Read the following Scriptures, placing yourself in the stories: Matthew 9:28; Matthew 21:28; Luke 8:25; John 18:34; John 21:15. Hear the questions like they were spoken to you. Let your answers lead you to encounter your heart and your God.

Ellie Lofaro

Humble yourselves, therefore, under God's mighty hand, that he will lift you up in due time. 1 PETER 5:6 (NIV)

The guest speaker told our congregation that Moses spent the first forty years of his life thinking he was somebody . . . the next forty realizing he was nobody . . . and the forty after that discovering that God could make a somebody out of a humble nobody. This analysis is of great interest to me, especially in light of the fact that I find myself in "the second forty."

Moving away from all that was familiar in New York was the beginning of a humbling process—a pruning season in my life. Nothing was familiar. My new town had no points of reference, warm fuzzies, or meaningful memories. I found it difficult to gain entry to hearts and homes. I decided the solution was to give my time and talent to the school, the church, and the community. Though I tried, I didn't find acceptance and unconditional love. I felt like I was in a dry, forsaken desert . . . and oh, so thirsty. *God, how could you bring me out here to die?*

His response came in bits and pieces, sometimes with a gentle brush stroke and other times with a fierce sword. I was forced to come to terms with some difficult truths. I had become smug and arrogant about avoiding the "deadly sins" and had no patience for those who lacked the strength and discipline to do the same. Compassion, mercy, and humility were *not* my trademarks. I had become "religious" and I was guilty of the *most* deadly sin: pride.

In Exodus 17, Moses comes to the place known as *Rephidim.* A mentor once told me that *Rephidim* represents the end of ourselves—the place where we learn the limits of our own abilities, where God alone can fulfill our needs. I have spent forty years avoiding *Rephidim* . . . but now that I'm here, I think I'll stay. It's a hard road, but a sure one. There'll be no more wandering for me.

Anita Lustrea

As Jesus was walking beside the Sea of Galilee, he saw two brothers, Simon called Peter and his brother Andrew. They were casting a net into the lake, for they were fishermen. "Come, follow me," Jesus said, "and I will make you fishers of men." At once they left their nets and followed him. MATTHEW 4:18-20 (NIV)

What does it look like to follow Jesus? How do you follow Him? I think of Mother Theresa and what following Jesus looked like in her life. There are countless others not nearly as famous as Mother Theresa who, day in and day out, quietly follow in the footsteps of Jesus. Sometimes I ask myself if I have any resemblance to them, any resemblance to Him.

I heard Dr. Rosalie de Rosset, a professor at the Moody Bible Institute, speak at a Bible conference in 1995. She said, "I wonder for how many of us do our souls any longer stand on tiptoe? What happens when people like you and me grow dull? When God is not real in our everyday lives. When the decisions we make are not affected by the presence of God. When the old, old story is simply that: old. When we relapse into a practical sort of atheism in which we pay lip service to our beliefs but we are out of touch with the three-dimensional living God behind them, who wants something of us, and makes it worth it if we know Him."

That quote from Dr. de Rosset's message jolted me into action. To be honest, at that point in my life I was flirting with sin. It was Dr. de Rosset's message that propelled me to action. I started digging into God's Word in a way I hadn't in a long time, and I started reading great authors whose writings informed my faith.

Where are you in your spiritual journey today? Do a self-assessment and journal a conversation with Jesus about where you'd like to be in your spiritual walk.

Lois Evans

Lead me in Your truth and teach me . . .
For You I wait all the day.
PSALM 25:5 (NASB)

Ecclesiastes 3:1 (NASB) tells us: "There is an appointed time for everything. And there is a time for every event under heaven." But there are moments in life where it is easy to forget the truth of this Scripture. We want our goals accomplished on our time; we want our needs met when we first feel them. Yet sometimes God's best for us doesn't mean right now, or even soon. Sometimes He asks us to wait on Him.

Our society is not good at waiting. We are accustomed to instant gratification. With our cell phones, fast food, and high-speed Internet access, we are used to getting what we want immediately.

When we pray and ask God to do His will in our lives, we must be prepared to operate on His timetable. The Creator of all life knows what is best for us, and His timing, just like all of His ways, is perfect.

The psalmist writes: "The LORD favors those who fear Him, those who wait for His lovingkindness" (Psalm 147:11 NASB). God promises to be with His people and hear their prayers. If it seems like you are stuck in the waiting room of God's blessings, take heart. He has not forsaken you; He is simply doing what's best for you. And it will be worth the wait!

Sharon Hanby-Robie

Offer hospitality to one another without grumbling. Each one should use whatever gift he has received to serve others, faithfully administering God's grace in its various forms.

1 PETER 4:9-10 (NIV)

Sadly, today, most of us equate hospitality with something only Martha Stewart can accomplish well. If we can't meet her standard, why bother? Flip through the pages of entertaining magazines and you will probably end up feeling depressed or at least inadequate. But is impressing others what Christian hospitality is all about?

I love the study of words: The Greek word *philozenia* is actually a combination of two words—*philos*, meaning "affection," and *zenos*, meaning "stranger." Affection towards strangers—how exactly does that translate today? In biblical times, it was absolutely something that was offered without hesitation. If a "stranger" came to your home in the middle of the night, you not only let him in, but you probably offered him your bed as well.

Having guests should not be an imposition that requires us to rearrange our lives—instead, it should be about inviting them into our ordinary, messy lives. It's about relationships—it can be about forging new relationships that are honest and open—messy kitchen and all. It's authentic. Hospitality is about cultivating intimacy and that requires honesty about ourselves, our homes and our lives.

What keeps you from offering hospitality? Often our excuses are more about what hospitality does *not* require rather than what it does require. Hospitality does require intentionality. True Christian hospitality also requires us to be willing to invite strangers into our lives—not just our homes. Inviting people into our lives is all about the heart and our willingness to let our true selves be known. As such, our biggest challenges might not be within our homes, but rather within our hearts.

Marcia Ramsland

"Well done, good and faithful servant! You have been faithful with a few things; I will put you in charge of many things. Come and share your master's happiness!" MATTHEW 25:21 (NIV)

One Monday morning I surveyed my teenage son's bathroom with dismay. The once gleaming tile shower walls dripped with shampoo "goo," the bathroom floor needed a good cleaning, and the bathroom countertop had seen better days. I can't believe he hasn't learned to clean up after himself, I muttered under my breath.

I made a mental note to talk this over with him when he got home from school and basketball practice. But since I wasn't in the mood to wait, I rolled up my sleeves and got busy.

My mind wandered as I began to scrub down the shower. *Why hadn't I checked up on him before? Did I neglect training my children to clean up a bathroom? Did it matter to anyone if I cleaned up the house today?*

Just then a thought crossed my mind about Jesus talking in a parable about people using their time and talents well.

"Well done, good and faithful servant! You have been faithful with a few things; I will put you in charge of many things," Jesus said in Matthew 25:21 (NIV). As I looked around I connected the principle with my current surroundings. God would be pleased if I was faithful in managing my home and promised to entrust me with meaningful things.

A clean home took on a new light. My work was worthwhile to God and that made it worth doing. In a few minutes more than the bathroom mirrors took on a new shine.

Invest fifteen minutes cleaning up a cluttered room today and reflect on the principle, "He that is faithful in little will be given much."

Lori Neff

Show me your ways, O Lord, teach me your paths; guide me in your truth and teach me, for you are God my Savior, and my hope is in you all day long. Psalm 25:4–5 (NIV)

My husband has a strong sense of justice. I love it and admire it. It can be annoying sometimes because he can't just "get over it" and move on as quickly as I can. Even though I would love for him to let things go, I think it's a great quality to pursue justice. I absolutely believe that since he is so passionate, that if he were to latch on to a cause that he believed in, he could really shake up the world!

I've noticed my own strong sense of truth—knowing it, living it, telling it. Throughout my life, I've been put into situations where I've been asked to know the truth, but live and tell something else. Needless to say, given my pursuit of truth, being asked to deny truth has been a big point of tension within me. I'm sure that people get frustrated with me and would like to tell me to try to get over it like I do with my husband. But, even though it's difficult and sometimes I want to give up, I can't deny it—I feel that God has given me a gift of being very aware of truth and maybe He wants me to speak up for truth. When I need some inspiration and a shot of courage, I visit Lynne Hybels' Web site and read over the Dangerous Women Creed. You might want to check it out: www.lynnehybels.com/dangerous_women_creed

Do you have a strong sense of justice or truth—or perhaps it's something else that grips your heart. Are you listening to that strong pull? How are you using this gift from God?

Margaret Feinberg

Well-formed love banishes fear. Since fear is crippling, a fearful life—fear of death, fear of judgment—is one not yet fully formed in love. 1 JOHN 4:18 (MSG)

There's one fellow in the Bible that I've always kind of wondered about. He's the guy who was given a single talent. While all his buddies got multiple talents, this poor fellow seemed to get the short end of the stick. He didn't complain, compare, or compete with the others. He was gripped by another vice: fear.

Matthew 25:14–30 tells us that this poor lad was so afraid of his master than he didn't have the courage to do anything. Rather than head down to the market or even the bank, he pulled out a shovel and began digging. Fear drove him to bury that talent.

On more than one occasion, I've thought, *What was that guy thinking?* But more recently, I've read the parable and recognized the same fear-driven tendencies in myself. I'm afraid that my efforts to serve and love God won't be enough. I'm afraid of how the scales will tilt on judgment day. I'm afraid I won't receive the approval from God that I so desperately desire.

My fears say more about myself and my insecurities than my knowledge of God. In fact, such honest confessions reveal that I don't really know God or the height or depth or width of His love. The Bible challenges this fear-driven thinking when it says, "Well-formed love banishes fear. Since fear is crippling, a fearful life—fear of death, fear of judgment—is one not yet fully formed in love" (1 John 4:18 MSG).

So like the man in the parable, I am given the choice to bury or believe. And no matter how many talents I am given, I pray for the courage to use them. No, not all the investments will yield a high return rate. But it's a risk worth taking, especially when it's made in the embrace of a loving God. Do any types of fear drive your life? If so, talk to God about them.

Carolyn Castleberry

An honest answer is like a warm hug. PROVERBS 24:26 (MSG)

Isn't that the truth? Some Bible versions say an honest answer is like a kiss. Either way, I'll take it!

I love spending time with friends who are real, honest, down-to-earth people. My best friends don't put up any pretense or pretend to have all the answers, and that's so refreshing to me. God wants the same thing. He wants you to come before Him honestly to deal with your past and to plan for your future.

Plus, He already knows. He knows how you feel about life, relationships, and money. If you're frightened, God understands. He isn't here to judge you, but to help you.

So we can agree with David: "O Lord, you have searched me and you know me. You know when I sit and when I rise; you perceive my thoughts from afar. You discern my going out and my lying down; you are familiar with all my ways. Before a word is on my tongue you know it completely, O Lord" (Psalm 139:1-4 NIV).

You cannot hide from God, so why try anymore? God is your Father. He's Dad. So why not work with Him and let Him work through you? This will happen only if you're completely honest with Him. Tell him this, as David did: "You deserve honesty from the heart; yes, utter sincerity and truthfulness. Oh, give me wisdom" (Psalm 61:6, TLB).

And He will give you that wisdom!

What are you hiding from the Lord? Bring this secret humbly before your loving Father. When we're completely honest with God, He shows up in *His* way, which is, of course, the right way.

Arloa Sutter

As he went along, he saw a man blind from birth. His disciples asked him, "Rabbi, who sinned, this man or his parents, that he was born blind?"

"Neither this man nor his parents sinned," said Jesus, "but this happened so that the work of God might be displayed in his life." JOHN 9:1–3 (NIV)

Like the inquisitive disciples of Jesus who were confronted with a man born blind, I want answers. "Whose fault is it, Rabbi, that this man was born blind?" Why is there so much pain and despair in the world? Why are there lines outside of shelters and soup kitchens in the wealthiest country of the world? Why can't I seem to get out of a difficult relationship or situation? Whose fault is it, Rabbi?

Jesus' response to the disciples' question about who was at fault for the blind man's troubles is an interesting one. He doesn't enter into the blame game at all. He doesn't even attempt to answer the blame question. Instead he claims there is a bigger story, a glory story that is about to be experienced. There is a healing that is about to take place that would never have been experienced apart from this man's great need. The man's difficulty becomes an opportunity for God to act. The negative circumstance is turned into a positive experience by the gentle hands of Jesus. A miracle would unfold that would bring healing to the nameless man born blind. It would involve the work of God being displayed in the man's world for all to see. His story would be remembered forever.

Is there a situation in your life that is in need of Jesus' touch? Do you trust God with the bigger glory story? How is the work of God being displayed in your life today?

Joy Jordan-Lake

When they saw the courage of Peter and John . . . they were astonished and they took note that these men had been with Jesus. ACTS 4:13 (NIV)

I was there when Mary was a new Christian, a young and feisty adult taking her early steps of faith—sometimes wide-eyed, with a "You have got to be kidding" look on her face.

I was there when Mary, a Caucasian and recently married to her African-American husband, pointedly returned the stares of fellow diners in an eerily all-white tourist town's restaurant. "If you've never seen an interracial couple before," she confronted one particularly rude, whispering diner, "let me offer: can you see well enough from there, or would you like a better view?"

I was there when she and her husband, Don, living in cramped graduate student quarters, staggered under the fresh, wholly unexpected news that they were expecting a child, and then later when they learned she was having a miscarriage. Young and inexperienced myself in ministry, I handled their grief with spectacular clumsiness. Still, it was a privilege to be there.

This summer, Mary and Don and their three children visited my husband and me and our three. They were on a vacation from where they were living in Egypt, where Don was heading the Egyptian arm of an international corporation. And as Mary spoke of her life there, and of her speaking eagerly of her faith anywhere and everywhere she could—despite the political dangers and restrictions—I was struck with how God has taken my friend's feistiness and fun-loving, unsinkable spirit and made her a person of tremendous spiritual courage.

By having been along for the long haul that is any real friendship, and any real journey of faith, I've gotten to be there to laugh, to learn, and to stand in awe of our God at work.

How might you help or learn from a friend today in your both becoming people of greater courage?

Christa March

But just as he who called you is holy, so be holy in all you do; for it is written: "Be holy, because I am holy."
1 PETER 1:15–16 (NIV)

I'm sure I smiled as I walked into the restaurant. It had been a long week and I was tired. The dark circles under my eyes showed how tired I was, but we made these dinner reservations with friends' months ago and we really didn't want to cancel just because I was tired. So, I was pleased to find the restaurant dimly lit. In the dim lighting I knew I didn't look so tired.

Sometime later a friend of mine reminded me of how often we Christians allow the bright light of God's holiness to be dimmed in our lives for exactly the same reason I liked the dim lighting in the restaurant; we don't want to recognize the sin in our own lives. When I know that certain things in my life do not honor or glorify my heavenly Father and yet I allow those things to be a part of my life I am "dimming" His holiness.

God has called His people to be holy in all areas of our lives; the areas that others see and our private lives as well. When we use His holiness as the standard for all that we do in our lives, we won't have to worry if others see our dark circles.

When the bright light of God's holiness shines into my home, what does it reveal? Does it bring to light books, movies, or Web sites that are not honoring to our heavenly Father? When God's holiness shines into my business life does it illuminate things that might dim my testimony?

Melinda Schmidt

A cheerful heart brings a smile to your face; a sad heart makes it hard to get through the day. PROVERBS 15:13 (MSG)

You probably already know what you could be unhappy about today, but what are you happy about? C'mon! Give it a try! For a million dollars . . . what would you say you are happy about today? What's your bright spot?

- the sun—it finally showed itself!
- your kids—what'd they do right recently?
- your sister—she's finally pregnant
- the new paint chip—you finally settled on a winner!
- your parents got accepted into the retirement community
- you have a new grandchild
- you found that lost beloved earring
- your son's team won his volleyball tournament
- you got a promising lead for a job
- your niece got a part in the school musical
- you went to a great concert last week

In the *Sound of Music,* Julie Andrews' character was convinced about the power of happy thoughts when she sang, "When the dog bites, when the bee stings, when I'm feeling sad . . . I simply remember my favorite things . . . and then I don't feel so bad!" King Solomon felt the same way—and he wrote it down long before Rodgers and Hammerstein: cheerfulness brings joy to the heart! (Proverbs 15:30)

Promise yourself you will NOT start each day for a week without thinking of three things you are happy about. Write them down and then try it again tomorrow! Start practicing thinking cheerfully each day and watch your spirit smile! (Proverbs 15:13)

Linda Clare

"I am the light of the world." JOHN 8:12 (RSV)

Some days, a wife and mother's life feels a lot like falling into a rabbit hole, doesn't it? Finances are tight, the house is a pigsty, the kids act up. You didn't get to the gym, again. There's too much work to be done and you're tired. God feels far away. If you're like me, you fall into a darkness that feels like a tunnel, with a pinpoint of brightness at its end. Balance and perception feel out of kilter as you tumble down, down, down your spiritual path. You feel like Alice in Wonderland.

And you're like the White Rabbit too. You're always late, running from soccer game to committee meeting, picking up dinner, the dry cleaning, and the kids. You haven't said more than three words to your husband in how long? This hole is getting deeper by the minute.

Plus, temptations pop up along the way—"Buy me," "Eat me," "Drink me." I grow large or small trying to fit everyone else's mold of who I should be. I feel as if I'm running backwards with Wonderland's Red Queen. In the darkness I finally stand still. The light's too far away. I can't go on. Maybe you've felt this way, too. You've told yourself you'll never make it. You may as well give up.

So we stand there, staring at that tiny light. Then we remember that Jesus *is* the light. The most curious thing happens: from far away the light rushes toward us, surrounds us, caresses us. The Light of the World shines truth and life and the way out of the rabbit hole. Are we ready to take God's hand and climb out into the sunshine?

You don't need one more thing to do! Delegate or ignore at least one chore this week that makes you feel as if you're digging deeper into that rabbit hole.

Linda Mintle . . . .

Now for this very reason also, applying all diligence, in your faith supply moral excellence, and in your moral excellence, knowledge, and in your knowledge, self-control, and in your self-control, perseverance, and in your perseverance, godliness
. . . 2 PETER 1:5–6 (NASB)

It is easy to feel hopeless and failed when it comes to losing weight and keeping it off. We diet, give in to the moment, and make unhealthy choices that defeat our purposes. In an age of abundance, we have choices to make that determine not only our spiritual health, but also our physical and emotional health. The question is, "When it comes to weight loss, can we really lose it and keep it off?"

Yes, if we commit to lifestyle changes that employ seven key spiritual principles. First, surrender to God. Without God's help, we are weak when it comes to making change and exercising self-control. The second principle is to accept the problem and acknowledge that changes must be made. In other words, stop making excuses. Third, we must confess our weaknesses and not hide the struggles we face. Fourth, we must take responsibility for the food we put in our mouths and all that is required to stay healthy. Fifth, we must forgive ourselves and others when we fail. Unforgiveness blocks us from moving forward. Sixth, allow God to transform our minds and struggles. Through difficulty, we build character and Christlikeness. He can use our difficulties to bring glory to His name. Finally, in order to preserve the changes we make, those changes must become part of our lifestyle and not some weight loss fad of the day. Changing habits and making lifestyle changes are not easy, but with God's help, we can lose it for life!

Anita Lustrea

One day some parents brought their little children to Jesus so he could touch and bless them. But when the disciples saw this, they scolded the parents for bothering him.

Then Jesus called for the children and said to the disciples, "Let the children come to me. Don't stop them! For the Kingdom of God belongs to those who are like these children. I tell you the truth, anyone who doesn't receive the Kingdom of God like a child will never enter it." LUKE 18:15–17 (NLT)

I went to see the movie *Finding Neverland* when it first came out and I cried. I'm not sure why. I rented it and watched it again to see if I could find some clues to the emotions it raised. Here's my best guess. *Finding Neverland* is the story of the writing of *Peter Pan*. It's a story about imagination and about childhood lost and childhood rediscovered. It conjured up good childhood memories and memories that aren't so good.

I walked away with all kinds of things stirring within me and I haven't resolved it all yet. But there is something that I am sure of. I want to continue to learn how to live my adult life well. In the process of being an adult, I never want to forget what it means to be a child.

Too many adults I know are too stiff, too unforgiving, too judgmental and have lost any sense of wonder and amazement. I don't ever want to lose my sense of wonder. I don't want to someday grow up and forget to be amazed by a glorious sunset. If that's what being an adult is all about I don't want any part of it.

Jesus told people there is something wonderful about a childlike faith. Reread Luke 18:15–17.

Grab your journal and make a list of those things that amaze you and cause you to wonder at God's greatness and His imaginative nature. I'll start. Rainbow trout, cotton candy, the ebb and flow of the tides. Now you keep going and when you're finished pray a prayer of thanksgiving to this great God of wonder for all the delights He brings into your world.

Nancy Anderson

. . . and let the wife see that she respects her husband.

EPHESIANS 5:33B (ESV)

My husband, Ron, always wanted my respect, but I thought he had to earn it and I had to feel it, before I could give it. Wrong.

We women are very good at pointing out our husbands' faults and failures and punishing them for not meeting our needs, but that only leads to discontent and distance in our marriages. We all know that yelling, nagging, and belittling are disrespectful and ineffective. So I'm suggesting a radical concept: *instead of waiting for him to earn your respect, behave respectfully and watch him grow into the man God designed him to be.*

Twenty-five years ago, our marriage was on the brink of divorce. I was controlling, critical, and disrespectful, so Ron was defensive and angry. We were both Christians but neither of us was living a Sprit-filled life. I was letting my emotions determine my actions and thought it was Ron's job to make me happy. But through a series of miracles (read my book *Avoiding the Greener Grass Syndrome* for the whole story) we made a decision to rebuild our marriage.

I began to live out the verse in Ephesians 5:33b (ESV), "and let the wife see that she respects her husband." I stopped nagging and started encouraging; I stopped complaining and started complimenting, and I stopped pushing him away and began inviting his touch. When I began to respect my husband, he was skeptical at first. However as he saw that I was committed to change, he began to treat me differently and we discovered a deep and true love.

Respect is both a verb and a noun, an action and an attitude; so begin today to respect your husband in thought, word, and deed. He will be more willing and able to give you the love and affection you need if he is respected and admired.

Kathy Koch

The next day John was there again with two of his disciples. When he saw Jesus passing by, he said, "Look, the Lamb of God!" When the two disciples heard him say this, they followed Jesus. Turning around, Jesus saw them following and asked, "What do you want?" JOHN 1:35–38 (NIV)

How would you answer Jesus' question? Why are you following Him? What do you want? What do you hope to gain because you're following Him?

Do you want more of His wisdom? His love? His forgiveness? His peace? Do you want the salvation He promises? Great! Or, like one of my staff responded when we discussed it, maybe you want to do something radical for Him.

In what ways have you recently become more like Christ because you're following Him? What do you hope to gain next? Ask God to make those qualities in Himself obvious to you so following and learning is even easier.

What about your children? Ask them what they want from Christ. What do you wish they wanted? Is there anything you can do to help them want the same things?

Here's another way to think about it. As your children follow you, what do you hope they gain? What do you want them to want from you? Your patience? Your integrity? Your passion? Your joy? Your teachability? Your curiosity? Your humility?

"Do what I say, not what I do," is really bad advice that doesn't work. It's a matter of integrity. Children will become like those they follow. Are you a safe person for them to learn from? Is there anything you should change about your life because they're following you?

Is there anything you should change about your life because you're following Jesus?

Leslie Parrott . . . .

You, my brothers, were called to be free. But do not use your freedom to indulge the sinful nature; rather, serve one another in love. GALATIANS 5:13 (NIV)

While sitting at a stoplight, Lorraine noticed a woman on the corner, slumped over a crate. There was a bundle in her lap; Lorraine could see a tiny arm sticking out. The woman was dozing off, and the baby was about to hit the ground. When the light changed, Lorraine drove past them, but then, about three blocks away, she decided to go back.

Gently touching the woman's shoulder, Lorraine handed her a piece of paper and told her if she needed help with her baby, she could take it to the address she had written on it. The address was her mother's apartment.

The next day the woman on the crate left her baby at Clara Hale's house. And as she did, Hale House was born. Since 1969, hundreds of children have found sanctuary in Mother Hale's brownstone in Harlem. In 1985, Ronald Regan said this about Clara: "Go to her house some night and you may see her silhouette against the window as she walks the floor talking softly, soothing a child in her arms—Mother Hale of Harlem is an American hero."

Since her mother's death in 1992, Lorraine has continued to honor her mother's legacy—providing a warm, loving, nurturing home for infants and young children in need.

In addition to being a temporary holding facility for children until their mothers can get help and resume care on their own, Lorraine's compassionate heart led her to establish Homeward Bound, a program that provides transitional housing and relapse prevention for former drug-addicted mothers. When asked why she works so diligently to meet these difficult needs, Lorraine said, "My mother's focus was that you've got to help other people in this world; otherwise why are you here?"

That's a great question. And it's sure to cause any of us to consider the difference we make when we serve others. As teacher A. F. Shelton said, "He profits most who serves best."

Victoria Saunders Johnson

[God] commanded the light to shine out of darkness . . .

2 CORINTHIANS 4:6 (KJV)

Christy's abuse began around eight years old. Each Saturday morning she got up early and watched cartoons. Her father began getting up too, while her mom slept late. One Saturday her father said, "I have something to show you that is more fun than cartoons." He made Christy promise to keep it "their secret." She could never get tickled with her mother around. As a child Christy didn't see anything wrong with this—it was fun to have a secret.

As Christy got older she began to feel this secret was dark and wrong. She began pulling away. Her father told her, "If you ever tell, no one will believe you, especially not your mom."

Christy suffered in silence for several years. Numerous times she attempted suicide and tried in vain to tell her mother. It was not until she became a Christian and told her pastor that this hideous secret came to light. Thank God for a pastor who believed Christy and stood with her as she confronted her parents.

One of the reasons God sent Jesus to come and live among us was to bring insight and understanding to confusing hurtful experiences. He's more than willing to shed His light into ugly midnight places in our past and present lives. Thank you Lord.

Now, twenty-three years later Christy has stopped asking, "Why God, why?" She is now saying, "What God, what? This has happened to me, what do I do now?" God is using her compassion to help teenagers open up about their hurtful situations. "The Lord has led me out of my darkness," Christy says. "Now I can help lead others out of theirs. I'm thankful."

Jan Silvious

The fear of the Lord is the beginning of wisdom, and knowledge of the Holy One is understanding. PROVERBS 9:10 (NIV)

Fear of the Lord is respect and awe of His all-powerful nature. Isn't it interesting that it is the "beginning of wisdom"? It almost seems as if you'll never be wise until you bend your knee to the fact that God is in charge and you're not. At that point, the door of your spirit opens to receive His insight. If you ever have wrestled with being angry with this God then you know that you have done a lot of "walking in place." Until you settle the fact that He is God and that He has the right to act in ways you don't understand, you can't operate in wisdom. I believe that's why the second part of this statement is so huge: "and knowledge of the Holy One is understanding."

The first lesson I was taught as a new Christian was the sovereignty of God—the fact that God reigns supreme. The second was His character—the fact that He always remains true to who He says He is. Those have been foundational truths that have anchored my soul in every storm that has raged in the last forty years.

When you know His character and His attributes, things are put in perspective and it is easier to accept His actions. I believe that getting to know Him by looking for who He says He is and what He is like enables you to accept Him and avoid some of the angry exchanges that truly get you nowhere. He has to be all-powerful and all knowing to be God. To argue with such a being and to presume to take your anger out on Him really does indicate a lack of wisdom. He can take it but is it good for you to give it? Think about that in the light of who He is.

Bethany Pierce

Sow your seed in the morning and at evening do not let your hands be idle, for you do not know which will succeed, whether this or that, or whether both will do equally well.

ECCLESIASTES 11: 6 (NIV)

In her book *American Childhood*, Annie Dillard writes about the pleasure of work: "There was joy in concentration, and the world afforded an inexhaustible wealth of projects to concentrate on . . . People cut Mount Rushmore into faces; they chipped here and there for years. People slowed the spread of yellow fever; they sprayed the Isthmus of Panama puddle by puddle. Effort alone I loved. Some days I would have been happy to push a pole around the threshing floor like an ox, for the pleasure of moving the heavy stone and watching my knees rise in turn."

Work is as much a gift from God as love, family, and friends. Granted, the work He gives us may not be glamorous. Maybe it will never get our names in print or inflate our bank accounts. Maybe our efforts will go unnoticed even by family and friends. Nevertheless, we must learn to see work as a gift and to do it joyfully, glad for the pleasure of a task completed to God's glory.

When I write this, I think of Brother Lawrence of the Resurrection, a humble lay Carmelite of the seventeenth century. At his monastery, Brother Lawrence was given a job in the kitchen, which he hated. But he resolved to complete his culinary chores out of love for God and his skills grew quite proficient over the years. By offering his efforts to God, his work was sanctified and made holy.

Whether we are doing work the world would consider noble or ordinary, that work is holy when made into an act of worship.

Kay Yerkovich

For we do not have a high priest who is unable to sympathize with our weaknesses, but we have one who has been tempted in every way, just as we are—yet without sin. Let us then approach the throne of grace with confidence, so that we may receive mercy and find grace to help us in our time of need.

HEBREWS 4:15–16 (NIV)

Have you been hurt in relationships? Perhaps your parent, a spouse, your friend, or child has wounded you. Do you need to talk to someone who really understands? Jesus knows exactly how you feel. Have you experienced betrayal? Judas was unfaithful to Jesus. He understands what it feels like when a trusted person is disloyal. Have you been embarrassed, humiliated, ashamed, or exposed? Jesus hung naked on a cross. He knows the experience of shame. Have you been afraid, overwhelmed, desperate for a way out, so distressed you felt as if you could not go on? Jesus describes all these feelings in the Garden of Gethsemane. Perhaps you feel alone and abandoned. All of Jesus' disciples deserted him at his hour of need. Maybe you even feel like God has left you. Jesus cried on the cross, "My God, my God why have you forsaken me?" Some of you have been physically or emotionally abused. Jesus suffered beatings and insults; He can sympathize with you. All of us face rejection or feel misunderstood at times. Jesus was rejected by many. He was opposed and falsely accused by the Pharisees. Life was not fair for Jesus. When you hurt, come with confidence to Jesus and talk to him. He knows exactly how you feel. He looks at you with eyes of compassion, and a heart that knows suffering. He longs to bathe your wounds in His mercy and grace.

Kendra Smiley

Therefore encourage one another and build each other up, just as in fact you are doing. 1 Thessalonians 5:11 (NIV)

It's my personal opinion that you cannot have too many encouragers in your life. I love to spend time with encouraging people. I am sure you have already noticed that, in general, our world is a not an encouraging place. It is as though some folks are reading a different, incorrect version of the Bible verse above. It would seem that the erroneous version states, "Therefore discourage one another and tear each other down, just as in fact you are doing." Those who are discouraging others are not doing what God has truly commanded. His desire, his instruction is for people, to be an encouragement to one another. We are to encourage and build one another up.

I find the last phrase of the Bible verse very interesting. Consider the words: "just as in fact you are doing." I wonder how long Paul, the author of 1 Thessalonians, had to wait before he could utter that expression. Read it again: "just as in fact you are doing." He waited patiently and when he saw them encouraging one another, he cheered them on. He was, in fact, doing precisely what he wanted the Thessalonians to do. Paul was encouraging and building them up.

How long would Paul have to wait to see encouragement in your home? How patient would Paul have to be? Do you live with others who are encouraging?

If you do not find yourself surrounded by others speaking "encouraging words," here is an idea. Be certain that you are modeling encouragement. Take the lead. Encourage those around you and build them up.

If you need encouragement yourself, read the word of God. Read the Word and hide it in your heart. That is the Next Right *encouraging* Choice!

Anita Lustrea

Then God said, "Let us make man in our image, in our likeness . . ." So God created man in his own image, in the image of God he created him; male and female he created them.
Genesis 1:26–27 (NIV)

I remember telling my son John one day, "You know, John, I gave you your best trait." "What's that?" he replied. "Freckles," I said. I loved his response. Without missing a beat he said, "Was that the best you could do?"

In all truthfulness, we are who we are because we are made in the image of God. I'm not necessarily talking about our physical features, though we are all unique. The physical characteristics are easy to spot, but what about the internal stuff, you know, our emotional makeup? We are equally unique in that design. I'm so thankful, and my husband and son are too, that there aren't a thousand "me's" walking around this world. We each have a specific contribution, a specific purpose to fulfill for the glory of God because we're made in His image.

Are you struggling to see your value today? Do you doubt your unique contribution to God's creation? Stand on the truth of God's Word and know that you are created in the image of God.

Try this exercise. It's a good way, if you have younger children, to show them they are unique creations. Grab a stamp pad—you know, the kind you use for rubber stamping. Get a clean piece of white paper, even a heavier card stock. Press your thumb into the ink and then press it onto the paper. You'll get a perfect thumb print that can only be traced back to you. Then draw a little squiggly tail on it and two little ears and then two dots for eyes and you'll see that you have a cute little mouse. This makes great refrigerator art that is '"unique" to you and to each of your children. You are an unrepeatable miracle of God.

Carol Ruhter

When you pass through the waters, I will be with you; and when you pass through the rivers, they will not seep over you. When you walk through the fire, you will not be burned; the flames will not set you ablaze. For I am the Lord, your God, the Holy One of Israel, your Savior . . . ISAIAH 43:2–3 (NIV)

Along North Carolina's Blue Ridge Parkway lies beautiful Graveyard Fields. It earned its name after a wildfire left a massive field of burned stumps resembling gravestones. The fire broke out on the first day of what promised to be a great trout season, as two hundred anglers fished the Yellowstone Prong. The wildfire's heat was so intense that it ignited leaves floating in the stream. Fishermen survived the inferno by immersing themselves in the icy stream and wrapping themselves with wet clothing. The charred landscape from which they escaped looked nothing like the one they entered. That year, barbershop stories about "the one that got away" featured fishermen, not fish.

Decisions, events, or words can ignite wildfires that completely alter our own life's landscape. That's not necessarily a bad thing. Fire is nature's way of clearing brush and enriching soil for future growth. Sweeping change can do the same in our lives. However, that doesn't negate the loss, discomfort, and fear we feel during fire's refining process. During those times, God, Himself, becomes our refuge and strength. In those flash-fires of life, the Savior immerses us in the cool, life-giving waters of His love and protection.

How does God allow raging wildfires to refine you, and yet not set you ablaze?

Joanna Weaver

Now the serpent was more crafty than any of the wild animals the Lord God had made. He said to the woman, "Did God really say, 'You must not eat from any tree in the garden'?" GENESIS 3:1 (NIV)

Satan's favorite ploy has always been to make humans believe that God doesn't really know what He's talking about. "Did God really say . . ." Satan hissed from his perch in the garden. And he hisses the same doubt and dismissal in ready ears today. "You will not surely die," he suggests, encouraging us to believe our eyes and our hunger rather than believe our God.

To a certain extent, Satan is right. Adam and Eve did not physically die that long-ago Eden day. As far as Adam could tell, the only real result from going against God's command was the rapturous look on Eve's face as she savored the juicy morsel. So when she offered him a taste, Adam didn't put up much of a fight.

However, with the partaking, Adam and Eve became aware of something that hadn't bothered them before. They were naked! But at least they weren't dead, they reassured each other as they sewed fig leaves.

But Adam and Eve were only partially right. While they still lived in the natural, something deep inside had died, the very life of God snuffed out and silenced. Simultaneously, a dark inheritance formed that would reign in all of us who would follow. A desire to do things our way, a propensity to believe the lies of the enemy, and a disturbing nakedness we spend most of our lives trying to hide.

Jesus died on the cross to restore what we lost so long ago. His resurrection shouts, "There is new life to all who'll receive!" But we must choose whom we'll listen to.

What lies has Satan been hissing in your ear? Identify and then reject them by writing a prayer of thanksgiving for the cross and all that Jesus has done for you.

Janet Thompson

Work willingly at whatever you do, as though you were working for the Lord rather than for people. COLOSSIANS 3:23 (NLT)

Arriving home from work one evening, my husband handed me a fifty dollar gift card. "What's this for?" I asked. "Being the 'employee of the year' in our office," he humbly replied.

I knew this distinction wasn't awarded merely for sales—but for attitude, going the extra mile, and being the most trusted, valued employee of the office—where he labors for a little more than minimum wage as a termite inspector. Gone are his days of corporate expense accounts, bonuses, and lavish trips as a reward for being the "top employee."

As I looked at my husband standing before me in his uniform and dirty work boots, my mind flashed back to the three-piece suits and polished shoes of his former high-powered career. What impressed me in that moment was the honor his current employer had actually bestowed on him. They see a man who gives his best to the company, even though he isn't getting big bucks and perks. What a witness that must be to his fellow employees, who know that he is a Christian, and what a role model it is for our children.

We may not always feel sufficiently paid or recognized for the work we do . . . and many times, we aren't. Especially in ministry or serving in our church or being a wife or mom. But what matters most to God is the heart with which we work. Is there some project you are working on now where you don't feel appreciated by others? Give it your best anyway, because God is the one who hands out the rewards when our work on earth is finished. If we are about His work here on earth, it is His "well done my good and faithful servant" we will receive in heaven. My husband and I are working for that bonus. How about you?

Anita Lustrea

The Lord had said to Abram, "Leave your country, your people and your father's household and go to the land I will show you." GENESIS 12:1 (NIV)

What would you do if your boss came into your office on Monday morning and said, "I want you to leave this place. I want you to leave this job and I want you to pack up your family and move two states away. I don't know exactly where you should go, but I'll be back in touch and tell you where to go."

That's exactly what God said to Abram in Genesis 12. Take a look. "The Lord had said to Abram, 'Leave your country, your people and your father's household and go to the land I will show you'"(v.1 NIV). Whoa . . . just up and leave and follow? The next verse after the command to leave holds the covenant God makes with Abraham. "I will make you into a great nation and I will bless you; I will make your name great, and you will be a blessing. I will bless those who bless you, and whoever curses you I will curse; and all peoples on earth will be blessed through you" (vv. 2–3 NIV).

How many of us have stayed put when we heard God speak, when He's prompted us to make a move, whether it's toward another person emotionally, or a physical move across the country or across the globe?

I'd like to challenge you for the next seven days to have a brief time of prayer sometime during your day, and then sit in silence for five minutes right after your prayer time. Start your time of silence with one simple question to the Lord. "What do you want me to do?" And then wait and listen. I don't imagine you'll be told to pick up and move across the country, but I would never presume to know the ways of God. What I do imagine will happen is a deepening of your walk with Christ as you put yourself in a different posture, a posture of listening for his voice. Enjoy the adventure!

Leigh McLeroy

God made everything beautiful in itself and in its time . . .
ECCLESIASTES 3:9 (MSG)

I was out of town on a Sunday—in a city I'd never visited before, and looking for a place to worship. I found one, too, but not by Googling "churches + Seattle." I met God instead at the aquarium on Pier 59.

At the aquarium, small sharks glided just inches from my nose, their skin like smooth, gray satin. In another tank a huge black seal swam underwater, broke the surface and did a "nose stand," half in the water and half out. For half an hour I watched four otters play, and more than once laughed out loud as they floated belly-up, rubbing their eyes and whiskers in small circles, like old men waking from sweet dreams. When they tired of the back float they chased one another, churning like a crazy load of "darks" in a slow wash cycle.

It was joy so pure it almost hurt.

There were no hymns at Pier 59. And no sermon. The price of admittance was twelve dollars, but if an offering plate had been passed I think I might have given more. The text for the morning was not from the prophets or the psalmists or the gospel writers . . . but from poet Gerard Manley Hopkins, who saw the Creator's "pied beauty" too, and captured it like this:

> GLORY be to God for dappled things—
> For skies of couple-colour as a brinded cow;
> For rose-moles all in stipple upon trout that swim;
> Fresh-firecoal chestnut-falls; finches' wings;
> Landscape plotted and pieced—fold, fallow, and plough;
> And all trades, their gear and tackle and trim.
>
> All things counter, original, spare, strange;
> Whatever is fickle, freckled (who knows how?)
> With swift, slow; sweet, sour; adazzle, dim;
> He fathers-forth whose beauty is past change: Praise him.

Set out today to "spy" and celebrate the dappled glory of God in the world. Worship Him for each wondrous thing you see.

Susie Larson

But small is the gate and narrow the road that leads to life, and only a few find it. MATTHEW 7:14 (NIV)

My boys are almost grown. Looking back, I recall many teachable moments when I had an open door to their soul. I seized every available opportunity. On several occasions, I shared this word picture with my sons:

The Christian life is like a winding, country road with deep ditches on each side. One ditch represents your rebellion, the other, your response to someone else's rebellion. Satan could care less which ditch he gets you into, he just wants you off the road.

Christ is the narrow road on which we come to salvation. And as the days grow evil, it'll be tougher to walk as He did. Many Believers are painfully pretending to be something they are not. In public, they *look* quite Christian, but behind the scenes they're embroiled in addictive behavior. Others are squeaky clean on the outside but their hearts are hardened with pride. As I pondered my analogy in light of the changing times, I pictured more and more of the road giving way, creating cavernous ditches on both sides, leaving a very narrow road on which to walk.

Daily we'll be faced with the choice:

Will I forgive or pick up an offense?
Will I love or hate?
Will I offer grace or hold a grudge?
Will I believe the best or assign a motive?

If we are committed to this walk of faith, we are committing ourselves to love and forgiveness, obedience and mercy. You may feel like you're walking alone at times, but you never are. Greater are those who are for you and with you, than those who are against you. Finish the race with grace and strength.

God is on your side.

Pay attention to your responses this week. Make allowances for the faults of others. Choose love and forgiveness every chance you get.

Janice Elsheimer

There is a time for everything and a season for every activity under heaven. ECCLESIASTES 3:1 (NIV)

My husband says I'm "a part-time teacher, part-time writer, and a full-time gardener." Whenever I'm home, friends and neighbors know where to find me: in the garden. This is where I find my joy. I'm happiest when I put my hand to something that rewards me by maturing and changing for the better. Teaching, child-rearing, and nurturing a marriage are like that; housekeeping is not. That's why I'm more likely to walk you through my gardens than take you into my house.

Working in the garden grounds me, makes me feel connected and whole. Being outdoors among the fragrance of flowers, herbs, and soil; hearing bees and birdsong; feeling rain coming on or sun on my shoulders: this is where I feel most alive. Even the chore of weeding, which neighbors greet with, "Oh, don't you just hate weeding?" connects me with God.

When I'm down on my knees weeding, I think about the things I need to weed out of my own life. Just as removing those energy-stealing weeds allows the desirable plants in your garden to thrive, weeding out the activities, people, and possessions that deplete your energy and resources is a life-affirming act. A garden full of green isn't necessarily healthy, and neither is a too-full life. A healthy garden requires weeding, and a healthy life requires weeding out the things that drain our energy so that we can make room for the things that are really important.

Make a list of things that deplete your energy more than they nourish you. Pray over your list and ask God to guide you in weeding out just one of these items from your life.

Nancy Sebastian Meyer

Therefore, as God's chosen people, holy and dearly loved, clothe yourselves with compassion, kindness, humility, gentleness and patience. COLOSSIANS 3:12 (NIV)

I used to love watching *Cinderella* when I was a child. In one of my favorite parts, the fairy godmother "poofed" Cinderella into that incredible ball gown, right in the middle of the pumpkin patch.

How many times have you looked into your closet and wished someone would "poof" you into the perfect outfit? Some things don't fit. Most are outdated. Everything looks old. Nothing is just right. Where is that fairy godmother when you need her?

We spend so much time on outer appearance, which is ultimately affected by our inner spirit. You've seen a lovely woman in gorgeous clothes who wasn't worth a second glance because her countenance spoils the effect.

So the question is: what is in your spiritual closet? These verses tell us compassion makes us beautiful. Kindness and humility compliment our features. Gentleness and patience are becoming.

Just the other day, I visited the cosmetics department of a large store at the mall to ask the clerk for a makeover refresher course. I came home with new tools to make myself beautiful and tried them out the next morning. As I left my bedroom with a final glance in the mirror, a little voice inside my head whispered, "Did you spend as much time looking into God's face this morning as your own?"

I certainly don't have a fairy godmother, but I do have a heavenly Father who is the source of all beauty and goodness. It's high time I remember to clothe my heart in His spiritual attributes and seek His face before I begin each day!

Check your spiritual appearance in the mirror of God's Word. Ask God if you need to add any accessories!

Sabrina O'Malone

Take my yoke upon you and learn from me, for I am gentle and humble in heart, and you will find rest for your souls. For my yoke is easy and my burden is light.
MATTHEW 11:29–30 (NIV)

A busy working mom's burdens aren't exactly "light or easy." And it isn't so simple to be "gentle and humble in heart" with so much to do every day. How can anyone with so many responsibilities lighten their load?

"Seek ye first the kingdom of God" (Matthew 6:33 KJV).

Ouch. That one hurt. Can you say that you always seek God's kingdom first? In my case I couldn't. In fact, the busier I am, the more often I tend to rush from one thing to the next; with barely a thought of anything except how little time I have to get things done. So what's the key to live the way the Lord wants?

"Trust in the Lord with all your heart, and lean not on your own understanding; in all your ways acknowledge Him, and He shall direct your paths" (Proverbs 3:5–6 KJV).

It's time to resign from the self-appointed (and imaginary) position as general manager of the universe. Thankfully, God's already got that covered. Trust Him and follow Him. He'll never lead you astray. Count your blessings—the very ones that keep you so busy. If you've got a family to take care of, a job that provides for your needs, and a home that needs your attention, remember that these are all gifts from the Lord. Be thankful instead of overwhelmed.

Pray regularly. Praise God often. And keep a sharp lookout for things to be grateful for. That's when you'll discover that the burdens that used to seem so heavy have become easy and light.

Melinda Schmidt

But if from there you seek the Lord your God, you will find Him if you seek Him with all your heart and with all your soul. DEUTERONOMY 4:29 (NIV)

If you've ever watched the movie *The Fantastic Four,* you'll see a group of superheroes that make meeting the challenges of life look so easy. Run into a bad guy? Transform into Invisible Girl and disappear. Or turn into a strong man with muscles of stone and strong-arm your troubles away.

Been there, and done it in my own way. Avoiding challenges, wishing them away, analyzing and worrying things into resolution—yeah, I know about that. Using my strengths to solve things quickly and easily—that's the way *I'd* like it to be!

The Fantastic Four never seem to run out of energy as they transform into their useful superpowers. Frankly, trying to be a superwoman has its appeal, but since God did not create me to be that woman, I tend to falter and get perplexed as I work to solve the puzzles of my days.

What situations did you start to solve or think about when you awoke this morning: son's college plans, daughter's grades, your mortgage rate, your husband's business trip to Milwaukee, a parent's health issues? What superhero were *you* trying to emulate as your mind ran through a myriad of perplexing issues?

Take a breath and meditate on Deuteronomy 4:29. Put your pride aside and humbly seek after God. Raise the white flag of surrender and affirm that you will trust Him with these concerns. Humility allows us to trust God with outcomes as we live our new day praising Him for the incredible power that He is—the capable Ruler of the world, including yours! (Psalm 103:19)

Katie Brazelton

"For I know the plans I have for you," declares the Lord, "plans to prosper you and not to harm you, plans to give you hope and a future." JEREMIAH 29:11 (NIV)

As a Life Purpose Coach®, I have talked at length with a woman I'll call Cynthia. She manages multiple roles—wife, mom, community volunteer, friend, women's ministry leader, household manager, kid's taxi driver, neighbor, sister, and daughter. She can't help but talk about feeling exhausted, unfocused, and like she is now "just going through the motions." Although she is very thankful for the relationships in her life, and the opportunities to serve her family, community, and church, she has lost her enthusiasm and passion for many of her day-to-day roles. She longs for clarity as to what God's broader and bolder purpose is for her. A vague feeling nags at her, leaving doubts as she asks me: "Are you sure that God has a unique plan for my life?"

What about you? Do you also long to be reassured that God has a specific and amazing assignment for you? Do you want to feel like your life matters in the greater scheme of things; that you are in sync with God's will; that you are *in your element*? Do you crave a divine urge or a fascination in your soul? If so, I can say to you with great confidence, based on God's Word, that indeed he does have a passionate purpose, tailor-made just for you!

Pray faithfully for one week to ask God to send you a Purpose Partner. Taking baby steps or quantum leaps down the pathway to purpose is much easier when you have a partner to encourage you each step of the way. Yes, without a doubt, we need cheerleaders along our journey, whether that's a friend, ministry partner, spouse, mentor, coach, or counselor. Let God choose someone to be your encourager, as you seek to fulfill his glorious and unique plan for your life.

Jill Briscoe

. . . Jesus, tired as he was from the journey, sat down by the well. JOHN 4:6 (NIV)

The sun was hot. The party had walked a long way in the Middle Eastern heat. Donkeys trotted past them, carrying their passengers. The disciples and Jesus were poor and had no extra money to hire the beasts, even though certain "women were helping to support them out of their own means."

Everyone was hungry including Jesus. Breakfast was a memory, and then there was the frustration for Him of sitting on a well and not having a bucket!

Of course, He who made the seas could have turned sand into water just as He could have, on another occasion, turned stones into bread. He had the power, but not the Father's permission to use His powers for Himself. So, he waited patiently for the disciples to come back from Sychar with refreshment.

Have you ever felt weary with the journey feeling you're walking in deep sand, frustrated with no means to help yourself? Jesus understands. Wait for the woman to come. Proverbs 11:25 (NIV) tells us, "He who refreshes others will himself be refreshed!"

Once Jesus had given the woman living water He forgot about His lunch! Don't be so absorbed with your own weariness you fail to see her need and realize this is a divine appointment.

If you are weary, tell the Lord; He understands. Ask Him to send someone to minister to even when you're tired. In the giving you shall receive refreshment of soul.

Janice Elsheimer

The sacrifices of God are a broken spirit; a broken and contrite heart, O God, you will not despise. Psalm 54:17 (niv)

"Do you have to use the restroom, Dad?"

"Nope," he says cheerfully. "I already did."

I looked down at his pants, which were soaking wet despite the adult diaper he now wears. I took him into the restroom to change him, just as the nurse called his name.

How do people do it? I, who haven't a nursing bone in my body, am caregiver by default for my Alzheimer's-afflicted father, yet I am completely inadequate to even the smallest task, like getting him to the restroom on time.

As we waited for Dad's name to be called again, I laid my broken spirit and contrite heart before God, asking for His help. I'm thankful for the small mercy of memory loss that allowed Dad to already forget about his accident.

Back with the nurse in the examination room, I finally fell apart. "How do people do it?" I asked her. "Just getting Dad in and out of the car is a major struggle. It takes two people, and there's only me to do it."

"You know," she says, "your dad might qualify for the Home-based Primary Care program. If he does, all the VA services he now gets will be delivered to him at the assisted living facility where he lives."

If Dad hadn't had the accident, if I hadn't felt broken and helpless and cried in front of the nurse, I would never have learned of this program, which is serving my dad today.

No matter how broken you are in spirit, believe God's promise to answer your prayers when we come to Him with the sacrifice of a broken and contrite heart.

Christa March

"And who knows but that you have come to royal position for such as time as this?" Esther 4:14b (NIV), emphasis added

Growing up in Sunday school I always loved hearing Bible stories. My favorites were the ones about women—amazing women like Ruth, Mary, and even Rahab. But my absolute favorite Bible story was that of Esther. The handsome king notices the pretty peasant girl and invites her to live in his palace. There is trouble in the kingdom and the pretty peasant girl, now queen, is the one who comes to the rescue. Yes, the story of Esther has everything that a little girl dreams about.

As I got older and read the story again there was one part of that story that really stood out. Esther 4:14b (NIV) says, "And who knows but that you have come to royal position for such as time as this?"

Esther could have been born at any time in history. But God determined that Esther should be born in that location and in that time so that she could be a part of His plan to save His people. Just like Esther, I came to realize, I was born in the place and time of God's choosing. Once I came to that realization, I prayed and asked God to make His plan for my life clear to me. He answered my prayer and I found my life's purpose.

Have you ever stopped to contemplate why God choose for you to live in this time in history? Just as He did with Esther, God knew that this point in history was where and when He could use you best, if you would let Him.

Look at where God has placed you. Is God calling you to care for someone specifically in your neighborhood or is there some way God could use you in your child's school? For such a time as this God has put you where you are. Find out why and get to work!

Anita Lustrea

Why, you do not even know what will happen tomorrow. What is your life? You are a mist that appears for a little while and then vanishes. JAMES 4:14 (NIV)

I'm closing in on fifty. In my lifetime I've lived in Maine, Pennsylvania, Georgia, North Carolina, Kansas, and Illinois. Lots of memories. Some nice. Some not so nice.

I wonder how many years I have left. Another thirty? Twenty? Ten? Five? One? We don't know, do we?

All I'm sure of is that I want to take what's left and make the most of it. I know I want Jesus to be the Lord of what's left. I want him to direct my path.

I know one thing: He loves me just the way I am, but not enough to let me stay that way. The question is whether or not I'll participate in what He has in store for me.

I think He still has some things for me to do.

I'm sure He'll put needs in my path that I'm uniquely able to fill.

I think He'll continue to be more concerned about my character than my comfort.

I think the best is yet to come

I think the Lord wants me to use whatever wisdom I've gained to contribute somewhere.

I'm sure I'm supposed to embrace change.

I'm convinced the Lord will want to take me out of my comfort zone.

I think I'll have to trust the Lord in ways I've never had to trust Him before.

I am excited about the future. What about you? Are you pumped about the future? Are you energized about what God has in store for you or are you dwelling in the past, angry about people and events, wishing you could go back in time?

Take some time and journal about what you think God has in store for you. What's your God-sized goal? What need are you being called to fill? How do you think God will continue to shape and form you? Pray through those questions and then wait and see what God has in store.

Shauna Niequist

Therefore do not worry about tomorrow, for tomorrow will worry about itself. Each day has enough trouble of its own.
MATTHEW 6:34 (NIV)

Right now, at our house, it feels like we're totally "in the meantime"—in between jobs, in between towns, even sort of in between lives, it seems. What I want to do in this in-between time is start packing even though we don't have any idea where we're going, use up canned goods and toiletries, watch the clock, and snap my heart shut like a locket, waiting for the future to arrive.

But that's not living, and that's not how I want to live. So I remind myself over and over to unclench my fists, unclench the muscles in my neck, and live in this life, in this house, in this town, in this very meantime. What that means for me today is that we're having a birthday party for my friend Andrew, because for right now, in the meantime, before our lives change and carry us away from this town, Andrew is our neighbor.

What it means for today is that I don't have to let the weight of an unknown future crush the slender stalk of today, the few hours I have to write, the few hours of pale sun slanting through this room that might not be my writing room forever, but has been for lots of good writing days and still is, in the meantime.

What it means for today is that I allow myself to be entirely here, now, in this place, in this beautiful meantime.

Have you ever felt like you've been "in the meantime"?

What do you do when you find yourself worrying about tomorrow instead of living in today?

Lori Neff

For you created my inmost being; you knit me together in my mother's womb. I praise you because I am fearfully and wonderfully made your works are wonderful, I know that full well. PSALM 139:13–14 (NIV)

You would think that since we're with ourselves 24/7 that we would inherently know ourselves, right? I certainly thought so. But, by the time I was in my early thirties, I was appalled that I didn't know myself at all. I felt like I spent most of my life fighting against how God made me so I could be what I thought other people wanted. There was a constant tension in my life that I couldn't explain and couldn't put my finger on. I knew that something was wrong and there must be more than this to life.

For years, I prayed for wisdom, for direction—for *something*. Then, subtly God began bringing people into my life who nudged me forward. A friend recommended a book about introverts, which helped me accept and even enjoy being an introvert. Another friend helped me take several steps forward by suggesting that I begin a daily exercise called Three Pages. This is simply writing three pages in a spiral-bound notebook each morning. Just writing whatever comes to mind. It revealed some bitterness that I didn't fully realize I was holding on to. It helped me sort out some complex issues that had rolled around in confusion in my mind.

God also brought wise friends into my life who continue to nudge me forward. God has shown me that He loves me and it's okay—and good!—to be exactly who He made me to be. Certainly, I have room to grow, but it starts with knowing and accepting myself and building on my strengths and understanding my weaknesses.

Jane Rubietta

For the Son of Man came to seek and to save what was lost.
LUKE 19:10 (NIV)

The counselor sat across from my young friend. "I want you to make a list of everything that was lost to you, stolen by the man who raped you. We can look at it next week."

At home, my friend began her list. Several pages later, she exhausted her inventory and the grieving began, again, through tears. The following week, her therapist read through the list, nodding. Then she looked into my friend's eyes.

"You can get all these things back."

Oh, what lightness, to realize that what the world, tragedy, violence, and loss steals, God can return to us. As I thought through the implications of Jesus' words to Zacchaeus, "For the Son of Man came to seek and to save what was lost," my mind reeled. What has the Enemy stolen from you, or your loved ones? Where have you experienced loss? Maybe you've lost a child, or childhood; a parent, or your past, or hope for the present and future. Maybe you've lost a spouse or house, or a breast, or a job.

This Scripture isn't promising the return of those people or positions. But Christ seeks and saves what was lost. He can bring you into a place of healing. My friend, who can never retrieve her innocence, has found in its stead a new love for other victims of pain, a miraculous ability to forgive, and the start of healing from the wounds of that trauma. God has brought into her life a remarkable man, who loves and cherishes her, and stands by her as she works toward new life.

What have you lost? Can you make a list? How can you invite God to save what was lost?

Kristen Johnson Ingram

Have mercy on me, O Lord, for I am weak; O Lord, heal me, for my bones are troubled. My soul also is greatly troubled; But You, O Lord—how long? PSALM 6:2–3 (NKJV)

On September 11, 2001, I listened all day to reports about terrorist attacks on the World Trade Center and the Pentagon. I am not a person who cries easily, so I was stunned and dry-eyed. But then two people, stranded in hellish fire at the Trade Center, joined hands and leapt out the window to their death.

The picture was suddenly personal and individual. I began to weep for those two, taking comfort from each other's hands. Not hundreds or thousands of bodies, but two frail humans who must have been more terrified of death by fire than death by falling. I imagined their watching the flames licking closer and closer, their faces getting hot, then their heading for the window, and finally silently joining hands. I hope they glanced some encouragement to each other.

And I hope they prayed. Just in case they forgot to ask God for mercy as they fell, I stood in my imagination on that windowsill, murmuring the words of today's Psalm: "Be gracious to them, O Lord, for they were languishing . . . their bones were shaking with terror . . ." *God, sometimes mass tragedy seems far away and impersonal,* I prayed. *Help me remember the hands joined in agony that make the story personal.*

In your journal, write a few words about something tragic that you read about in the newspaper. Allow yourself to feel grief, and write down a short prayer for that person.

Glynnis Whitwer

I am the true vine, and my Father is the gardener. He cuts off every branch in me that bears no fruit, while every branch that does bear fruit he prunes so that it will be even more fruitful. JOHN 15:1–2 (NIV)

"Mom, wouldn't it be weird if someone only had five dollars, then bought a five dollar wallet?"

My son Robbie meant it as a joke, but I couldn't stop thinking about the idea of someone spending their last dime on something, only to be unable to use it properly. One day I realized God was speaking to me through that comment. I was that woman who bought a five dollar wallet with her last five dollars. Only it wasn't about money—it was my life!

I had invested so much of my time in "good" activities that I had no margin in my days. My overloaded schedule left me drained and empty. My husband's business was growing, which left me assuming most of the household responsibilities. Add to that the needs of our five children, my own work, volunteer roles, writing and speaking, and I knew I was on overload.

So I started praying and asking the Lord to reveal the things that needed to be dropped. A few things were obvious. I had to ask for help in a few areas of my life. There's more to be pruned, but the last options are big and I need to be sure of the Lord's direction before I eliminate something based on frustration.

My son's innocent comment has become a profound guiding principle in my life. I don't want to be the woman with a beautiful, but empty, wallet. I know Jesus came to give me an abundant life, but that meant spiritually, not an overflowing to-do list.

I think I'll keep that "five dollars" and forgo the "wallet." I'd rather have the margin (and the spiritual, emotional, and relational health that comes with it) than more great opportunities.

Consider if your schedule is overcrowded. Ask God to reveal one responsibility that can be delegated or released. Then act upon His answer.

Miriam Neff

Praise be to the God and Father of our Lord Jesus Christ, the Father of compassion and the God of all comfort, who comforts us in all our troubles, so that we can comfort those in any trouble with the comfort we ourselves receive from God. 2 CORINTHIANS 1:3–4 (NIV)

Troubling times don't define us, but they certainly refine us. We have no choice but to change. Our character either grows or shrinks. Our arms either fold or reach out.

When I knew my husband's diagnosis, I called a woman who had been down this path before me. She answered any question I asked, wept with me, and most of all, understood. I soaked up comfort from her like a dried sponge. God's compassion for me was often delivered through her words, her prayers, her hugs.

A few months into my life alone, a woman emailed me from another state. "May I call you?" And God, in his beautiful way, let me pass His comfort forward to someone I have not yet met, though we have talked for hours on the phone. She is on the journey of ALS with her husband. I understand.

On one of her very hard days she called me. "Will I get through this? When it's over will I still be standing?" Her voice, knees, and heart were quaking.

"You're talking to me," I answered softly. "I'm still here."

I love the word *all*. He comforts us in *all* our troubles, the ones we created ourselves, and the ones that happened just because this is the world. The comfort He provides is transferable, not just to someone in the same circumstance (though often we have those opportunities by His design), but in *any* trouble. You see, it's His comfort we are passing on, not our own. That's why it works anywhere.

Pray for God to use your troubles to create trophies.

Tracy Groot

This is the confidence which we have before Him, that, if we ask anything according to His will, He hears us. And we know that if He hears us in whatever we ask, we know that we have the requests which we have asked of Him.

1 JOHN 5:14–15 (NASB)

God desires truth in the innermost being (Psalm 51:6), and will not cheapen our attempts at change by falsifying results. He loves us too much for that.

How easy would it be for God to snap His fingers and make me a size 10? Yet I know Him better than that—He will give me truth, not gilded gifts. If I pray, "God, help me to lose weight," I'll hear crickets in an empty expanse, and maybe, if I listen hard enough, a voice whispering, "Try again." He wants me to get as close to truth as I can when I pray. If I pray this instead, "God, I know this will cost me, but please, help me not to use food to cope; help me to get hungry before I eat," I'll have God's instant attention.

We have to come to truth if we are going to pray God's will. He will settle for getting as close as we can, because sometimes we don't know what the truth is. We have to get quiet for it, or wait for it. When it comes to our understanding, and lights a recess of our heart, we have hope; and hope does not disappoint. We then take our findings to God in prayer: "God, I think I've been a jerk with my son. Maybe he's not the one who has to change . . . maybe it's me. If so, show me. Give me courage."

David refused to offer to the Lord that which cost him nothing (1 Chronicles 21:24). Genuine prayer may cost as much as truth. Give God something genuine to work with, so He can produce genuine results. As some smart person once said, "There are no shortcuts to any place worth going."

Nancy Kane

Greater love has no one than this, that one lay down his life for his friends. JOHN 15:13 (NASB)

A reference in a *Newsweek* article to the slaying of five Amish children by Charles Roberts in a Pennsylvania schoolhouse had the effect of stumbling on a land mine for me. According to survivors, after Roberts bound the girls' feet, Marian Fisher, age thirteen, told Roberts, "Shoot me first."

Amish children are raised to identify themselves as a part of a larger group of believers where love and sacrifice are the very fabric of life. In this environment "I" is subservient to "we" and the "we" is subservient to "God." They are taught to follow in Christ's footsteps, to love as he loved and ultimately to offer their lives as a gift of gratitude for all of what God has done for them.

How little I think in terms of "we" and "community" and being a representative of the larger body of Christ. But there is no place for Christlike love in this self-reliance and personal independence. To be a follower of Christ is to be initiated into an eternal family of fellow sons and daughters of a perfect heavenly Father who together, in the grit and grind of daily life, make Christ visible to the world.

I can't help but believe in that moment for Marian Fisher all of the lessons came rushing forward that she had seen and heard in this tight knit Amish community—setting aside one's own interests, considering others better than yourself, and to show one's love of Christ by loving others in sacrificial ways.

I believe Marian Fisher had made room in her soul for God to grant her the grace to respond so courageously. Rita Rhoads, one of the survivors of the slayings, said that Charles Roberts's final words were "Pray for me."

"That's kind of interesting because he said he hated God," Rhoads told ABC News. "He must have recognized the faith in them, God in them."

We see here more than the tender life of Marian Fisher cut short. We see Christ in a distressing disguise.

Linda Mintle

Each one should test his own actions. Then he can take pride in himself, without comparing himself to somebody else, for each one should carry his own load. GALATIANS 6:4–5 (NIV)

Have you been hurt by someone, taken advantage of, wounded by words or treated unfairly? If so, it is easy to feel like a victim. After all, you have been wronged! The problem is that being a victim and blaming others for your pain keeps you stuck. It is not part of kingdom living. Better to get unstuck by taking responsibility for your actions and reactions.

Here is how. You can't control what other people do or say to you, but you can control how you react to what they do and say. So carry your load by refusing to be a victim. You don't have to deny the negative things that have happened to you, rather choose a different path. Let go of any anger and unforgiveness that has built up because of injustice and hurt. Turn the people who have hurt you over to God and forgive them. Let God be their judge. God is for you and will work all things according to His purposes in your life, but you have to cooperate with God.

So right now, examine your heart. Do you harbor ill feelings towards anyone? Are you secretly hoping they get a taste of their own medicine? Are you holding judgment against them? If so, release the injustice to God so you can move forward and start living again. Get out of that victim role and take responsibility for putting yourself there! God is bigger than any injustice you will ever experience. If you let Him, He will move on your behalf.

Christine Wyrtzen

May the Master pour on the love so it fills your lives and splashes over on everyone around you.

1 THESSALONIANS 3:12 (MSG)

Some of you sell your souls to get the love you want. You prostrate yourself, promise things you have no right promising, all for the prospect of someone's affection. Others of you are saying good=bye to an aging parent and you're realizing the window of time is short for getting the love you've always craved. Perhaps all your efforts, day and night, are trying to figure out how to turn their heart toward you. Oh, how we dream of sitting in their shade, satiated and content.

Jesus promises all that and more. He's beckoning to us to sell our souls and call Him "Master." He knows that if we willingly give up our life, we will find it. A soul who abdicates his right to a self-proclaimed identity and then blends into Jesus only finds that his true self emerges.

The beloved John spoke of the barrier to love. It is fear. If I open up my heart completely, no secrets, to someone as big as God, and then He rejects me, I would find it unbearable. To play it safe, I open my mind to the thought of His love while I seal away my heart in order to protect it.

To open ourselves completely takes faith. We must believe Him when God tells us what He is like. We must also believe Him when He tells us the truth of what we're worth to Him. If we allow the Master to love us without restrictions, it will fill us up and splash over onto the very people upon whom we've been waiting upon to love *us*! That's the irony and the miracle.

What present relationship brings you the most pain? Why? What are you doing, within the dynamics of that relationship, try to get what you want? Are you willing to transfer your needs to Jesus? Write Jesus a letter and tell Him about it, in detail.

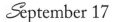

Melinda Schmidt

Where does my help come from? Psalm 121:1b (NIV)

It struck me as rather pathetic—who would buy booklets for sale at an airport for some last minute help for "the perfect phrases for the sales call" or tips on perfecting a performance review, being a more articulate executive, achieving goals, or the saddest of all: how to dismiss an employee. Who was going to be the victim of that last-minute advice some boss read on a random flight? Admittedly the insights could be helpful in the workplace, but the book kiosk just seemed to scream desperation to me.

How many of us, moving through life's complexities, snatch at some last-minute thought from a Scripture verse, book, a friend, a "sign," or even a devotional like this one? We are so desperate to get it right, get it fixed, get some wisdom, that we begin to snatch, snatch, snatch for that nugget that will take care of it all. Might God be asking us to get still before our heavenly Father, learning His promises of wisdom and help? Perhaps God is calling us to sit in His wonder, His mystery, watching and waiting for Him (Psalm 121:1–2).

Many might recall times when godly wisdom was quickly needed and miraculously found. But don't miss developing a relationship with God and His Word that gives the continual wisdom needed as we travel through life.

Ask the Lord to help you to seek Him in the challenge in front of you, to help you to lean on Him and trust Him for what you need. We all need patience to wait for His help. May we not snatch at a quick fix, but really come to know God's abiding wisdom and promise of care in days ahead.

Beverly Hubble Tauke

"Praise be to the Lord, the God of Israel, who has sent you today . . . May you be blessed for your good judgment and for keeping me from bloodshed . . ." 1 SAMUEL 25:32–33 (NIV)

Family treachery was a way of life for the Hebrew beauty Abigail. Her rich, powerful, alcohol-soaked husband, Nabal, was radioactive at home and in society. Predictably, his evil attracted destruction to his own family (Proverbs 17:13).

Nabal publicly insulted local "Guardian Angels" protecting his workers and property. Bloody retaliation against obnoxious Nabal and his estate was planned by legendary giant killer and future king, David—not one to suffer fools (1 Samuel 25).

Terrified workers pled for Abigail to save their lives. Astutely, she declined power encounters. Her family crisis called for wisdom encounters—which she executed brilliantly.

• **Emotional Wisdom (James 3:13-18):** Inoculated by peace and integrity rooted in God's wisdom, Abigail resisted anxious, fearful, angry reactivity.

• **Strategic Wisdom (Proverbs 22:3):** Radar for engaging both volatile Nabal and retaliatory David guided Abigail's successful conflict resolution strategy.

• **Communication Wisdom (Proverbs 29:11):** Honest, wise speech appeases kings (Proverbs 16:13)—and also *future* King David, who celebrated Abigail's skillful diplomacy. Savvy Abigail also carefully timed her candid report to alcohol abusing Nabal.

Abigail was neither the helpless sort nor the type to fly by the seat of her pants in the name of "faith." She chose, instead, to navigate family treachery with the reliable rudder of godly wisdom.

What toxic personalities or behaviors wound your family? How can you better protect yourself and your family with greater emotional, strategic, and communication wisdom—promised by God to those who seek such gifts from him (James 1:5)?

Rosalie de Rosset

All discipline for the moment seems not to be joyful, but sorrowful; yet to those who have been trained by it, afterwards it yields the peaceful fruit of righteousness. HEBREWS 12:11 (NASB)

In the great seventeenth-century classic *Robinson Crusoe*, British novelist Daniel Defoe presents the doctrine of sovereignty in the most beguiling way. Most people, however, mistakenly believe that this is just an adventure story about a man stuck on a desert island. Instead, what God does with the wayward Crusoe, who against his father's injunctions keeps jumping on ships because he has wanderlust, is to allow him to be shipwrecked on a remote tropical island where he must work to survive and where he meets God in a stunning personal way. Ironically, the confines of the island and the discipline of work and hardship, of terror and uncertainty, teach Crusoe more than he learned in his vast travels around the world. Beyond learning how to survive physically (an amazing process), Crusoe becomes a grateful Christian who depends on His maker for all his needs.

Listen to his words in a key quote from the book: "So little do we see before us in the world, and so much reason have we to depend cheerfully [sic] upon the great Maker of the world, that He does not leave his creatures so absolutely destitute, but that in the worst circumstances they have always something to be thankful for, and sometimes are nearer their deliverance than they imagine; nay, are even brought to their deliverance by the means by which they seem to be brought to their destruction."

Perhaps, like Robinson Crusoe, we are metaphorically shipwrecked, unable any longer to follow the wanderlusts we have rationalized: material comfort, addictions, or intellectual laziness. In order to survive as sturdy Christians, we may have to work at spiritual survival and in that discipline develop passionate and grateful hearts toward God, certainly a kind of deliverance into true faith.

Nicole Bromley

Praise be to the God and Father of our Lord Jesus Christ, the Father of compassion and the God of all comfort, who comforts us in all our troubles, so that we can comfort those in any trouble with the comfort we ourselves have received from God.

2 CORINTHIANS 1:3–4 (NIV)

In a world plagued with abuse, betrayal, addiction, and brokenness, we are surrounded by people who are silently hurting and feeling alone. Many of us have been there ourselves. But, no matter what we have experienced in life, we are not alone. There are others around us who are going through the same thing and are in need of comfort. God asks us to reach out to them in whatever way we can. He asks that we give to others from what He has given us.

You may feel you have little to give, but what you do have may be exactly what someone else is desperately searching for. You may think you haven't received enough comfort yet to comfort others. But you have received some! You may think you have nothing to say. But you have a story!

Has the Lord met you in the valleys of your life? Has He carried you through pain? Have you been comforted in your troubles? If so, you are now equipped to comfort *anyone* going through *anything* because of the comfort you have already received. God's healing waters have showered you, and you now have a well for others to draw from.

Ask the Lord to give you His eyes and ears to see and hear the needs of those around you who are hurting. Ask Him to help you respond out of the love and comfort He has already given to you.

Victoria Saunders Johnson

... he will joy over thee with singing. Zephaniah 3:17 (KJV)

"Mary Bethune. Rosa Parks. I can do this. I'm a strong black woman."

I lay back on the abortion table waiting, wanting the procedure to end.

Once I found out I was pregnant I determined, "I'm not calling on Jesus. I'll fix it." So here I am recalling black history women to strengthen me. "Corretta King. Harriet Tubman. They're tough. I'm tough."

Eight hours later I woke up, the deed done. I watched darkness fill my room. I reached down feeling my empty womb. "One pain pill put me to sleep all afternoon," I reasoned, "half the bottle should kill me." Twenty minutes later, I watched my death pills floating in throw-up. "God's not going to let me die." Depression, shame, and guilt stood like little toy soldiers around my bed.

I still determined—no Jesus. I knew, if I asked, He'd come, but how? Shaking His finger in my face? Serving up punishment because I murdered my baby? I refused to extend my hand.

But then, He came—anyway. Knocking the toy soldiers off the bed and lining up angels to sing me love songs. They sang me to sleep and gave me the courage to make it to class the next day. They're still singing thirty-four years later.

Ever done something so bad, you think, "I won't call Him"? Take it from me, listing historical leaders is useless. Having an abortion at nineteen seemed like the worst thing I could have ever done. And maybe it was. But it didn't matter to Jesus. He came and loved me through one of my darkest days.

His angels are present right now. Ask Jesus to unplug your ears, your heart, and listen.

Carolyn Custis James

Be imitators of God, therefore, as dearly loved children and live a life of love, just as Christ loved us and gave himself up for us as a fragrant offering and sacrifice to God.

EPHESIANS 5:1–2 (NIV)

Every year Hollywood holds its breath as Oscar nominations are announced and actors anticipate the annual Academy Awards. It's one thing to create a fictitious character or recreate someone from the distant past. The achievement is significantly greater when the Oscar is awarded for accurately portraying someone everybody knows.

In 2007, Helen Mirren won the Oscar for Best Actress for her portrayal of Queen Elizabeth II. Her performance was so believable, it was easy to forget you were watching an actress and not the real queen. Not surprisingly, even Queen Elizabeth II herself watched Helen's performance.

No doubt it helped that Helen is British and has been observing the queen all her life. But her performance was no accident. Nor did she coast on her natural talent. Helen acted like the queen because she made the queen her study. She scrutinized the monarch's voice inflections, mannerisms, moods, facial expressions, and body movements and imitated what she saw.

In an interview, Helen recounted the moment she finally mastered the queen's way of walking. She was in her front garden, talking with a neighbor, when she finally got it right.

As God's image bearers, we are called to imitate Jesus. It is a tall order that takes us well beyond our natural abilities. We have to make Jesus our study—scrutinizing his character, his teachings, his interactions with people, his heart for the world, his self-giving love. And then we must strive to imitate what we see. Little wonder the apostles urge us to "Fix our eyes on Jesus" (Hebrews 12:2), who is both our example and also our help.

The actress who takes home the Oscar may have reached the pinnacle of her acting career, but the Oscar we seek is to be known as the heart and hands and feet of Jesus in this world.

Lynne Hybels

Is not this the kind of fasting I have chosen; to loose the chains of injustice and untie the cords of the yoke, to set the oppressed free and break every yoke? Is it not to share your food with the hungry and to provide the poor wanderer with shelter—when you see the naked, to clothe him, and not to turn away from your own flesh and blood? ISAIAH 58:6–7 (NIV)

Several years ago a friend challenged me to read Isaiah 58 every day for thirty days. I did and it turned my life upside down.

In this passage the Israelites complain to God because they're fasting and praying and going through all their detailed rituals, and yet God doesn't seem to be blessing them the way they think He should. He responds by condemning them for the way they behave on their fast days, exploiting their workers, fighting with one another, and generally forsaking His commandments.

God then describes the kind of fast he desires, explaining that if they spend themselves on behalf of the hungry and satisfy the needs of the oppressed, then "their light will rise in the darkness, and their night will become like the noonday" (v. 10). And God will guide them always and satisfy their needs.

I don't know how Christians got to the point where we thought we could please God without actively caring for the poor. Twentieth-century evangelicals made a lot of noise about a lot of issues, but we sure didn't spend ourselves on behalf of the hungry. Thankfully, we seem to be waking up in the twenty-first century. All over the world I've been meeting Christians who are committed to living lives of compassion and fighting for justice.

We each have a choice to make. Will we be the kind of worshipers to whom God says, "I am not impressed with your empty rituals"? Or will we become lights that shine his goodness into the world.

If you read Isaiah 58 each day for thirty days, I bet I know what choice you'll make.

Ellen Vaughn

There is no fear in love, but perfect love casts out fear. . . .
1 JOHN 4:18A (ESV)

What are you afraid of?

Wait, before you turn the page to get away from that thought, let me ask a different question. Would you like to be free of fears and anxieties? If you're like me, you're saying *YES, yes, yes.*

Many of us who've been following Jesus for a long time still struggle with anxiety and fear. Maybe we think it's inevitable, that a certain amount of dread is just part of being a human being.

What would life look like, free from fear? What would it feel like not to wake up in the night stabbed by dark dismay, not to feel anxious about relationships, work, finances, spouses, family, and children, not to mention global warming, terrorism, and, er, the end of the world as we know it?

Bad fear is a result of the brokenness that came when Adam and Eve went their own way in Eden. But in the same way that God provided a cure for sin and the fall, He also provides a way for us to be free from fear.

Ironically, freedom comes when we learn a different kind of fear: the fear of the Lord. When we see God as He really is—immense, magnificent, holy, so high above us—we are filled with reverence and spine-tingling awe.

The great paradox is that this awesome, glorious God loves us. He is love. And the more we learn of His heavenly love, the more that perfect love casts out the fears of this world.

Today, whenever you feel a stab of fear or anxiety, intentionally focus on God. Focus on His incredible, liberating love for you . . . let its immensity crowd out your cares.

Marcia Ramsland

The sluggard craves and gets nothing,
But the desires of the diligent are fully satisfied.
PROVERBS 13:4 (NIV)

Do you have a full email inbox? Would your life be easier if there wasn't so much email coming in?

I just trained a staff of two hundred people to simplify their work life and was surprised at the problem the email inbox is. My one-on-one visits to each desk reminded me that we have compounded our paperwork and interruptions issues with email problems. Here's what I found:

# of Inbox Emails	Leadership	Staff
0–20 emails	54% of leaders	20% of staff
20–100 emails	15 % of leaders	25% of staff
100–400 emails	8% of leaders	50% of staff
400–2,200 emails	10% of leaders	3% of staff

The fact that more than 50 percent of the leadership had fewer than ten emails in their inbox means they are decisive and have honed the habit of clearing their inbox daily. The staff who had one hundred to four hundred read emails, but were bogged down in responding.

So how can we move to a "Leadership" rating? The answer is found in the successful life principle in Proverbs 13:4. Put quite simply, it is the diligent person reading and responding to email right away that is satisfied at day's end. The sluggard in us would love to have that same result, too, but we have to work at it. It's a matter of living faithfully each day to get better and better. So start by pressing that delete button often!

Today find a friend that's good at clearing email, create folders and filters, and create a diligent lifestyle on your computer. You'll be glad you did.

Nancy Sebastian Meyer

No discipline seems pleasant at the time, but painful. Later on, however, it produces a harvest of righteousness and peace for those who are trained by it. HEBREWS 12:11 (NIV)

This is my "diet verse." I love food. I hate exercise. For years I've prayed, "Lord, help me want to diet and live a healthy lifestyle." For years I've failed.

Prayers are just words unless we follow through with obedience. So last May, at age forty-five and fifty pounds overweight, I asked God for help and immediately began obeying as I waited for His answer.

I collected everything I'd learned about eating and exercise, as well as information about my personality and motivational needs. I brought it all before God and we reviewed it together. Suddenly I recognized a missing factor—an accountability person. I asked God, "Who?" (Since He revealed the need, He must have a specific answer). A name came to mind. When I called and she agreed to help, I felt renewed hope.

To say that the road these past nine months has been quick or smooth would be a lie. "No discipline is pleasant at the time, but painful." However, today I weigh thirty pounds less than I did nine months ago and I'm still working on the other twenty. Although I still love food, I have found joy—yes, joy—in exercise. My body craves it, and I'm healthier at forty-six than ever before. This is good . . . right . . . righteous! And my mind is at peace—I'm not carrying shame, guilt, or discouragement.

Although difficult from moment to moment, disciplined obedience truly yields righteousness and peace for the long haul.

In what area of life does God desire your renewed obedience? Bring everything to Him and examine the pieces together. See how He will help you become disciplined in this area of your life—and then obey!

Anita Lustrea

A new command I give you: Love one another. As I have loved you, so you must love one another. By this all men will know that you are my disciples, if you love one another.
JOHN 13:34–35 (NIV)

My husband, son, and I tried to fly to Florida from Chicago in December a couple of years ago. There was a horrific storm that afternoon and evening. After hours of delays we had boarded our flight and just pushed away from the gate. Then the pilot's voice came, once again, over the intercom. "Midway Airport has been shut down indefinitely. We are going back to the gate for you to deplane, go to baggage claim and get your luggage." What we learned not long after was that a plane had slid off the end of the runway causing a fatalitiy; therefore everything was shut down pending an investigation.

Taxi and transportation services in and out of the airport had been halted. With no way to get home, we called John, one of our "3:00 a.m. friends"—those you can call in the middle of the night—and he graciously came. The normally twenty-minute trip from his house to the airport took him two hours. Then he could only get within a mile of the airport because of street closures due to the airplane accident. So we had to walk a mile with our suitcases over sidewalks that still had eight to ten inches of snow on them with more coming down. To this day my son talks about the night we trudged through the snow and what an "awesome adventure" it was. What I remember was the sacrificial love of our friend John, who drove two hours to the airport, another two to get us home, then another hour to get back to his house.

Take some time today to make a list of your 3:00 a.m. friends and thank God for them. If you find your list blank it may be time to risk a little and start opening yourself up to relationships that God can use in your life in a significant way.

Kristen Johnson Ingram

It is like a mustard seed, which a man took and planted in his garden. It grew and became a tree, and the birds of the air perched in its branches. LUKE 13:19 (NIV)

Mustard, at least in this country, doesn't become a tree, but it does furnish some cheerful yellow flowers on a tall stock in early spring, and its ruffled leaves dance under rain showers. I like to walk down an old logging road where I can find crisp, fresh spring greens to take home and cook with a little bacon. On my way, I see other harbingers of the season, like wild blue and yellow violets, pink spring beauties, and oak leaves bursting open. And I hear the song of at least a hundred frogs, who have dug out of their muddy winter home.

My home garden is beautiful, but the wild one, with its amphibian music, is spectacular, a celebration with wake-robins and avalanche lilies leaping from the moist soil like butterflies. I have to work hard in my garden, but the one around the logging road requires no human intervention, and though I want my garden to have its colors in neat clumps, I also love nature's sprawling excess. God is a talented gardener, one I'd like to copy. Maybe I'll start with a mustard seed.

God cultivates many wild things besides flowers and weeds. Start a journal of birds you see: even in a city apartment, you can spot pigeons, finches, ravens and starlings. Can you hear their songs and calls? Take some time to be thankful for creation.

Christa March

Put on the full armor of God, so that you will be able to stand firm against the schemes of the devil. EPHESIANS 6:11 (NASB)

Several years ago a Christian woman, who served with me in ministry, began talking about me behind my back. Before I knew it, her words had turned others against me. When I learned what she had done, it felt like she had stabbed me in the back. How could someone I trusted so much hurt me so badly?

During this time, in my daily quiet time, I was reading through Ephesians. Something in the sixth chapter of Ephesians stood out to me. Chapter six is where the Apostle Paul talks about putting on "the full armor" of God, so we can "stand against the devil's schemes." I read the passage over and over again. In those verses, I found something to protect many different parts of my body; the belt of truth for my waist, the breastplate of righteousness for my chest, and the readiness that comes with the gospel of peace that covers my feet, the shield of faith, and the helmet of salvation and the sword of the Spirit.

"But Lord, what about my back?" There was nothing mentioned to protect me from attacks aimed at my back by my fellow soldiers. Why doesn't God's armor provide protection for my back? After several days of crying out to God in pain and anger, God used another friend to clear up my confusion. God never intended for His people to fight each other. We are called to fight against Satan and not each other. When we fight each other, we leave our backs open to the real Enemy.

Psalm 32:10 (NIV) says, "Many are the woes of the wicked, but the Lord's unfailing love surrounds the man who trusts in him." If I trust in God, I don't need to worry about my back; God is protecting me with His love.

When a fellow Christian has hurt you, do you retaliate or do you trust God to protect you? Do you believe God "has your back"?

Shaunti Feldhahn

Finally, brothers, whatever is true, whatever is noble, whatever is right, whatever is pure, whatever is lovely, whatever is admirable—if anything is excellent or praiseworthy—think about such things. PHILIPPIANS 4:8 (NIV)

Most of us dreamed of the day when we would finally marry, and be able to journey through life together as one; we couldn't imagine ever losing that passionate thrill.

But just as life goes in seasons, so do our emotions—and sometimes we hit a season of discontent. We didn't expect it, but our feelings have changed. It turned out Mr. Perfect had some flaws. Maybe those flaws hurt us and we are dealing with pain and negative thoughts about our husband; or maybe it's just that the joy and exhilaration has dwindled, leaving politeness but no passion. How do we turn it around?

Sitting in a prison, the apostle Paul wrote one of my favorite passages in the Bible—and helps us answer that question. A few verses earlier, Paul says to "rejoice" in all things, then tells us how: concentrate on those things that are good and positive.

As fallen human beings, it's really easy to focus on the negative things. It's easy to wish things were different, to dwell on some very real hurt, or just to let boredom take hold. Try this wonderful prescription from Nancy Leigh DeMoss instead: For the next thirty days, don't say anything negative about your husband—either to him, or about him to someone else. And also for the next thirty days, find at least one positive thing a day about your husband to focus on and tell him.

I guarantee you will find your feelings changing, in a wonderful way. We all know that the more we focus on the negative, the more discontented we will be—and thankfully, the more we focus on the praiseworthy in the man who is most important to us, the more we will see those things all around us.

Mary Whelchel

Make sure that nobody pays back wrong for wrong, but always try to be kind to each other and to everyone else.

1 THESSALONIANS 5:15 (NIV)

Paul wrote to Timothy that ". . . the Lord's servant must not quarrel; instead he must be kind to everyone . . ." (2 Timothy 2:24 NIV). Sometimes, however, we behave as though the Bible said, "Be kind to everyone who is kind to you. Be kind to the people you like. Be kind when you want to impress someone, or when there's something in it for you."

It's easy to be kind to people who deserve our kindness, but the Bible says we are to be kind to *everyone*. That includes strangers, people who irritate us, people who are not kind to us, coworkers who don't do their job right, managers who have too many last minute emergencies—everyone includes everyone!

I remember being unkind to a hotel clerk who was not very efficient at her job. Her lack of efficiency inconvenienced me just a bit, and I'm sure the look on my face and my body language was most unkind. The Holy Spirit convicted me strongly as I walked away from that hotel clerk. How easy it would have been for me to say something kind to her, to make her feel a little more comfortable. I blew the one chance I had to show her what Jesus is like, by treating her kindly even though she was inefficient.

I'm praying specifically now that God will help me be kind to strangers, for that seems to be an area where I often fail.

To whom do you often fail to be kind? Shore that area up with prayer, and ask God to help you to be kind, as the servant of the Lord should be, to EVERYONE.

Janet Thompson

"For I know the plans I have for you," says the Lord. "They are plans for good and not for disaster, to give you a future and a hope." JEREMIAH 29:11 (NLT)

Have you heard it said God never wastes a hurt? His plans are for good and not for harm. Even in the worst circumstances, God's plan is still to bring out the best. I clung to those promises when I heard the dreaded diagnosis that I had breast cancer. Initially, it was hard to imagine how God could bring any good out of such a devastating situation, but because I believed that God had a purpose for everything that happened in my life, I was open to let Him work out His perfect plan. And you know what—He did and He will do the same in your life.

Maybe you too have just received devastating news and you wonder: Where is God? Rest assured that He is going through this crisis with you, and He will not only provide a way out of your pain, He will bring good out of your suffering. Perhaps someone observing you will draw closer to the Lord, or there will be a refining of your own heart and compassion, but rest assured a pearl *will* rise out of the mire. You can count on it.

Crisis helps us put our life into perspective. We evaluate our goals and accomplishments and determine if they are in line with the way God wants us to live. It's a time to ask ourselves what needs changing to live a more balanced life: one that truly puts God first. As you pray today, let God reveal His focus and purpose for your life during and after the difficult situation. How can you use what you learn to help someone else going through something similar? Remember the first step in healing is helping.

Linda Clare

Jesus said to him, "Feed my lambs." JOHN 21:15 (RSV)

On a perfect October afternoon, Hannah, a petite middle-aged woman, stood in the middle of a parking lot, clutching a trash bag full of second-hand clothing I'd given to her. We'd just emerged from a bookstore after an hour or two. In the store, Hannah had zipped and unzipped her purse, trying to stuff a bunch of no-good-news mail inside, looking shell-shocked about her no-good life, explaining all these disasters to her mother and me. And now, in the parking lot, she'd lost her car.

She stopped talking abruptly—her red, raw hands tight on the bag's drawstrings. Out in the Indian summer Technicolor parking lot, the world paused. Head down, she let go tears and wailed, "Is God even in the area?"

Her mother and I instinctively put our arms about her. Our murmurs floated on the still afternoon air like a prose lullaby. "God loves you," we whispered. "Something will happen, you'll see." Hannah wept and we tried to comfort her.

The red car finally showed itself—aided, I'm certain, by our prayers. Hannah's other problems weren't so easily handled, but I came away a different person. I'd glimpsed Jesus alive and real and working to help those who need it most.

That day I learned that the area code for God is a toll-free number that will lead me out of busyness, past the search for everything I've lost and into the cradle of stillness. There, the only thing to do is let go and listen. Listen for the sound of someone singing, someone crying.

Put your arms around the despaired, bang on heaven's door and ask for Jesus. He'll prove God's love is a bigger and wider place than we can ever imagine.

Find someone who is down on their luck. Be Jesus for that person—listen, hug, act, and love as Christ would.

Dannah Gresh

"... *I am the Lord, who heals you.*" EXODUS 15:26 (NIV)

Have you begun to explain away "the God who heals"? Have you relegated his healing only to the emotional and spiritual realm? And that, you see less and less frequently, dousing your faith in doubt.

Well, draw close.

I just witnessed a miracle last week.

It started months ago with a phone call from my dear friend Erin. She told me she'd just had her first ultrasound. It didn't go well. The baby had a terribly distended bladder and Erin was on her way to a neonatologist. Would I pray?

I did. She called me a few days later.

"The neonatologist wants me to abort my baby," she said matter-of-factly. "She says he may not survive to term and if he does, he'll live a short and miserable life, most likely on dialysis."

Seeming to disregard the words she just told me, she continued.

"We're going to name him Elisha," she said. "It means 'the God who heals.'"

In the days and weeks to come, we prayed over Elisha. I laid my hands on Erin's rounded belly. We hoped. We believed. We asked for forgiveness when our faith waivered.

Erin was scheduled for a C-section so the baby could be taken into emergency surgery upon birth. The surgery would enable him to ... ah, well, pee. But on the day of the C-section, I never heard from her.

They didn't do the C-section. Instead, they waited two days for the baby to deliver the old-fashioned way. When he did, he came in not screaming ... not crying ... but peeing!

Our God heals!

Today, I challenge you to pray in faith for one person in your family or circle of friends who needs healing. Lay your hands on them as Scripture encourages and exercise your faith.

Pam Farrel

*We will not hide them from their children; we will tell the next **generation** the praiseworthy deeds of the Lord, his power, and the wonders he has done.* PSALM 78:4 (NIV), emphasis added

We never have asked our kids, "What did we do wrong?" because as two people that came from very dysfunctional (at times violent) homes, we know we have had baggage to overcome. One family holiday we did ask, "What did we do right?" Our kids replied:

- "You disciplined us. When we entered high school, our peers couldn't achieve their dreams because they lacked the self-discipline to make them happen."
- "You prayed for us. We knew every day that you or dad would pray for us. It was like 'a force field that kept us from evil.'"
- "You created time for memories. You were both in ministry but we could always count on the annual father-son trip, or that you two would be the parents at school events and trips."
- "You gave us traditions to look forward to: *Learner and Leader Day* each August before school started where we signed the Privileges and Responsibilities Contract and got a cool present that applauded our passion; the Gift to Jesus where you helped us take our eyes off ourselves at Christmas; the lighting of the candle and personal blessing each Thanksgiving; and the sixteenth birthday dinner complete with the ID bracelet and car keys inscribed with 'Until the Day' that reminded us to be pure."
- "You lived it. You were the same at home, in the grocery store, and in the pulpit."

At times, people have commented on our parenting style, which to some seems so planned out and structured. The comment we hear is, "It just seems like so much work." But that day, it didn't seem like work at all, it seemed like God's mercy and grace.

What proactive parenting or mentoring step can you take to pass the baton of faith?

Lori Neff

Do not speak in the hearing of a fool, for he will despise the wisdom of your words. PROVERBS 23:9 (NASB)

Silence first
Then inquiry
Do you really want to know my inmost thoughts
Or is this a polite expression of interest?
If I answer, will you understand?
Will you care?
If I entrust my dreams to you,
Will you keep them?
Will you think I'm foolish?
If I expose my heart to you,
Will you treat it carefully?
If I tell you my concerns,
Will you realize how important they are to me?
Will you say that it's stupid?
Trust?
Take risks?
I choose to remain silent.

I chose to remain silent for many of my young adult years. I was hurt again and again when my dreams and concerns were brushed aside or laughed at. I was so hurt that I shut down and attempted to not let anyone in. I didn't understand at the time that there is wisdom in knowing who we can share our heart with—not everyone we encounter will treat it with care. After years of silence, I am learning to open up and take a few risks. To my surprise, I've found that when I'm authentic and transparent with others, I usually see heads nodding in recognition and agreement. That's given me the courage to cautiously speak up more even when I feel uncomfortable and think people might look at me as if what I said was lame. I'm beginning to believe in myself (see myself as God sees me), not take myself so seriously and believe that perhaps I do have something to share. I pray that when I open my mouth, my words would be life-giving and wise. How will your words today offer hope and life to others? Do you need to risk opening up more and sharing from your heart?

Joanne Heim

Tremble, O earth, at the presence of the Lord,
at the presence of the God of Jacob,
who turned the rock into a pool,
the hard rock into springs of water.
PSALM 114:7–8 (NIV)

Have you ever been stuck between a rock and hard place—with no exit anywhere in sight? In a place where no matter which direction you turn you come up against something hard? In a place where you feel trapped, caught between two equally horrible situations or choices?

It's uncomfortable and it feels hopeless because though you're spinning in circles looking for a way out, the view stays the same—simply put, you're up against a wall.

I've been there—in that trapped place. I've fought against it, beating my head against the rock until I'm exhausted and ready to give up. And when I stopped fighting against it and fell to my knees in surrender and silence, God began to speak.

He reminded me that He is with me wherever I go, that I cannot hide from His presence. That there's no spot too tight into which he cannot come. He showed me that I can find rest in him wherever I am, whatever wall I'm facing—that he is God and can turn the "rock into a pool, the hard rock into springs of water."

That place where you're stuck—between a rock and hard place—just might turn out to be a place of rest and refreshment, a place to encounter God and experience his rest and provision. Stop banging your head against the wall. Sit still and invite God to speak.

Never forget that our God is awesome. Rocks pour forth water and stones turn to bread with Him. He is there to refresh you, to offer you rest. Even—maybe most especially—between a rock and a hard place.

What wall are you facing today? Instead of fighting against it, have a seat and ask God to turn it into a place of refreshment.

Sabrina O'Malone

Be still, and know that I am God. PSALM 46:10 (NIV)

This is one of the most difficult Scriptures to live by, especially when you are busy. As a working mom with five young children, there's always something for me to do. "Being still" is the exact opposite of my purpose-driven inclination to get things done. Nevertheless, stillness is one of the things God requires. At the very least, it gives you the opportunity to recharge and focus on the Lord and His agenda.

Your thoughts and prayers lay the groundwork for great things to come. But you will need to consciously dedicate some of your time to do it. This is the best way to stay in step with God's plan for your life. Otherwise, if you continually handle urgent (not necessarily important) things first, it will tend to leave less and less time for the things that really matter.

You need to slow down. Especially if you've been entrusted with the care of children. Starting today, why not eliminate just one time-waster that saps your time, energy, or money? Instead, take some time to make rest and downtime a priority. Even if it's just a microbreak—take it! And resist the urge to mentally run through your to-do list.

Take a deep, cleansing breath, bow your head, close your eyes, and ask the Lord to direct your thoughts and actions. Pray for wisdom, peace and the courage you'll need to cut out the things that aren't really beneficial for you or your family. And reflect upon all the good things God has already done for you through the years. Finish by praising Him for His goodness, faithfulness and love.

This is the best recipe I know for gaining energy, focus, and joy. Try it!

Erin Smalley

Therefore encourage one another and build each other up, just as in fact you are doing. 1 Thessalonians 5:11 (NIV)

Have you ever wondered why women have such a deep longing for female friendships? The answer is simple. Just like the Lord desires to be in relationship with us, we desire relationships with others. Although both men and women were created for relationships, women "crave" relationships innately and are driven to be in relationships in a way most men will never fully understand or need.

I love to look at the precious female friendships that are found in Scripture. Ruth followed Naomi to a foreign country, giving up all she ever knew. In Ruth 4:15 it says that the love and commitment Ruth showed Naomi was truly amazing—better than seven sons! Isn't it fascinating that the first person Mary goes to when she finds out that she is carrying the Messiah was Elizabeth—another female. In true female fashion, Elizabeth then offers Mary much comfort, joy, and wisdom.

Unfortunately, when we get overly busy with family and work, we often put our friendships with other women on the back burner or let them go completely. This is a tragic mistake because women are such a source of strength, healing, rejuvenation, and encouragement to one another—not only emotionally but also physically.

Spend some time today asking the Lord if there are some healthy friendships that you have neglected lately that need to be rekindled—for their own good and yours. Furthermore, pray that the Lord will prompt you to reach out to some women in your church, community, or from your past who are in need of some loving support and encouragement.

Ultimately, I hope that this will lead you to discover the "true gift" that God has for you through your female friendships.

Christa March

For I am convinced that neither death nor life, neither angels nor demons, neither the present nor the future, nor any powers, neither height nor depth, nor anything else in all creation, will be able to separate us from the love of God that is in Christ Jesus our Lord. ROMANS 8:38–39 (NIV)

Is there a sin in your past that you've asked God's forgiveness for but you can't seem to forget about it? Even though you know that you've been forgiven, you somehow let the memory of that sin hold you back from having a close, truly intimate relationship with Jesus Christ.

I've met several women who fit that description perfectly. These women were amazing wives and mothers and yet, all of them felt that some sin they had committed years ago remained an invisible wall between them and God. Yes, they considered themselves Christians, albeit in their minds "second rate" Christians because of their particular sins.

Romans 8:38–39 (NIV) says, "For I am convinced that neither death nor life, neither angels nor demons, neither the present nor the future, nor any powers, neither height nor depth, nor anything else in all creation, will be able to separate us from the love of God that is in Christ Jesus our Lord."

There is nothing that can separate you from God's love that's been made available to you through Jesus Christ. No matter how bad your sin might have been, the blood of Jesus is still more powerful. He has forgiven you and desperately wants that intimate relationship with you. Let this verse be the weapon you use as you crash through your own invisible sin wall.

Memorize Romans 8:38–39. Satan has a way of reminding us of the things we did before the blood of Jesus cleansed us from all unrighteousness. But nothing defeats Satan more than Scripture. So, every time he reminds you of that sin from long ago, quote Romans 8:38–39.

Kristen Johnson Ingram

. . . the one who is in you is greater than the one who is in the world. 1 JOHN 4:4 (NIV)

Who did this? Who planted the bomb, caused the pollution, loaded the gun, or built so shoddily that the building collapsed? Who brought the disease to town or fed drugs and pornography to our children?

Not knowing who to blame or who to punish can leave everybody feeling pretty helpless, but Ephesians 6:12 (NIV) tells us that "our struggle is not against flesh and blood, but against the rulers, against the authorities, against the powers of this dark world and against the spiritual forces of evil in the heavenly realms." Maybe you believe in the Devil as an active force of wickedness, or simply that evil is an inevitable part of humanity. Either way, you know the Devil is out there. The word "antichrist" can make you remember scary movies and terrible threats from self-styled prophets, and your feeling of impotence may increase.

Should I punish the evildoer or the dope dealer or even God? Should I sue someone, bomb someone, put someone in jail? Shall I shake my fist at heaven or quit believing, deserting my faith in anger? I feel overwhelmed by evil.

But I'm not helpless. St. John went on to say, " . . . the one who is in you is greater than the one who is in the world" (1 John 4:4 NIV). God within us does constant battle with the Enemy, and girds us for both the spiritual and the physical battle. So "Who did this?" is not as important a question as, "Who will help us?"

Martin Luther answered that question this way: "God plus one is a majority."

With a friend or two, talk about resisting evil.

Matthew 6:13 (NIV) says, "And lead us not into temptation, but deliver us from the evil one."

Kay Yerkovich

And the Lord said, "Simon, Simon! Indeed, Satan has asked for you, that he may sift you as wheat. But I have prayed for you Simon, that your faith may not fail and when you have returned to me, strengthen your brethren. LUKE 22: 31–32 (NKJV)

Sifting or threshing wheat is an aggressive process of beating, shaking, and tossing to separate the grain from the straw and chaff. Satan asks specifically to "thresh" Peter hoping to separate him from his Lord.

Jesus' response to Satan's bold request? Prayer! Jesus could have prayed for countless things as Peter faced the dark days ahead. Jesus did not pray that Peter wouldn't fail, for He knows what a valuable teacher failure can be. He did not pray that Satan could have no influence. In fact, Jesus does not refuse Satan's request and during Peter's threshing he struggles to the point of denying His Lord. Yet, even the schemes of our Enemy are tools in the hand of a mighty, sovereign, God. Satan desires to destroy and indeed the Devil's work may tear down and expose, but God is ready to rebuild to His glory.

Jesus prays for one thing; that Peter's *faith* wouldn't fail. Faith: clinging to Jesus when nothing makes sense and the dark places inside us lay exposed. Eventually, faith enables us to return to Jesus after every failure with a deeper awareness of who He is and who we are.

We face the same Enemy. Like Peter we must learn that we all have the capacity to deny our Lord when life gets difficult, our prayers are unanswered and our hopes are dashed. When you can't go on, when you feel like giving up on Jesus, He is praying for you that your faith will not fail. When His prayer is answered and you return to Him, strengthen others.

Melinda Schmidt

Nothing in all creation is hidden from God's sight.
HEBREWS 4:13A (NIV)

He couldn't bring himself to tell the scope of his wife's mental and emotional illness, and after he died, their family and friends began to realize the stress he had long carried on his shoulders. He alone had met her needs, cared for her, carried her.

An explosive family ordeal was misunderstood by others as they kept quiet for decades the pain one of their own inflicted on them. Keeping the secret with smiles and superficial conversation about this person, friends understandably did not agree with the boundaries they began to set with this volatile family member.

I was surprised to find numerous columns devoted to the word *truth* in my Bible's concordance. Truth is important to God for it expresses His character. Jesus said, "I am the way and the truth and the life" (John 14:6 NIV).

Because a husband wouldn't tell the truth about his wife, no one could help share his wearisome burden and after his death, family and friends were left to fill the void his widow believed only he could fill adequately.

Because the dysfunction of a family member was covered up, others were unable to empathize and help support them over the years and doubted their integrity when they drew boundaries. Their actions appeared unfeeling and cruel.

Who could blame the outcomes of these situations? Truth had not been told. Authenticity along the way could have brought understanding and prevented much hurt.

While we have to be wise in what we share, covering up can backfire. Is there something in your life, that if you told the truth about it, others could be given an opportunity to support you and understand what your life is really like?

Joy Jordan-Lake

All the believers were together and had everything in common. Selling their possessions and goods, they gave to anyone as he had need. ACTS 2:44–45 (NIV)

Any of us who've long been on a journey of faith need to be knocked over the head sometimes by those new to the path.

The scrappy little Massachusetts congregation—full of college students who'd begun asking God-questions only since leaving home and homeless people looking for warmth of a physical and spiritual nature—didn't feel like any church I'd ever known. Only a couple of us had grown up memorizing the order of the minor prophets to earn shiny dimes and Krispy Kreme doughnuts. Most of the congregation was experiencing grace and mercy—and Jesus—for the very first time.

At one of the first Bible studies I attended here, we read from Acts, the early church's attempts to live as a community of faith. I knew this passage like the scars on my own kneecap: all too familiar.

But Rick, a young Navy sailor studying to be a doctor, asked quietly, "I'd like to ask a favor."

We all nodded, happy to oblige.

"I'd like to pass around my checkbook and my credit card statements. I'm afraid I'm spending too much money on myself, and I know that as a Christian now, that's not an option. I need your feedback. And, in fact, maybe we'd *all* like to pass around . . ."

Which was the end of my being happy to oblige. I was appalled. Partly because his suggestion broke all good mind-your-own-business rules of proper social behavior and church-people decorum. And partly because his suggestion, humbly asked, struck me as precisely the kind of openness we all ought to learn.

No matter where you are on your own journey of faith, how might you learn today from someone newly resurrected or perhaps still seeking?

Dee Brestin . . . .

But his delight is in the law of the Lord, and on his law he meditates day and night. PSALM 1:2 (NIV)

I discovered a powerful secret in prayer many years ago—a secret that has transformed my prayer life from rowing upstream to catching the wind of His Spirit in my sails.

Pray the psalms. Dietrich Bonhoeffer, in *Psalms: The Prayer Book of the Bible*, writes:

> It is a dangerous error, surely very widespread among Christians, to think that the heart can pray by itself . . . Prayer does not mean simply to pour out one's heart. It means rather to find the way to God and to speak with him, whether the heart is full or empty. No man can do that by himself. For that he needs Jesus Christ. If we wish to pray with confidence and gladness, then the Words of Holy Scripture will have to be the solid basis of our prayer.

Sometimes you can simply pray a psalm verbatim. More often, you read a verse and let it lead you into prayer. If the psalmist is praying against his enemies, think of our unseen spiritual enemies, and pray against them. Let me show you a few examples:

"But his delight is in the law of the Lord, and on his law he meditates day and night" (Psalm 1:2 NIV). *Lord, please help me delight in your Word, so that I want to meditate on it day and night.*

"Keep your tongue from evil and your lips from speaking lies" (Psalm 34:13 NIV). *Lord, forgive me for the hurtful things I said today. Please keep my tongue from evil.*

You will find you are praying more for your character and more for things you have neglected in your past prayer life. You will also always be praying within the will of God and experience His wind in your sails.

Christine Wyrtzen

O continue Your lovingkindness to those who know You.

Psalm 36:10 (NASB)

When a man sits in a foxhole on the frontlines of war, how is he strengthened? He remembers his lover at home. He relives their many memories together, times they connected that were especially poignant. It might mean recalling an evening they had watching a sunset, or a long talk they enjoyed on the phone late one night, or a romantic dinner and the sound of the first time she said, "I love you." These experiences, stored away in his heart, will be the fuel by which he is able to access courage.

My relationship with Jesus can work identically. It has taken me a lifetime to learn this. Education about Christ through His Word is no substitute for experience. Just as education about a person, like facts on a resume, would never transcend the experience of living life with him, I need an internal inventory of memories, experientially, that I am able to access when the stresses of life hit me. *I remember when Jesus said this, or did that.* It is only these recollections that make the heart strong in adversity.

My life needs to be one exercise after another of cultivating memories and refining the art of biblical meditation. I want to experience the company of Jesus in many settings. Just a few words from Him will be enough to counter the challenges ahead. Growth, demands, deadlines, oversaturation in ministry—these all contribute to a malaise of the soul and fatigue of the body. Only spirit sustenance will be the cure-all, the fuel that will allow my soul and body to soar. All for His honor. All for His glory.

Isolate the most meaningful moment in your history with Jesus. When did you hear Him speak, discern His presence, or feel His miraculous touch. Close your eyes throughout today. Relive it. Allow it to strengthen you.

Ginger Kolbaba

He will yet fill your mouth with laughter and your lips with shouts of joy. Job 8:21 (NIV)

Several years ago, my husband, Scott, left me a voice mail message at work: "Hi, just wanted to let you know you're the proud owner of a VW convertible. Bring home money."

What's he talking about? I wondered.

I soon found out: he'd found a 1992 VW Cabriolet convertible with 92,000 miles on it for less than $2,000. He looked it over and took a test drive. It was in good condition—it just needed a good cleaning and some TLC. So we paid cash for it, brought it home, and fixed it up.

The first night we had our new convertible, we drove around for hours with the top down. And when the chill of night descended, we simply rolled up the front windows, blasted the heat, and kept driving. I've never had so much fun or laughed more. Our "love bug" has brought us many evenings of relaxing joy and laughter as we clip along country roads.

Too many times we make marriage all about *work* and forget that God created us in marriage to experience joy and laughter. Our relationship shouldn't be just hard work. We need a good balance. When my marriage gets a little too difficult, I look out into our garage and think about the fun we have in our VW.

Have you allowed work to take over the fun you used to have in your marriage? What's one simple thing you can do to bring back some joy and fun in your relationship?

Janice Elsheimer

Forget the former things; do not dwell on the past. See, I am doing a new thing! Now it springs up; do you not perceive it?
Isaiah 43:18–19 (NIV)

Habits. We need them to survive, to keep ourselves from having to reinvent our daily lives every twenty-four hours, to stave off chaos. Habits—like brushing our teeth, covering our mouth when we cough, saying "please" and "thank you," putting things back where we got them—are good and necessary parts of living with ourselves and others. Habits are good.

Unless they're not. Think about your "bad habits." We all have them. They can start as small pleasures or indulgences and grow into compulsions, obsessions, or addictions—habits run amuck. And when they start controlling us instead of helping us, we may feel helpless, unhealthy, and ashamed.

Our bad habits and addictions didn't come on in a day, and we won't overcome them in a day. But at least we can start. We built our habits one day at a time, and that's how we can dismantle them. Experts tell us it takes twenty-eight days to break a habit that may have taken years to cultivate. In ancient times, people prayed and fasted for forty days, a "quarantine," which literally means "a forty-day period of separation." In our own way, in today's world, we can still go into "the wilderness," we can quarantine ourselves from our destructive habits and focus on God's admonition to forget the former things and join Him in doing something new, healthy, and wise.

Choose one habit you want to break. Know that God can help you break it, that all things are possible through faith. Just for today, fast from that habit and join God in "doing a new thing!"

Anita Lustrea

Come, all you who are thirsty, come to the waters; and you who have no money, come, buy and eat! ISAIAH 55:1A (NIV)

I think Jesus asks some curious questions in the gospels. As an interviewer I'm always intrigued by interesting questions. Think about Jesus' question to blind Bartimaeus. He asks, "What do you want me to do for you?" At face value we think, "He wants you to heal him of course." But Jesus is asking something deeper. He wants Bartimaeus, and us, to come face-to-face with the deep desires and longings within us.

Isaiah 55:1-3a (NIV) issues an invitation to those of us with deep longings. "Come, all you who are thirsty, come to the waters; and you who have no money, come, buy and eat! Come, buy wine and milk without money and without cost. Why spend money on what is not bread, and your labor on what does not satisfy? Listen, listen to me, and eat what is good, and your soul will delight in the richest of fare. Give ear and come to me; hear me, that your soul may live."

I don't know about you, but I see this amazing invitation issued to me yet still find myself looking for fulfillment in counterfeits. Maybe it's food, maybe it's vegging out to TV too many nights or hours in a row. Maybe it's that little spending spree that isn't in the budget that I think will make me feel better about a bad day at work. What keeps you from responding to this invitation to quench your thirst? What stands in the way of true satisfaction in your life? Take some time today to do a little internal work and sit with these questions. It might be just what you need to get unstuck and move forward into the inviting arms of Jesus.

Kathy Koch

Now faith is being sure of what we hope for and certain of what we do not see. HEBREWS 11:1 (NIV)

The student yawned and I knew he was creative and smart!

I was almost finished explaining some of Christ's excellent teaching techniques when one student at the seminary in Kiev, Ukraine, raised his hand. He knew enough English to formulate his question. He asked me to demonstrate some of my ideas by pretending they were children and I was their teacher. Oh, my!

Not knowing how all the Ukranian adults would respond, I decided to try it. When teaching that we must make sure our students understand our lessons and don't just finish them, I asked the adults to stand and pretend to be children. They nervously smiled as they stood.

"Boys and girls (some shy giggles after translation), we've been talking about Daniel's great faith in a great, big God even when he was in the den with hungry lions. How do you think he was standing in the den? Remember, he had great faith in a great God. On the count of three, show me how he might have been standing. Ready? One—two—three!"

Some of the students did nothing—they just stood casually. Some assumed a worship posture and others pretended to be praying. All of these were sensible responses. One young man's response was extraordinary.

When I said "Three!" he remained standing and faked yawning. Pretending to be Daniel, it was clearly no big deal to him that hungry lions were nearby. He knew his God and there was absolutely nothing for him to worry about.

If you had been in the lions' den, how would you have stood? How much faith do you have today?

Leigh McLeroy

If we live by the Spirit, let us also walk by the Spirit. Let us not become boastful, challenging one another, envying one another. . . Bear one another's burdens, and thereby fulfill the law of Christ. GALATIANS 5:25–26; 6:2 (NASB)

I spied the elderly couple leaving the county courthouse together on a cool fall morning. He wore a jacket and a soft hat and she a simple skirt and blouse. As they moved toward a short flight of steps I noticed that both of them were limping. She placed her left foot cautiously, as if perhaps she'd had a stroke. He favored his left knee, moving with a definite "hitch" that mirrored hers. I feared what might happen when they reached the steps, but I needn't have.

Approaching the first step, he grasped both of her hands firmly in his. Then he planted his "good" right leg below him and she followed suit, trusting him with her weight and moving down with her own right leg. As soon as she did, he swung his left leg down, and she carefully slid hers to meet his own. They never hesitated. These two collaborators had obviously done this dance before. Six steps later their errand was complete, their descent was sweet, and the lesson they taught was mine to keep.

We do well to need each other.

Alternating strength for weakness step by step, we can achieve far more together than we might alone. But most of us are not so adept at revealing our weaknesses, or so graceful being helped by another's strength.

There's a quiet beauty in the dance of compensating flaws . . . in hands grasped together in a common task. All that's required is that we uncover our shortcomings and let them be balanced by another's strengths. It only costs us a dash of humility, and a bit of determined love.

Step by step, together we can make it. Shall we?

How have you danced the dance of compensating flaws to the glory of God?

Ellen Vaughn

. . . there is terror on every side . . . but I trust in you, O Lord; I say, "You are my God." My times are in your hands . . .

PSALM 31:13–15A (NIV)

David wrote many of his desperate psalms when he was pursued by people who wanted to kill him.

We may not be on the run, but we can often feel like David, that stresses and fears are pressing in from every side.

But David challenges us to make a choice. We can believe that God is with us, and that He allows troubles for our eventual good and for His glory . . . or we can live as if life is just a random series of events over which God has no control. Either our times are securely in His hands, or they are just ticking away on some cosmic clock, without purpose or meaning.

Hebrews 11 defines faith as the assurance of things not seen. We can't yet see God, but we can sure see the things that threaten us each day. But we have the opportunity, like David, to trust in God, to lean into Him and believe He holds us, that He loves us and has given Himself for us.

The nineteenth-century pastor E. Paxton Hood wrote, "The hand of Jesus is the hand which rules our times. He regulates our life clock. Christ is for us and Christ is in us. My times are in his hand. My life can be no more in vain than was my Savior's life in vain."

Today, set the alarm on your phone or some other device to go off quietly once each hour. When it does, fix your attention on God, and thank Him that your times are in His hands. Pray that He will increase your trust in Him!

Mindy Caliguire

Forget the former things; do not dwell on the past. See, I am doing a new thing! Now it springs up; do you not perceive it?
ISAIAH 43:18–19A (NIV)

As winter approaches, the trees gently surrender their leaves to the wind. They float away one by one, eventually to earth below. The true structure of the tree, invisible in full leaf, is now visible—and, to me, it is beautiful.

I silently appreciate these sterile beauties in photographs, paintings, in fields nearby. Some (okay, most) friends think this is a bizarre or poorly developed aesthetic. "That's crazy, Mindy . . . trees without leaves are a sign of the fall (meaning original sin, not autumn!)." But as years pass by, I love leafless trees more and more.

Some ask, "Why?" but how can you explain a favorite color, a favorite view? I'll offer my observations:

- they symbolize an ability to survive harsh seasons, appearing dead, yet fully alive.
- the true structure becomes visible—branches elongated and symmetrical, twisting, meandering in a confused tangle, displaying their unique personality. Fluffy, vibrant, green no longer hides their character.
- the gentle releasing of the leaves reminds me of life's seasons when I, too, must surrender to the harsh winds of life, the declining sunlight, the chill. I *let go* of what my life appears to be, trusting myself to the season. Sometimes I let go one lonely leaf at a time; sometimes in droves. Bare and naked, the source of my life sustains me.

Have you endured a harsh season—waiting for God to do a new thing? What have you noticed lately about your own true, God-given, essence beneath a leafy exterior? What have you released recently? What needs to be let go as you trust God to sustain you through a season of change?

Kendra Smiley . . . .

Offer hospitality to one another without grumbling.
1 PETER 4:9 (NIV)

John and I used to live in a thirty-by-thirty-foot house. Imagine this: two adults, three active boys and two home-based businesses all under that very small roof. Now expand your imagination and see if you can add this to the mix: two eight-foot Sunday school tables elegantly (?) set for the main course of a Bible study progressive dinner. Does that stretch your imagination? It definitely stretched my hostess skills!

If you cannot imagine it I wish you could have seen it. We served a wonderful dinner to sixteen hungry, Jesus-loving adults and then sent them down the road for dessert. This hospitality was not necessarily easy, but the cramped space did not stop the fun.

Too often we think that we can only extend hospitality when we have a big, beautiful home. "I'll be *more* than happy to host a small group after we redo our family room." You don't need to "redo" your family room. Instead I would suggest redoing your attitude and perception of hospitality.

Recently I was present at a wonderful celebration dinner in the home of a missionary in Vienna, Austria. The dinner followed a "Day Out for Women" and there was truly much to celebrate. The room where we gathered was not large nor had it been recently redone. We balanced our plates on our laps as we ate and talked and laughed and celebrated the day we had spent together, encouraging and equipping the women who had attended the event. Hospitality reigned . . . just as the Lord commanded.

When was the last time you had the opportunity to extend hospitality to someone? Did you hesitate and make excuses or did you relish the occasion with joy? Offer hospitality . . . no grumbling allowed . . . the Next Right Choice!

Miriam Neff

Therefore, my brothers and sisters, you whom I love and long for, my joy and crown, stand firm in the Lord in this way, dear friends! PHILIPPIANS 4:1 (TNIV)

Stand firm in the Lord? I really don't feel like that every day! With your job, your circumstances, you might not either. Just who does God think I am that I can stand firm today? If you work in a public high school, as I did for many years, you are weighed down by the needs of teens in an increasingly dangerous world, where adolescent decisions can have life-changing consequences—often not good ones.

It's hard to stand firm as a parent, a marriage partner, or a caregiver. It's hard to be single. It's hard to have integrity in many work environments. In fact, there are few easy journeys in this life.

Stand firm, Lord? How in this world?

The answer is in the "therefore." This not so spiritual-sounding word is there for a significant reason. It means, "Based on what I just said, the following is true."

In the previous paragraph in Philippians, God tells me that I am a citizen of heaven. And I am here waiting for Jesus. He's coming. And He is going to transform my sagging body. (Which sags more on some days than others.)

Therefore.

Just who does He think I am? A citizen of a higher country. A woman with future-oriented expectations. Standing firm because of who I am, regardless of what's coming down around me.

Thought to ponder: today is just the right day to stand firm.

Sharon Hersh

Commit to the Lord whatever you do, and your plans will succeed. PROVERBS 16:3 (NIV)

During a trip to Israel with a group from my church, we visited a cave thought to be that of the demoniac in Mark 5. There, Jesus orders the demons that held this man in bondage to go into a herd of pigs which promptly ran over a cliff and into the Sea of Galilee.

My pastor encouraged us to find a rock and write on it something we wanted to surrender to God. We were to step to a cliff overlooking the Sea of Galilee and throw our rocks into the sea. I looked at my rock, not sure of what to write. *What would you write?*

I initially wrote my destructive addiction, alcoholism. Then I wrote people-pleasing, which erodes my soul and robs me of joy. Finally, I wrote the addiction that just wears me out: workaholism. What my life would be like without these? Tears streamed down my face and Jesus impressed on my heart, "Sharon, I never asked you not to drink or work or try so hard. *I just miss you when you do.*"

Our sin separates us from God. In that moment, I felt God's presence. In surrendering to Him, I felt the awe and wonder of knowing that He missed me.

This week, when you stop working, taking care of others, and planning your next move or when you begin to feel lonely, restless, or empty, surrender that moment to Him. Don't do it so that He'll make the loneliness, restlessness, or emptiness go away. Surrender to not craving something from God—but craving God. And in that sweet surrender discover that God doesn't want something from you. He wants you!

Nancy Kane

. . . for where your treasure is, there your heart will be also.

MATTHEW 6:21 (NASB)

"When I finally realize my (fill in the blank—career goals, financial independence, lifestyle, etc.) then I will truly be happy." We all can get caught in the quest for "happiness." Most of us have seen the credit card commercials that show couples sunning themselves on a white sandy beach in an exotic location, or the family driving a well-equipped minivan with a built in DVD player showing the kids in DVD paradise as mom and dad drive along on the vacation. The intended message of these images is that when we enjoy these things we have "arrived" and are truly happy. So we are enticed to work increasingly harder to attain more only to realize a less lasting reward. How often we find that the happiness we experience when we attain something lasts only for a moment; like eating junk food when our bodies are longing for a balanced nutritional meal.

Christ knew our propensity to allow material things to dominate us and to be slaves to money. He encourages us to not store up treasures for ourselves here on earth because where our treasure is so our hearts will be also (Matthew 6:19–22 NASB). Jesus' question and encouragement to the disciples is relevant for us today. . . .

"Is not life more than food, and the body more than clothing? . . . And why are you worried about clothing? Observe how the lilies of the field grow; they do not toil nor do they spin, yet I say to you that not even Solomon in all his glory clothed himself like one of these. . . . But seek first His kingdom and His righteousness, and all these things will be added to you" (Matthew 6:25–33 NASB). So, today, may we be seekers of Christ and trusting that all of our complex daily needs are opportunities in which God Himself will show us His provision.

Virelle Kidder

The disciples went and woke him, saying, "Master, Master, we're going to drown!" He got up and rebuked the wind and the raging waters; the storm subsided, and all was calm. LUKE 8:24 (NIV)

Jesus' disciples learned quickly that He was full of surprises. Whether paying taxes from a coin in a fish's mouth, or feeding thousands with a boy's meager lunch, no one thought Him ordinary.

Luke records an extraordinary surprise. While crossing Galilee with his disciples, Jesus fell sound asleep when suddenly a storm came up and began to swamp the boat. "The disciples went and woke him, saying, 'Master, Master, we're going to drown!' He got up and rebuked the wind and raging waters; the storm subsided, and all was calm. 'Where is your faith?' He asked His disciples" (Luke 8:24-25a NIV).

I picture them standing in the boat, trying to process what they'd witnessed. "Who is this? " they wondered. "Even the winds and the water...... obey Him."

I'm still amazed at answered prayer. Will I ever get used to miracles? I hope not.

About half way into our kid's college years, our finances dried up. Long gone were our modest savings. Steve's job at the state education department provided a steady income, but it was never enough. Some nights I'd watch him praying with his head down on the dining room table with our bills spread out in neat rows. Daily I prayed, "God, please don't let us dishonor you with our finances. Help us pay our bills, Lord."

The call came on my birthday. My elderly second cousin in California died that day and left me a hefty bequest, her executer said. *Could this be real? Dare I believe it?*

It was real. God not only paid our bills, but gave us the joy of giving liberally, too. I'll never forget the feeling.

Do you know someone who needs an overflow of God's miracle provision, too? What a great thing to pray for today!

Carol Ruhter

. . . and do not give the devil a foothold. EPHESIANS 4:27 (NIV)

The vinca groundcover was getting a little sparse under the lofty pine trees in my backyard. So when I noticed clover growing in its midst, I didn't pluck it. What's the harm in a little clover? After all, I reasoned, the clover's attractive greenery blended in to make the vinca look fuller. For a while. Over time, the clover tendrils began intertwining with the vinca, aggressively re-rooting where they touched soil. When I finally realized the clover was overtaking my garden bed, it had choked out much of the vinca. Like other weeds, clover thrives where there is lack of attention, mulch cover, and other growth. Eventually it destroys what we've planted.

Is there such a thing as a *little* sin? It often blends right in, intertwining itself into our lives like clover in the vinca. Once given a "foothold," sin's tendrils aggressively re-root where there is lack of attention, prayer cover, and spiritual growth. Those little sins that appear so attractive and harmless can quietly overtake our lives. We must not fail to identify sin as a foothold for Satan. If we do not immediately uproot sin, Satan will choke out our relationship with God and all He has planted in our lives.

Will you ask God's Holy Spirit to search your heart and show you where sin has taken root?

Anita Lustrea

Love the Lord your God with all your heart and with all your soul and with all your mind and with all your strength.
MARK 12:30 (NIV)

As a kid, I used to love trick-or-treating. To me, trick-or-treating wasn't an event as much as it was an art form!! This was about avoiding the cheap candy homes and zeroing in on the good stuff on each block. This was about covering lots of ground. It was about a candy stash. This was about greed and gluttony.

It's funny to think back about what motivated me as a kid. Thank goodness candy is no longer one of my primary motivations. I've paid plenty of penalties for my addiction to sweets.

What motivates me now? In large part, Mark 12:30-31 (NIV): "Love the Lord your God with all your heart and with all your soul and with all your mind and with all your strength. The second is this: 'Love your neighbor as yourself.' There is no commandment greater than these."

My prayer is that I'm motivated to love God and to do good for others. Although I have good motivations I sometimes fall short on the follow-through. Instead of loving God I often choose to like Him a lot. There's a difference. My desire to do good for others is limited by an almost insatiable desire to take care of myself.

When I was a kid I was motivated to be a world-class trick-or-treater. It's not about candy anymore. I want to be a first-class lover of the Lord and lover of other people. When you trick-or-treat it's easy to measure success. When you want more of God and an influential life you measure things differently. It's about quality more than quantity, it's about relationship not acquisition, it's about soul care and touching lives. It's about a peace that passes understanding and the knowledge that you do, indeed, walk your talk. It's about Jesus whispering in your ear and saying, "Well done. . . ." There's nothing better than that—nothing.

What motivates your life? Journal about that today.

Mary Whelchel . . . .

Give everyone what you owe him: If you owe taxes, pay taxes; if revenue, then revenue; if respect, then respect; if honor, then honor. ROMANS 13:7 (NIV)

The Bible tells us that the works of God reveal to us what kind of God He is (Psalm 19:1). The beauty of His creation, the majesty and grandeur of His universe give us a clear view of His character and His personality.

That's true of us, as well. Your job performance reveals what kind of person you are. Suppose someone was asked to write a description of you based upon an audit and inspection of your job performance. What would that audit reveal?

Are you careful to do your job with thoroughness? Or would the inspector conclude that your work is sloppy? Do you think the inspector would conclude that you care about other people, based on your attitude toward your coworkers? Or would it reveal a callousness toward others, not bothering to be kind and considerate toward them?

As I look at the work of God's hands, I know so much about His loving, caring nature. I see all around me evidence that He is a merciful and bountiful God, a God who wants to bestow blessings and goodness on me. His work reveals His character to me.

My work reveals my character as well. At the end of each day I need to ask myself what kind of impression my job performance has left behind me. What do other people know about me based on my work?

Would you be pleased to have someone describe you based on the way you performed your job this past week?

Anita Lustrea

Be still and know that I am God. PSALM 46:10 (NIV)

I've been thinking lately about the pace of life. More precisely, the pace of my life!!! Some of you remember going to a circus and watching a performer running around with crazy spinning plates. No sooner does he get one spinning when another begins to wobble. By the end of the act the performer was breathless and so was the audience. That plate-spinning circus act is a metaphor for life. Run fast, spin the plate, correct the wobble, run faster, spin some more plates, correct the wobble, run, spin—aaah!!!

That's not the way I want to live. Our church recently did a sermon series called "Living inSanity." It's a great play on words. How do we want to live? Insanely? Or in sanity?

The pace of my life is, for the most part, the result of my own decisions. I am the author of my living insanity. I crowd my calendar, get involved with too much, and don't say no. The problem with this insanity is that I end up edging out the relationships and responsibilities that breathe life into my soul. That's not the way I want to live. Stephen Covey once said, "You will never be able to say no until there is a greater yes burning inside of you."

I need to rediscover my "yes."

Yes to Jesus.

Yes to my primary relationships.

Yes to my calling.

Yes to Sabbath.

Yes to eating right.

Yes to exercise.

Yes to solitude.

What about you? What do you need to say yes to? What will bring life into your heart and soul? If you don't say yes to something noble, be prepared to live a plate spinner's life.

Take some time to reflect on what's really important. You'll find it much easier to say no to that which is unimportant.

Adele Calhoun

Be careful that you do not forget the Lord, who brought you out of Egypt, out of the land of slavery.

DEUTERONOMY 6:12 (NIV)

Christianity is a faith that remembers its history. God directed the Israelites to "Remember when I chose you . . . delivered you from slavery . . . fed you manna . . . gave you the law and the Promised Land." He wanted them to remember forever their unique bond.

Years ago a Boston billboard announced, "Come visit our planetarium, you small insignificant speck in the universe!" Listen, you are *not* some insignificant forgotten speck in the universe. God remembers you and comes to you in your story of addiction, weakness, and limitations (read: slavery) to deliver you and set you free.

As my friend Jackie's husband was dying of Alzheimer's, it was excruciating to watch his memories dry up as he lost his life's story. One day Jackie asked him, "Do you know who I am?" He reached out to her and said, "I don't know your name, but I know you belong to me." The memory was gone but the relationship held. How comforting to know God can never forget us.

We have choices about what and how we remember. Don't just read the story of Israel's deliverance from Egypt millennia ago. Tell *your* story of deliverance. Others will remember a God who is always working on relationship, both then *and* now.

Joshua had Israel build stone memorials as memory joggers. Resolve to fight your selective memory and spiritual amnesia by stacking up your God sightings and memories. Drop marbles in a bowl every time you see God show up. Draw a life timeline on paper and mark where God showed up for you. Repeat to others the goodness of God in the real events of life. Let God's story be the touchstone for your memories.

Katie Brazelton

Do not be anxious about anything, but in everything, by prayer and petition, with thanksgiving, present your requests to God. And the peace of God, which transcends all understanding, will guard your hearts and your minds in Christ Jesus. PHILIPPIANS 4:6–7 (NIV)

The plague of our times is troubled minds. Some doctors estimate that at least 75 percent of their patients are suffering physical effects caused by fear, worry, and anxiety.

Nothing on this earth can rip the joy right out of us quicker than an anxious spirit. Our worry affects us physically, emotionally, mentally, and spiritually. I became the Queen of Worry in the mid eighties after my husband walked out of our marriage when our children were four and six. My counselor said that my rapid, extreme weight loss indicated I was letting worry "eat away at me." Yikes! With that mega-amount of worry, it's hard to believe that I ever survived single-mothering, a corporate downsizing, and the death of my ex-husband. How did I pull through?

All I can say for certain is that I distinctly remember reading the good news of Philippians 4:6–7, day after hopeless day, until its anti-worry prescription finally took hold!

Here's where the rubber meets the hot pavement of life. We have a choice. We can block inner peace through worry, or we can promote peace through prayer. How amazing it is that God provides this precious gift of worry-releasing prayer to quiet our souls. Accept your heavenly Father's invitation to enter his peace today. What have you got to lose . . . except worry!?

Decide to do all your worrying in a half hour each week by scheduling a time to write down all your worries and put them into a nicely decorated Worry Box. The rest of the week, pray with thanksgiving instead of succumbing to worry. You will be surprised to find that most of the items in your Worry Box will be handled effortlessly by God!

Robin Chaddock

He took the five loaves and two fish, lifted his face to heaven in prayer, blessed, broke, and gave the bread and fish to the disciples to hand out to the crowd. After the people had all eaten their fill, twelve baskets of leftovers were gathered up.
LUKE 9:16–17 (MSG)

Do you ever have those funny little conversations with a friend where one thing leads to another and—Boom!—a terrific (or terrifically silly) ideas pops into your head, just based on the conversation?

Most of mine happen over bagels and coffee, and one such time was with my friend Kelly. We were talking about people using their giftedness for the good of the community. We are, essentially, given our gifts for no other reason than that they be used to benefit God's creation, make a difference in God's world. And each one of us is uniquely gifted to make a unique contribution.

I don't know. Maybe it was because I was eating at the time, but the image of the little boy with his little lunch popped into my head with the phrase, "What's in your lunch bag?"

So what IS in your lunch bag? Your own lunch bag. The lunch bag you have right now. Nothing more, nothing less. That's the stuff God is waiting to use for transformation, for difference-making. You are in charge of knowing what you have, God is in charge of distribution. Peek inside that sack and delight in what you see. That's the ultimate response to God's call.

Melinda Schmidt

Answer me when I call you, O my righteous God. Give me relief from my distress; be merciful to me and hear my prayer.
PSALM 4:1 (NIV)

Caregivers are the hands of God—reaching out to hold a hand, stroke an arm, feed a meal, change an adult diaper, order a hospital bed, push a dad in a wheelchair, make call after call to siblings, insurance agencies, doctors, home health care companies, always searching the Internet to better understand the diagnosis, weeding through parents' mail and paying their bills, grieving a life that is being snuffed out slowly by disease, cleaning a shunt site, and always . . . hoping.

Caregiver, please know that if the one you care for was emotionally, physically, mentally able—they'd say, "Thank you, dear."

Caregivers can feel isolated, a part of a world that no one can possibly understand. And, truthfully, no one else really can. The trials of the one they care for can become their own and threaten their other personal relationships—family, friends, spouse, children, peripheral family. Caregiving can become a parallel universe one lives in while living what everyone else calls "real" life. And one world can suck the life from the other. It is an exhausting journey but caregivers will often tell you they wouldn't do it any other way. Or at the very least, it's just the right thing to do. They are heroes.

If you know a caregiver, will you care . . . for them? A phone message to say you are thinking of them and the hard task they are doing, a carryout meal, a card, an email, flowers, an earnest prayer? Let them tell their story over a cup of coffee. Don't think for a moment that their world couldn't become your own . . . in an instant.

Nicole Bromley

He took a little child and had him stand among them. Taking him in his arms, he said to them, "Whoever welcomes one of these little children in my name welcomes me; and whoever welcomes me does not welcome me but the one who sent me."
MARK 9:36–37 (NIV)

Children are precious to God. Over and over Jesus shows His love for children by welcoming them into His presence and giving them special attention. He went out of His way to show others the importance of children. When we show love, care, and concern for others, especially children and those who the world considers insignificant, we are bringing Christ into this world.

Many children, and even adults, have never experienced the welcome Jesus speaks of. Many children are not even welcome in their own homes. According to Jesus' words here in Mark 9:37, our society rejects Jesus every day by devaluing the life of a child through things such as abuse, neglect, and abortion. As followers of Christ, therefore, we must be committed to welcoming, honoring, and protecting children, here in our own communities and across the world.

Jesus takes this message even further, scolding the disciples and explaining that to *not* welcome the children would be to reject Jesus Himself. When we welcome and embrace children, we are welcoming the kingdom of God into our midst.

Ask yourself: What is my attitude toward children? Have I welcomed children, and those the world considers insignificant, as Jesus instructs? What am I doing to make a difference in the life of a child today?

Kay Yerkovich . . . .

You turn things upside down, as if the potter were thought to be like the clay! Shall what is formed say to the one who formed it, "You did not make me"? Can the pot say to the potter, "You know nothing"? ISAIAH 29:16 (TNIV)

He is the potter, I am the clay,
A heap of broken shards, I lay.
All vestige of beauty lost,
What good can come at such a cost?
Now each shard He carefully takes,
And something new He slowly makes.
Each jagged edge fits just in place,
With brokenness He now creates.
New colors form as He designs,
With endless patience He refines.
My wonder mends the pain and ache.
Now tenderly my hand He takes,
And bids me touch . . . another's broken place.

I wrote this during a difficult season in my life. Sometimes life rips us up, tears our hearts and leaves us feeling broken beyond repair. During difficult times we wonder, "What good can come from such pain?" Our Lord Jesus is a master designer and He looks into the future and pictures the finished vessel in all its beauty and splendor. He alone can create beauty out of our brokenness. At times, only by faith can we submit to the loving hands that mold and shape us into the unique vessel that ultimately will display our Father's amazing workmanship.

Nancy Kane

There is a time for everything, and a season for every activity under heaven. ECCLESIASTES 3:1 (NIV)

Someone has said that the life of the follower of Christ can be divided into three books of the Bible: Ecclesiastes, Job, and Song of Solomon. Most of us spend a good portion of our lives in Ecclesiastes, always searching for what is meaningful, striving and seeking for more. Our days are spent in busyness and hurry, relentlessly running after our goals and dreams. While we may realize that this doesn't satisfy, somehow we keep trying.

Inevitably, at some point in all of our lives we encounter the second season which is the book of Job. Perhaps not to the magnitude of what Job experienced, but a time of unrelenting testing and trials. It is in this season that we see that we are unable to control the outcomes of our lives and are helpless to fix ourselves. We feel powerless and vulnerable and begin to recognize in a deeper, more profound way, God's sovereignty over everything.

This then leads us, if we learn our lessons well, to the third book—Song of Solomon. We realize at this stage that we no longer are praying for God's help, rather we want more than anything, God himself. We long for His presence; we realize that our only real satisfaction in this life can be found in resting in Him. We set our sights on knowing him, learning how to walk with Him moment by moment and loving him as an end all to itself. May God grant us the grace to live our entire lives as a love story dedicated to Christ Himself. So we can say with heartfelt devotion, "I want to know Him, and the power of His resurrection, and the fellowship of His sufferings becoming like Him in His death."

Leslie Vernick

As far as it depends on you, be at peace with all men.
ROMANS 12:18 (NIV)

I hate conflict. It seems easier to just let something go, shove it under the rug, or put up with it than to risk disapproval or rejection by bringing it up. But I've learned that there are times in my relationships I have to be willing to risk conflict in order to bring about genuine peace.

My girlfriend, Sharon, did something that bothered me and I couldn't seem to let it go. I begged God to help me forget it, to lay it down, to forgive her, but I couldn't. Eventually I found myself distancing myself from her because I'm not a good pretender. I felt hurt and was avoiding her because I didn't want to be honest. I was afraid.

When you're in this kind of dilemma, the only biblical way out is the way of a peacemaker. You must be willing to enter into potential conflict in order to bring about true peace and reconciliation. Otherwise, the relationship will deteriorate because of unresolved hurts and anger.

A biblical peacemaker always prepares for this kind of conversation with prayer. Ask God for His wisdom and a humble heart. Next, write out what you want to say. By planning your words it's more likely that they will communicate exactly what you want to say. Practice saying what you've written out loud. Notice your tone. Is to too harsh, too weak? Aim for a neutral voice tone. Lastly, pick a time and place where it is most likely you will have the time and energy to talk this through. This is too important a conversation to do it on the fly.

Is there someone you need to talk with to make peace? Go. Don't put it off. Obey God and do your part. Jesus says, "Blessed are the peacemakers, for they will be called sons of God" (Matthew 5:9 NIV).

Sandra Glahn

[The Lord] has shown his favor and taken away my disgrace among the people. LUKE 1:25 (NIV)

My friend Celestin Musekura tells what it was like for his mother to be an infertile woman in Rwanda. She "could not go to the fountain to fetch water or sit with other women. Children sang about her inability to produce. After two years, when a woman could not bear children, usually her husband chased her away or married a second wife to bear children, just as we see in the Old Testament. My father had given my mother the final word that she had three months to leave, when she discovered she was pregnant. I was that child." Celestin's mother gave him a surname, Musekura, which means "Savior," because her son saved her from her shame. Later Celestin trusted Christ, and God used him to lead his mother to the True Savior.

In both Old and New Testament times, people looked down on the infertile. Once she conceived, Hagar despised Sarah (Genesis 16:4). The same thing happened to Hannah when Elkanah's second wife conceived (1 Samuel 1:6–7). And then there's John the Baptist's mother, Elizabeth (Luke 1:5–25). She and Zechariah had more wrinkles than an elephant when an angel appeared to him to say, "She's having a baby." And when Elizabeth was "showing," she exclaimed, "[The Lord] has shown his favor and taken away my disgrace among the people" (1:25 NIV).

Having endured a decade of infertility and pregnancy loss, I love in Elizabeth's story the reminder not only of God's power but that much of our shame isn't from God at all, but from others.

When life hurts, we might think God is punishing us, but Elizabeth reminds us to separate our status with people from our standing before God. In Him, through our true Savior, we stand accepted, loved, and unashamed.

Beverly Hubble Tauke

He who fears the Lord has a secure fortress, and for his children it will be a refuge. PROVERBS 14:26 (NIV)

As human steamrollers, controlling personalities rumble through life squashing independent conscience and judgment of those around them. Biblical characters Rebecca, her brother Laban, and King Saul were all this breed.

Rebecca engineered the betrayal of her son, Esau, and blind husband, Isaac. Laban connived to exploit nephew Jacob financially after sticking him with an unwanted wife. King Saul tried to violently coerce his son Jonathan into a homicidal plot against treasured friend and future king, David.

What was achieved by such family controllers?

Rebecca's plot backfired, as pet son, Jacob, fled for his life and never saw her again (Genesis 27). Repeatedly whacked by his own schemes, Laban drove his two daughters, grandkids, and Jacob to move far away from his meddling (Genesis 29–31).

Violent controller King Saul alienated his son, seeming to deepen Jonathan's dedication to David, so despised by Saul (1 Samuel 20).

Even well-motivated family controllers can train wreck families. Advice comes from Richard Foster in *Celebration of Discipline*: "Lay down the everlasting burden to set others straight, [made possible] when we genuinely believe that inner transformation is God's work and not ours."

Agonized by a daughter's decisions, author Patricia Raybon reported similar direction from God. During prayer, she was surprised to sense this response: *"Love her. Trust me. And have some peace. Stop turning yourself inside and out, trying to run my business."*

Well, now. Wasn't it sage old Solomon who urged distrust of mere human understanding (Proverbs 3:5–6)? And didn't he promise ultimate family protection through reverence for God, not through personal control?

Do we *get* this? That is the question.

Linda Mintle . . . .

Your beauty should not come from outward adornment, such as braided hair and the wearing of gold jewelry and fine clothes. Instead, it should be that of your inner self, the unfading beauty of a gentle and quiet spirit, which is of great worth in God's sight. I PETER 3:3–4 (NIV)

A typical day begins before the mirror. I say to myself, *if I could lose just five more pounds, I would feel better about myself.* For the moment, I believe this crazy thought. Yet this type of thinking leaves me restless and feeling inadequate. I revisit the thought. If I could lose a few more pounds, my life would somehow magically improve. Deep down, I know this isn't true. My weight doesn't define me unless I allow this to be the case. Only when I grasp how God thinks about me does my esteem improve. His thoughts are right and true, not distorted. And He has already told me what He thinks of me. There is no qualifier like "just five more pounds!"

"Come just as you are," he calls.

"Just five more pounds to lose and I'll be ready."

"Come just as you are," He patiently replies.

It seems too good to be true. God wants us just the way we are. But isn't God like everyone else—ready to judge us by our appearance, our weight, or by how successful we are? Can we really come to Him just as we are—flawed, confused, distracted with worry, and even overweight?

"Yes," He calls. "Come just as you are."

No judgment. No criticism. He's not thinking, "If she only lost five more pounds . . ." Weight loss is not God's focus.

We are the apple of His eye, the one He cherishes. He wants our devotion, our hearts. When we finally give in to the call, we can rest in His acceptance and no one else's matters. Five more pounds melt away, not by dieting or tricks, but by the love and acceptance we receive from a God whose unconditional love esteems us in a way nothing else can.

Anita Lustrea

He reached down from heaven and rescued me; he drew me out of deep waters. PSALM 18:16 (NLT)

Have you ever felt like you were in a black hole and couldn't crawl out? Some would call that having the blues, or depression. That's where the psalmist spent some time. Maybe you can identify with this Scripture. I know I can.

Psalm 18:16-19 (NLT):

> "He reached down from heaven and rescued me; he drew me out of deep waters. He rescued me from my powerful enemies, from those who hated me and were too strong for me. They attacked me at a moment when I was in distress, but the Lord supported me. He led me to a place of safety; he rescued me because he delights in me."

Why is it hard to admit we are depressed? I remember going to a doctor for some tests because I thought I was entering menopause. The doctor ordered a complete blood workup and then before sending me to the lab said, "Would you be opposed to taking an antidepressant if the blood work doesn't show any hormonal imbalance?" I immediately started to cry and mumbled something about being willing to do it, but I was sure my emotions were a mess because of menopause.

I found out I was depressed because I had virtually no vitamin D in my system. Today I take large doses and get sunshine when I can and I'm fine. I was surprised that I reacted so emotionally to the suggestion of medication for depression. I had no problem supporting friends who needed help. But for me to admit I might have a problem was really difficult.

What about you? Are you trying to pull yourself up by your bootstraps one more day? Are you struggling to make it? The psalmist offers great help, but sometimes we need a medical doctor to check us out and offer other kinds of help. Don't be afraid or ashamed. Do what you need to do to get help today.

Miriam Neff

The horse is made ready for the day of battle, but the victory rests with the Lord. PROVERBS 21:31 (NIV)

Plan ahead. Use calendars, paper and pencil, BlackBerrys, iPhones. Plan by the month, year, and have a five-year plan as well. It's all good. Scripture advises that we wisely use our time, budget our money, and be ready for both what we expect and what we don't. Thankfully the saying "God helps those who help themselves" are not God's words. What bad news that would be for the poor and weak, the widows, and orphans.

We live with the mystery that God asks us to plan, but not promise a scripted, predictable outcome.

We live with the paradox that God is all powerful and controls all. And at the same time He gives us freedom and resources as puny humanoids to use or misuse. If I am consumed in this life by "readying my horse" for battle, and life certainly has many battles, I'll lose faith and become bitter when those events come that shake and change my world. At this stage in my life, I have learned that many are beyond my strength, wealth, or sphere of influence to determine a good outcome. And my choice of outcome might look smart for the moment, but foolish for the future.

We may be worrying about the battle preparations living without patience, kindness, thoughtfulness, or generosity. God warned the children of Israel through Hosea that the battle would go against them "because you have depended on your own strength and on your many warriors" (Hosea 10:13b NIV).

If our battle-ready horse is a source of personal pride, we've lost.

Pray, instead, that the Lord will give you the resources for your battles, and that He'll move the people you cannot move. Ask Him what you can do to further His kingdom in this particular situation. Trust in Him.

Margaret Feinberg

If any of you lacks wisdom, he should ask God, who gives generously to all without finding fault, and it will be given to him. JAMES 1:5 (NIV)

As a child, anything and everything around my eighty-two-year-old great-grandmother's home became a source of wonder—from knickknacks to the house cat. But one thing that I'll never forget is a simple prayer she kept framed in her living room known as the Serenity Prayer, which reads: "God grant me the serenity to accept the things I cannot change, courage to change the things I can, and wisdom to know the difference."

My great-grandmother found solace in these words, and now, I am beginning to find them too. This prayer sums up the greatest areas of my spiritual and emotional struggles—knowing my boundaries, discovering my limits and learning to accept whatever God's hand and my choices bring into this life. When I pray the Serenity Prayer, I am reminded that God's peace is still available in a storm-tossed world.

The Serenity Prayer has provided comfort to millions and is a humble acknowledgment that God is God; we are not. And in that epiphanous moment, we can hand over the control of our lives that was never really ours to begin with.

In *How People Grow*, Dr. Henry Cloud and Dr. John Townsend make the following observation: "So many of people's problems come from trying to control things outside of their control, and when they try, they lose control of themselves. It is no wonder that praying 'The Serenity Prayer,' knowing the difference between what we can change and what we cannot, leads to people regaining control of their lives."

It's a truth my great-grandmother discovered long ago. One day I hope to not only have a copy of the Serenity Prayer framed in my home but also in my life—acceptance, courage, and wisdom.

Lori Neff

Be still, and know that I am God;
I will be exalted among the nations,
I will be exalted in the earth.
PSALM 46:10 (NIV)

Each Sunday, my church observes a time of silence. I have to be honest—at first, it made me really antsy and uncomfortable. I spent those minutes worrying that a child might suddenly cry or wondering how long it would be until the next part of the service. Then, as the months went on, I found that I couldn't wait to get to church to experience those few minutes of silence. I come each week stirred up like a snow globe and then as we sit in silence, the flurry of thoughts settle and I can see more clearly.

One Sunday I felt discouraged and defeated. I sat in silence, just listening, settling my heart and feeling sad. Out of the blue, I felt God quietly whisper to me, "I love you." That took me off guard—I very rarely sense God telling me something and I certainly didn't expect to hear Him say He loved me since I felt like such a failure. And the words washed over me, I was moved to tears. How did I forget that God delights in me? I had filled my life with so much noise and activity from morning to night that it took a moment of silence to pause and be reminded of God's tender love for me—and that's exactly what I needed at that moment to have the strength to keep going.

I may not hear God tell me something every time I engage in silence, but I have found it to be such a helpful practice to keep perspective and be open to what God wants to teach me. I try to build intentional times of silence into my life now.

If you're ready to give silence a try, begin with two to three minutes a week of complete silence before God.

Christine Wyrtzen

Even if you should suffer for the sake of righteousness, you are blessed and do not fear their intimidation and do not be troubled. 1 PETER 3:14 (NASB)

A good translation of this verse would be, "Do not fear what they fear. When they curse you by their gods, there is no reason to panic. Though they fear the gods and swear by them, your God is the one true God and is more powerful."

"The power of life and death are in the tongue," Scripture says (Proverbs 18:21). Without applying the power of the cross against the words spoken against us, we fall prey to the language of others' tongues. We are assaulted by the words of someone who lives afraid. What makes him cower comes out through his speech and easily invades our peace if we let it. "Don't you understand that we're going to be bankrupt?" "If you don't go to college, you'll never make a good living." Each is a threat based on fear.

I am responsible for my internal world, for what I receive into my spirit and what I reject. Just because something has been spoken against me doesn't mean I am its victim. I must not let it take root or the spirit behind their words will infect me. When things are spoken in my presence that would not be words Jesus would speak, I go into action. I handcuff them, examine them, and decide what to own and what to throw away. My heart is a garden for which I'm responsible and God's promises are snuffed out by the barrage of negativity I failed to keep at bay.

Let's be guardians of our heart today. The internal world of God's child is never dull, never off duty. We are soldiers guarding the fortress of our tenuous faith.

With God's help make a list. What are the top ten most hurtful comments spoken to you across the breadth of your lifetime? They could be nicknames, a label, a negative prediction. List them, then renounce them and put them under the power of the cross. Take back your life.

Anita Lustrea

Yes, the Lord pours down his blessings. PSALM 85:12 (NLT)

Sometimes the holiday season really gets to my husband. To him Thanksgiving doesn't feel very thanks-filled and Christmas looks more like a blur of activity rather than a focus on the birth of Christ. I love the holidays, but struggle with the frenetic pace that accompanies them.

Stopping long enough to count blessings reminds me that God does indeed watch over me. Stopping long enough within the blur of holiday activity helps me to remember the *why* behind all the stuff that we do.

I've been blessed. I know I'm loved. I have a job that brings me great satisfaction. I work with great people. I live in a good country. The freedoms I have here can never be dismissed. My home life is sweet.

So what do I do with those blessings? Is it a starting point or an ending point? Do I look at those blessings as something I deserve or as a building block so I can *become* a blessing to others? I choose the latter. My life counts when I'm not resting on either my laurels or disappointments and when I'm not so busy counting my blessings that I forget to look beyond myself to the needs of others. That's where the action is. Psalms 85:11–12 (NLT) reads,

> "Truth springs up from the earth, and righteousness smiles down from heaven. Yes, the Lord pours down his blessings. Our land will yield its bountiful harvest."

Sometimes the holiday pace does get to me. When that happens, I carve out some time to see the blessings of God all around me. To spend some time talking with Jesus and reconnecting, remembering His goodness, looking toward Bethlehem and the promise of new life, new birth, and resurrection. Then the holiday season makes sense. It isn't just a whole lot of activity. It becomes a response to the Lord, who has showered blessings on me because He loves me. Guess what? He loves you too. More than you can possibly imagine.

Janice Elsheimer

In the morning, O Lord, you hear my voice; in the morning I lay my requests before you and wait in expectation.
PSALM 5:3 (NIV)

I woke up this morning with the start of a poem on the tip of my memory, a birthday gift from God. I made a stab at capturing it with my pen, a stab at the start of something that felt like it might be good.

Why is it so hard to remember every image, every word from our dreams, no matter how soon we rush to put them on paper? Perhaps it's because God intends our dreams to be *prompts* and not *dictations*.

Here's the prompt I received this morning: *To rise on the wings of the morning: that's how a good day begins . . .*

And here's what came once I started stabbing:

A Good Day

To rise before dawn on the wings of the morning,
To cherish each hour as the gift that it is,
To welcome the work that is laid out before me,
To rest in the midday and wake up refreshed,
To love and to cherish the people I love
And treat with compassion the people I don't,
To slide into sleep on a prayer of thanksgiving
With hopes for another sweet, simple good day.

Not a perfect poem yet, but a start. Sometimes that's the best thing to hope for: a good start. And often, that turns out to be enough. Just by journaling our prayers and petitions, our confessions and our worries, even our poems, our day can take a turn for the better.

When you wake up tomorrow morning, write down your first thoughts of the day. Start your day with the knowledge that God hears your voice, then wait in expectation to hear His.

Ginger Kolbaba

Ruth replied, "Don't urge me to leave you or to turn back from you. Where you go I will go, and where you stay I will stay. Your people will be my people and your God my God." RUTH 1:16 (NIV)

A few months ago I met a woman whose husband is serving a two-year sentence in prison. They've been married nearly thirty years. Now twice a month, she drives a six-hour round trip to visit him.

As I listened to her story, I asked her how she was coping, and how their marriage was doing.

"Everyone's told me to divorce him—even most of the people in my church and my counselor," she told me. "But until God frees me from this marriage, I need to stay put. Yes, what my husband did was awful—but do I forget all the good things he's done? Do I throw away everything when marriage gets tough? Does God do that to me when I mess up?"

After our visit, I thought again about the bravery of this woman. She'd made huge sacrifices—of her time, love, and finances—for someone who, according to society, is unworthy.

What a picture of loyalty and Christlikeness. You can learn to love somebody in good times and bad. But you can't understand the real meaning of loyalty until it's challenged. Then it teaches you quickly about your character.

When was the last time your loyalty in marriage was tested? How did you do? How would you respond if you were in the same situation as the woman above?

Carol Rukter

. . . for it is God who works in you, to will and to act according to His good purpose. PHILIPPIANS 2:13 (NIV)

This morning I discovered the chrysalis of a tiger swallowtail butterfly. The small brown pod looks nothing like the delicate yellow swallowtail that will soon grace gardens and quiet streambeds . . . or what its caterpillar looked like a few months ago. As a caterpillar, it ate so voraciously that it burst through several skins. After shedding its last skin, the inner skin hardened into the chrysalis. Inside, the protected caterpillar is now in its transformational stage and resting; it doesn't even eat or drink. When it's almost time for the new butterfly to emerge, the chrysalis will become transparent. Breaking through the chrysalis will be an arduous but vital process for the butterfly. When the swallowtail finally emerges, wrinkled and wet, it will pump body fluids into its wings until they unfold and dry. Only then will it fly.

When I hear God calling me to serve Him, I want to take wing. Immediately. I prefer advancing directly from the caterpillar stage to flying . . . let's skip the skin-sheds and chrysalis, please. Funny thing about God though. Before He creates change *through* us, He must create change *in* us. Experiencing that transformational period in our lives might feel dark and confining—much like a chrysalis—until we recognize whose hands are reshaping us. Then, it becomes an intimate period of God's protection, preparation, rest, and transparency. Like the butterfly, God allows us to struggle as we emerge, before He unfolds our wings and guides our flight.

Are you willing to embrace the transformational period and become what God intends you to be?

Susie Larson

The Lord is wonderfully good to those who wait for him and seek him. LAMENTATIONS 3:25 (NLT)

With a warm cup of coffee in my hand, I snuggled in the chair with my Bible and read the thirty-second chapter of Exodus. Moses was up on the mountain having a face-to-face encounter with God. His followers hadn't heard from him in a while and got bored waiting for him.

Let's look in at their response: "When the people saw how long it was taking Moses to come back down the mountain, they gathered around Aaron. 'Come, make us gods who will go before us. As for this fellow Moses . . . we don't know what has happened to him.'" (Exodus 32:1 NIV).

When God asks us to wait longer than we'd prefer, we get impatient, and we wonder about Plan B.

A backup plan sounds good when God takes too long to deliver our breakthrough.

During the waiting season we often get bored and lose heart. As a result, we minimize God's involvement in our process. When we do that, we are only a step away from building a counterfeit with our own hands.

The *time in between* is like the tide that pulls back to sea and reveals the garbage on the beach; it reveals our raw motives, our ugly intentions, and our flawed character.

God hasn't forgotten us. He doesn't ever accidentally look away when we take our leaps of faith. He catches us when we jump. He lifts us up when we stumble. *And when He makes us wait, it's because He's making us ready.*

Waiting is a true test of our hearts.

And that's why the time in between is so important.

No matter what breakthrough you're waiting for, *trust that God is always good* and be faithful in the waiting.

Consider this time of waiting as an opportunity to know God better. More than the gifts He gives . . . determine to know the heart with which He gives them.

Arloa Sutter . . . .

Therefore, since we are surrounded by such a great cloud of witnesses, let us throw off everything that hinders . . .
HEBREWS 12:1 (NIV)

Irving was on a mission. His mind was disabled by schizophrenia, but he was convinced if he lived frugally and saved, he could amass enough wealth to eradicate the national debt. He bought government bonds with his disability checks, and ate at our homeless service center every day to save money.

I invited Irving and another of Breakthrough's homeless service center guests to my house for Thanksgiving dinner. I prepared a wonderful feast with all of the holiday delights. Irving was a diabetic so I knew he wouldn't be enjoying pie and ice cream with the rest of us. I found a package of six sugar-free ice cream sandwiches for him. At the end of the meal his eyes lit up as he savored what for him was a rare treat. As he left I gave him the other ice cream sandwiches to take home and he gratefully accepted.

The next day Irving was at my door. He handed over the ice cream. "Here, take these," he growled. "They make me want to have them all the time."

As I reflect on Irving's ice cream I am inspired by his willingness to sacrifice his pleasures for his cause. However misguided he was in his mission; he was committed to it and willing to give up momentary pleasures to reach his goal. When he died in 2000 he left our ministry $500,000, convinced that the way to eradicate the national debt is to provide employment opportunities for the unemployed.

Irving's ice cream has become a symbol for me. What am I willing to sacrifice to advance the kingdom of Christ? What's your mission? Is ice cream getting in the way?

Joanne Heim

Teach us to number our days aright, that we may gain a heart of wisdom. Psalm 90:12 (niv)

How many lists do you have for today—groceries, errands, chores that need to be done. Chances are you could think of two or three more—at least!

Despite our lists, it seems like days when everything gets crossed off are rare. Will we ever catch up on all that needs to be done?

There is hope! God is concerned with all the details of our lives—including our to-do lists. And, when we ask Him to, He's ready and willing to teach us how to use them most effectively—and to become wise in the process.

That's what Moses is praying in Psalm 90. As the leader of the Israelites, Moses knew something about a huge to-do list! Sometimes caring for the needs of my family of four feels overwhelming. Can you imagine poor Moses trying to manage all those people?

That's why he asked God to teach him to number his days the right way. The Hebrew word for number means just what you think it does—to count, reckon, appoint, assign. Exactly the stuff of to-do lists.

With only so many hours in a day, it makes sense to ask God for help in making appointments, filling the calendar, planning what needs to be done and prioritizing your lists, to show you what's most important and what can wait until later.

As I've done this, I've been amazed at how God has rearranged my lists. Often he brings other people to mind, and a phone call to a friend ends up being the most important part of my day. Other times, the things I thought were pressing turn out to be not as important as spending time with my children, or taking some time to rest.

Try it. Sit down with your to-do list and ask God for help with it. Ask him to point out those things that you may have forgotten, or things that should wait. Ask him to shine through you as you make phone calls or have lunch with a friend.

Melinda Schmidt

. . . think about such things. PHILIPPIANS 4:8 (NIV)

The institution of Thanksgiving Day has a meandering history. In 1777 the Continental Congress declared the first national day of thanksgiving after a victory over the British at Saratoga. By 1941, President Franklin D. Roosevelt signed a bill that firmly established the fourth Thursday of November as our national holiday of thanksgiving.

Thanksgiving Day may have lost some of the national spiritual fervor and intentionality around celebrating a corporate day of thanks to the Almighty, but can be personally useful as a place of spiritual mind-renewal. Along with thankfulness, ("And be thankful," Colossians 3:15 NIV), what does God direct us to harbor in our minds?

- ". . . we take captive every thought to make it obedient to Christ" (2 Corinthians 10:5 NIV). Do I habitually monitor what I allow and entertain in my mind?
- "Let us come before him with thanksgiving and extol him with music and song" (Psalm 95:2 NIV). Do I spend time regularly expressing thanks and worship—throughout the year —focusing on God's character and loving care in my life?
- ". . . a prudent man gives thought to his steps" (Proverbs 14:15 NIV). Am I carefully considering, not impulsively or with feelings alone, that next step?
- "I thank my God every time I remember you" (Philippians 1:3 NIV). Do I thank God for those dear ones he has placed in my life?

On this day dedicated to gratefulness, take some time to examine the nature of your daily thoughts. How would you characterize them—life-giving or life-defeating? And most importantly, do they follow God's directives?

Lois Evans

. . . He who began a good work in you will perfect it until the day of Christ Jesus. PHILIPPIANS 1:6 (NASB)

Are you tired and worn? Plagued by doubt and helplessness? Do you wonder if you are competent to fulfill the responsibilities God has placed on your life? I invite you to journey with a man who is frequently remembered as the weeping prophet, Jeremiah, often timid and rather afraid, yet whose life was changed when he experienced the touch of the Lord.

I remember the day my husband, Tony, announced that God was calling him to serve as a pastor. I did not share his enthusiasm, since initially he had told me that he was going to become an evangelist! Now I wanted to do a wonderful job as a pastor's wife so I plunged into numerous activities aimed towards strengthening the church, and, in time I began to experience exhaustion and despair. Why? I was looking at the faces of the people and trying to please them, rather than turning my eyes towards Jesus and allowing Him to touch me and use me in a way that only God could use *me*.

God reached out His hands to touch Jeremiah's mouth so Jeremiah could proclaim God's message to people who terrified him. Yes, you and I may be doing all the "right" things, yet we are getting burnt out because those right activities aren't necessarily God's will for our lives.

Look, you don't have to become like the person next to you to experience joy and peace. God used Jeremiah to deliver a specific message to a certain group of people during a definite time span. God has a unique plan for you and He will qualify and enable you for what He has called you. Let Him touch you.

Amy Norton

Defend the cause of the weak and fatherless; maintain the rights of the poor and oppressed. Rescue the weak and needy; deliver them from the hand of the wicked. PSALM 82:3–4 (NIV)

We have many powerful moments with our children as they grow up. Moments that are humbling and stay in our minds as a time they learned something important, a life lesson.

I was sitting at my computer looking at photos from a recent trip to India. They showed the tremendous needs and poverty among the children we had visited. One of the most powerful photos was from a slum we visited in Delhi. It showed little toddlers who were very dirty and half-dressed standing in front of a trash-filled pond in which was a huge black pig. Behind the pond were the straw huts the children lived in with plastic roofs made with trash and old tires. I had no idea my nine-year-old daughter was behind me looking over my shoulder until I heard her burst into sobs. She could not stop crying and asking how God could allow anyone to live in such poverty. She thought that God should let everyone live like we did, with a home, clothes and food to eat.

I had to teach my precious daughter about the painful things of this world, about being blessed with so much when others have so little. How we are to bless others with what we have, to visit the poor and share God's love with them. We all need to realize the simple blessings the Lord gives us each day that we many times take for granted like food, a home, and warm water. Many times we are so busy thinking of our own needs it's hard to think about those around us.

Find opportunities to bless others through the blessings the Lord has given you.

Miriam Neff

So do not throw away your confidence; it will be richly rewarded. You need to persevere so that when you have done the will of God, you will receive what he has promised. For in just a very little while, "He who is coming will come and will not delay. But my righteous one will live by faith. And if he shrinks back, I will not be pleased with him."

HEBREWS 10: 35–38 (NIV)

Does God's "little while" ever seem like an eternity to you? I wait for Him to show up in a situation. And I wait, and I wait, and I wait. How can I persevere when I'm not sure what will work? I'm guessing at the next step to take.

It may be a dry or ruined marriage, a financial mess, a testy or even hate-filled teenager, or a failing career.

Getting busy when I know the steps to a guaranteed outcome doesn't require faith. Faith is that tenacity to put one foot before another when you cannot see the earth your foot will rest on, when there is simply no guaranteed Plan A. That's when God sees our perseverance as faith. He promises to reward our God-confidence with something beyond the immediate resolution to today's problems. We cannot even imagine what the reward will be.

We should not be surprised that we have days, or weeks, months, or bleak years where we wait. Hurrying through O'Hare Airport, I step on a path with an automated voice that repeats, "Keep walking." That message, though ever so ordinary sounding, offers spiritual advice. Just keep walking, dear sister, keep walking.

God's word to you today: *I will bring resolution. I see your tenacity. But most precious to me, daughter, I see your faith.*

Janet Thompson

"Give me children, or I'll die!" GENESIS 30:1 (NIV)

Rachel's cry of barrenness still echoes around the world as one in six couples experience infertility. You may be one of those couples or know someone who is struggling with having a baby. Two of my daughters know this pain, and my husband and I have spent countless hours on our knees praying and fasting for God to bless them with children.

Most little girls grow up playing house, and one of the first gifts they receive is a baby doll. This past Christmas my two-year-old granddaughter abruptly stopped opening presents after unwrapping a toy stroller. She promptly put her new doll in the stroller and for the next hour pushed her baby around the house. Nurturing is innate in a woman's soul, and many women feel that being a mother is their purpose in life. God made them to have babies and if they can't then they feel lost . . . sad . . . maybe even like Rachel, suicidal.

When we were praying for our daughters, my husband and I prayed for them to become parents—we didn't pray exclusively for them to get pregnant. When one daughter realized that she wanted to be a parent more than she wanted to be pregnant, she knew there was a baby somewhere needing a home, and she and her husband soon adopted our precious grandson Brandon. Miraculously, God later blessed her with two pregnancies.

There is no reason to give up the dream of being a mother. Motherhood might not come the way you planned, but it might be exactly how God planned. There are many options to parenthood today, and there are many children, like our precious Brandon, who God wants to bless with a loving family.

When you accepted Christ into your heart, God adopted you into His family. Is it possible that God is now calling you to be an adoptive or foster parent?

Marcia Ramsland

Every good and perfect gift is from above, coming down from the Father of the heavenly lights, who does not change like shifting shadows. JAMES 1:17 (NIV)

Did you know the holidays are the one time of year when people write more lists than any other time? And there's the famous annual list to write—a Christmas gift list. Seeing that it is the time we celebrate the birthday of Christ, I wonder what would happen if we each put "Jesus" on the top of our Christmas gift list? We could start a new habit and put Jesus at the top of the list and prayerfully ask God what we should give each year.

The first year I did this God challenged me to give of my time to play the piano for a preschool Christmas program—all five classes of them. (Why couldn't He have asked me to perform Handel's *Messiah* instead?) The school was happy to have a pianist, and God changed my reluctance into a generous spirit. Because of it I was able to share my faith with the director.

Another year I met my writing deadline as a gift to Jesus. I needed His help to write my *Simplify Your Time* book at the busiest time of year. I chuckle at the irony of God's request and knew I had to depend on Him to complete the gift in time. To know what to give Jesus as a gift, reflect on all the good gifts God has given you this year—His faithfulness, His mercy, His love—and all the specific ways He demonstrated that.

Put Jesus on the top of your Christmas gift list and reflect God's generous giving of a "good and perfect" gift that He inspires.

Kendra Smiley

. . . the angel said to him: "Do not be afraid, Zechariah; your prayer has been heard. Your wife Elizabeth will bear you a son, and you are to give him the name John. He will be a joy and delight to you, and many will rejoice because of his birth, for he will be great in the sight of the Lord. He is never to take wine or other fermented drink, and he will be filled with the Holy Spirit even from birth. Many of the people of Israel will he bring back to the Lord their God. And he will go on before the Lord, in the spirit and power of Elijah, to turn the hearts of the fathers to their children and the disobedient to the wisdom of the righteous—to make ready a people prepared for the Lord."

Zechariah asked the angel, "How can I be sure of this? I am an old man and my wife is well along in years."

LUKE 1:13–18 (NIV)

Some of the phrases of parenthood are timeless. They span generations and have been uttered by mother, grandmother and great-grandmother alike.

One of my favorites is "because I said so . . ." That is the final answer by the overwrought mother who has already answered the question "Why?" thirty-six consecutive times. That is the ultimate reply of frustration and authority. "Because I said so . . ."

I have yet to discover that phrase in the Bible, but I imagine that on more than one occasion, it could have come from the lips of God. Take the account of Zechariah when the angel announced he would become the father of John the Baptist. "How can I be sure of this?"

"HOW?" Because God said so.

Do you believe what God has said? Believe it. That's the Next Right Choice.

Anita Lustrea

"Go," said Jesus, "your faith has healed you." Immediately he received his sight and followed Jesus along the road.
MARK 10:52 (NIV)

Have you ever had a craving, a strong desire for something? Think back to when you were ten, twenty, thirty, forty, fifty. How have your desires changed? I wanted a bicycle when I was ten; when I was thirty I wanted a baby. Our desires mature, don't they?

Desire is much about connecting with God. But it's in that desire that we sometimes become fearful. What if God doesn't hear my heart, or see this desire that is weighing so heavily on me? What then?

Read Mark 10:46–52 and put yourself in the Gospel story, to become the character Bartimaeus and consider how you would answer the questions Jesus poses to him. Jesus was traveling through Jericho and the blind man Bartimaeus heard that Jesus was nearby, so he began to shout out, "Jesus, son of David, have mercy on me!" "Be quiet!" some of the people yelled at him. But he only shouted louder, "Son of David, have mercy on me!" When Jesus heard him, he stopped and said, "Tell him to come here." So they called the blind man. "Cheer up," they said. "Come on, he's calling you!" Bartimaeus threw aside his coat, jumped up, and came to Jesus. "What do you want me to do for you?" Jesus asked. "Teacher," the blind man said, "I want to see!" And Jesus said to him, "Go your way. Your faith has healed you." And instantly the blind man could see! Then he followed Jesus down the road."

Take some time today, maybe over the course of several days to ponder how you would answer Jesus if He were to stand before you and ask, "What do you want me to do for you?" Spend some time asking Jesus to bring you face-to-face with the deepest desire of your heart.

Kathy Koch

Moses said to God, "Suppose I go to the Israelites and say to them, 'The God of your fathers has sent me to you,' and they ask me, 'What is his name?' Then what shall I tell them?" God said to Moses, "I AM WHO I AM." Exodus 3:13–14 (NIV)

One of the identities I encourage children and adults to claim is this one: "I am a human being."

After my audience says it after me, they laugh. I'm sure they're wondering why I think it's so important. Why is it important? Because we're not human doings. Praise God! Who we are is more important than what we do because everything we do springs from everything we are. Our being drives our doing. We must pay attention to who we are and to who our children are.

At the end of the day, maybe we shouldn't just ask our children, "What did you do today?" Maybe we should ask, "Who were you today?" One mom who tried this got a puzzled response from her nine-year-old daughter.

"What do you mean, mommy? I was Alexis."

"I know that, but which Alexis showed up for school today? The pleasant, confident Alexis or the whining, complaining Alexis?"

"Oh . . ."

Let's purpose to think about God this way too. He does what He does because of who He is. How would you complete these sentences?

Because God is love, He ______________________________. (see 1 John 4:8)

Because God is faithful, He ____________________________. (see 1 Corinthians 10:13)

Because God is powerful, He ___________________________. (see Psalm 147:5)

Because God is the Provider, He ________________________. (see Genesis 22:14)

It's appropriate to praise God for who He is and thank Him for what He does. Both are important. Why not spend some time adding to the above list?

God is our everything! Is there a specific Someone you need Him to be for you today? Let Him know.

Susie Larson

You both precede and follow me.
You place your hand of blessing on my head.
Psalm 139:5 (NLT)

Ever had one of these days? You're behind on emails and you miss a deadline. Laundry spills over the basket and your piles of paperwork make you want to build a bonfire. Instead of feeling on top of your circumstances, you feel buried beneath them.

Does that ever happen to you? Well, I have some good news. Psalm 9:10 (NIV) says,

"Those who know your Name will trust in you, for you, Lord, have never forsaken those who seek you."

What beautiful promises we have here! Though we waver . . . He is steady and strong.

Though we forget . . . He is mindful of all things. Though we fall short . . . He goes the distance for us. His strength trumps our weakness. At the end of the day, it is good to look over our shoulder, acknowledge our missteps, and then *look up*. With simple trust and a believing heart, we can enjoy peace in spite of ourselves.

Of course if we are lazy, irresponsible, or consistently unprepared, that's a problem. We can't kick back and "trust" that God will encourage such behavior by covering for us. But, when we sincerely love Him, and thus, take serious our call to be faithful to the things to which He has called us, we must also know that He's made room for our humanity.

He knows our frame. He knows our capacity for weakness, failure, and even for greatness. He is intimately acquainted with our needs and He even redeems our mistakes. We have every reason for faith. We have every reason to trust Him. When we carry today's share, we can know and trust that He carries us. His yoke is easy and His burden is light. Have joy and trust Him today.

Try this once. Turn your back on worry. Refuse to entertain one worrying thought today. Determine to trust Him.

Lori Neff

For to me, to live is Christ and to die is gain.
PHILIPPIANS 1:21 (NIV)

Bonnie and I were roommates in college. I was really shy at the time, and her exuberance and zest for life pulled me out of my shell. Bonnie was also a few years older than I was, and I looked up to her in many ways. We often stayed in our room in the evenings instead of going out, and we talked—about boys, life, classes, hairstyles—everything. She wasn't afraid to talk about anything. When I think of Bonnie, I think of her curly hair and how she gave the best hugs and how she loved people. She had a mischievous smile and a sparkle in her eye that I saw often. Of course, we had our disagreements, too. She used to get so mad at me for hitting the snooze button too many times in the morning. And I would get upset when she would borrow my stuff without asking.

A few years after graduating, Bonnie and her husband went to serve in Lebanon. She wrote to me that, though it was difficult to adjust to the language and culture, she knew that was where she was supposed to be. Soon after I received her letter, Bonnie was shot and killed as she was opening a clinic where she worked. Devastated and stunned, I tried to make sense of this tragedy. Now, a few years later, I still don't have many answers. But Bonnie's death has been a constant reminder that tomorrow is not guaranteed for any of us. There's no time to waste—this, right this very moment, is your life that God has given to you. Live for the glory of God.

"The glory of God is a person fully alive."—St. Irenaeus

Carol Ruhter . . . .

Comfort, comfort my people, says your God.
Isaiah 40:1 (NIV)

My footsteps crunching the snow startled a deer. I watched as the doe bounded through the woods and across a frozen lake, until the ice gave way and she plunged into frigid water. The lake was miles from the nearest road, which would have made it difficult for rescuers to reach her, even if they chose to try. So until the sun set an hour later, all I could do was pray for God's mercy as I watched her futile efforts to get her feet back onto the ice. The next day I found the gash in the ice refrozen, with no trace of the deer or her struggle.

For more than a year, I pondered why God allowed me to witness that troubling drama. Then He opened my eyes to the people all around me who may need rescue or comfort. They've fallen through life's cracks and are desperately struggling to get back onto their feet. The enormity of need is overwhelming, and my capacity to provide comfort is limited. But I trust God, who is without limit. I pray for God's mercy, knowing *He'll* provide comfort.

I'm not sure how God answered my prayers for the doe that wintry evening. After I left, it's possible He surged her with strength to escape. Perhaps He allowed her to quietly slip below the surface rather than to later starve or feel a hunter's bullet. But I've since learned that God looks to my heart—not just my hands—when calling me to comfort any of His living things. And sometimes, the greatest comfort we can give is prayer.

Who—and how—is God calling you to comfort?

Christine Wyrtzen

And now you will be silent and not able to speak until the day this happens, because you did not believe my words . . .

LUKE 1:20 (NIV)

Zachariah was told that his wife, Elizabeth, would bear a son. John the Baptist would be born and would grow to prepare the way for Jesus' ministry. He stumbled in disbelief at the incredible news. Zachariah and Elizabeth were both old and had suffered a lifelong marriage marked with barrenness. How could such a thing be? Perhaps he felt God toyed with their dreams.

Upon hearing the good news of impending blessing, Zachariah was incredulous. He asked Gabriel if he could possibly expect him to believe such news! He paid a price for his unbelief. For nine months, he was struck mute, unable to speak about the wondrous miracle taking place inside of his wife's womb. His speech was crippled because of his lack of faith.

So is mine, when I fail to believe the promises of my Father. Speech is always affected by unbelief because words are born in the heart, the place where beliefs are cemented and doubts are festering.

Mutually exclusive beliefs can't coexist. "God has forgotten me" cannot be vocalized simultaneously with "God takes care of me because He loves me dearly." "God can't forgive me for this" cannot be articulated alongside "God's mercies are new every morning." The most important work I will do today is the work I do in my heart. Faith is not conceived on a day when the sky is blue and all is going well. It is set against the backdrop of unbelief. I must choose sides.

I want to believe God all the time, even when circumstantial evidence is against Him. I pray that He will make me a woman of faith.

Nancy Sebastian Meyer

Do nothing out of selfish ambition or vain conceit, but in humility consider others better than yourselves. Each of you should look not only to your own interests, but also to the interests of others. PHILIPPIANS 2:3–4 (NIV)

When I open the Internet, news instantly appears on my homepage. There, in all its splendor, is the depravity of man. Politicians slam each other. Actors sue, swindle and sleep with one another. Even sports heroes defame themselves with drugs and DUIs.

My email inbox overflows with ads offering instant fame and fortune for only a few start-up dollars. E-catalogues tantalize with more ways to become beautiful, fit into the latest fashions, and waste time and money on . . . well . . . *me!*

Turning off the computer and looking in the Bible, I find in Philippians a different perspective. I am reminded of the little acronym I learned as a child: JOY is spelled Jesus, Others, then You. God promises that when seek His face first and then serve others, He will bring into our lives far more fulfillment and joy than we can imagine.

My seventeen-year-old daughter recently complained about the incredible immaturity of kids at school. As we wrestled with the problem, I brought up those infamous politicians, entertainers, and athletes, and the get-rich quick, care-only-about-yourself ads. We recognized the immaturity of the kids at school actually aligns quite closely with self-centeredness displayed the world over.

Becky and I came to the conclusion that maturity isn't so much about age as where you put your focus. Together we decided to buy into God's definition of maturity, found in Philippians 2:3–4, which tells us to get beyond our own concerns and see life from an others-centered perspective.

Putting your own concerns in Jesus' capable hands, today how can you spend your thoughts and resources on others around you?

Kristen Johnson Ingram

The flowers appear on the earth; the time of singing has come, and the voice of the turtledove is heard in our land.

Song of Songs 2:12 (NKJV)

Even on the darkest, soggiest winter day, the promise of spring gives me patience. I'd like to be outdoors, planting gladiolus bulbs or weeding the flower beds, but the cold air and hard ground signal, "Not yet." So after I fill the bird feeders and watch the sun disappear, I curl up on our couch with a stack of seed catalogues and gardening books. I picture my beds full of marigolds and zinnias, and in my imagination I can see an apple tree blossoming. Meanwhile, winter does have its roasted chestnuts and magnified snowflakes, after all.

If I couldn't imagine spring, winter could be unbearable. And life on earth could be too hard to stand, if God hadn't left me a stack of promises.

Waiting for Jesus is like anticipating spring. He'll come with myriads of angels and shining with glory. I can see him with my mind's eye, victorious and joyful, calling us into his light forever. And the "catalogue" I read to help me imagine that day is the Bible. Just as garden magazines make me long for real flowers, Scripture lets me imagine the joy I'll feel when Christ returns.

Even so, Lord Jesus, come quickly.

Go to a nursery or plant store, and buy a packet of seeds. Even if you have no yard, you can plant a little pot of chives or basil for your kitchen. Water the pot and give it a spoon of coffee grounds; and meanwhile, remember that "I am with you always, even to the end of the world."

Anita Lustrea

But by the grace of God I am what I am, and his grace to me was not without effect. No, I worked harder than all of them—yet not I, but the grace of God that was with me.

1 CORINTHIANS 15:10 (NIV)

How good are you at extending grace to others?

I interviewed Miroslav Volf a couple of years ago on *Midday Connection*. He is a Croatian immigrant and professor at Yale Divinity School. We were talking about giving and forgiving in a culture stripped of grace.

Dr. Volf told an amazing story of grace that day on the program. He was one year old and his brother Daniel was five when they were under the care of a nanny who got distracted one day. Daniel slipped through the gate in the courtyard of their apartment building and went to a nearby military base about two blocks away. He found some soldiers in training, and one of them put Daniel on a horse-drawn bread wagon to give him a ride. As they were passing through the gate on the bumpy cobblestone road, Daniel leaned sideways and his head got stuck between the door post and the wagon and the horses kept going. Daniel died on the way to the hospital. The story is horrific, heartbreaking.

What was so amazing about the story was the forgiveness that Volf's parents extended. The nanny, on whose watch this happened, was an older widowed lady that the Volf family had taken in. The Volfs forgave her and she continued to live with them and care for Miroslav while his mother worked in a factory. At the trial of the soldier Mr. Volf stood to say that he and his wife had forgiven this soldier and said that they didn't want to press charges.

After the soldier was discharged from the army, Miroslav's father went to visit him, even though it took two days of travel. He was concerned for the soldier and wanted to talk to him once more about God's love and grace. Could you extend that kind of grace? Could I?

As you journal today, write about the score you've been keeping with your spouse or good friend, or your boss. Will you offer grace instead of scorekeeping?

Ellie Kay

Bring the whole tithe into the storehouse, so that there may be food in My house, and test Me now in this, says the Lord of hosts, if I will not open for you the windows of heaven and pour out for you a blessing until it overflows.

MALACHI 3:10 (NASB)

I had my first business at the age of seven. I found a wind-up hand buzzer in a box of Post cereal and I was the first student in my second grade class to own one. Thus, the "Handshaking Business" was born. I decided to charge the girls a nickel and the boys fifteen cents for the trouble. The boys cost more because of the agony of having to touch their hand!

I made ten dollars in the first two weeks—that's a lot of handshakes! My mom told me that 10 percent of that was the Lord's tithe, so I took my dollar to Sunday school to pay the tithe. I can still vividly remember the feeling of joy in putting that dollar in the offering plate. I learned that the sweetest dollar I ever made was the one I could give away. But I soon learned that not everyone wanted to talk about "the tithe."

In fact, most people would rather discuss their latest root canal than talk about money—it can be a painful topic. But the Bible gives us some very practical financial information that can help us as we navigate our budgets, monthly bills, and even our debt load. There is only one instance in the Bible where God challenges us to "put Him to a test" and it occurs in relationship to how we share our money. This verse in Malachi gives us a practical way that we can help our finances by bringing the tithe into the "storehouse" for a very special reason—so that we will be blessed. It was true for the seven-year-old entrepreneur that I was and it's true for you—the sweetest dollar you'll ever make is the one you can give away.

Robin Chaddock

I'm leaving you well and whole. That's my parting gift to you. Peace. I don't leave you the way you're used to being left—feeling abandoned, bereft. So don't be upset. Don't be distraught.
JOHN 14:25 (MSG)

You know, I am completely amazed by my ability to ignore the reality of Jesus in my life. I hear His words in this passage in John's gospel and I think they are just beautiful. I drink them in for a moment during quiet time, sitting in worship, or discussing them in Bible study.

But when the rubber meets the road, I'm pretty much a loser at application.

I still get upset beyond necessity over the gnawing sensation that no matter what I do I'll never be finished and it will never be enough.

I still fret over my children's futures, the money that is or isn't in their college funds, the glitches in their character as they are developing through the teenage years.

I still allow myself to get distraught pondering the next moves in my career.

What's the deal?

Jesus' parting gift is meant for me especially in these times. Jesus knew that I would need to hold to a greater reality than I let myself experience when I am so self-absorbed in my own little world. The reality of what he was leaving was the Holy Spirit, the Comforter, the Guide, the Teacher.

If Jesus' words aren't real in the everyday, they just aren't real.

Where do you need peace? Real peace? What clearer understanding of God and God's hopes and dreams for you and for the world can bring the perspective you need to be at peace? It's there. It's available. It's Jesus' parting gift. It's the best of reality.

Ginger Kolbaba

For this reason, since the day we heard about you, we have not stopped praying for you and asking God to fill you with the knowledge of his will through all spiritual wisdom and understanding. COLOSSIANS 1:9 (NIV)

I'm not a big fan of winter. I don't like being cold. I don't like that the days are shorter. And I especially don't like the added poundage to my thighs from eating the heartier winter food! But there's one thing I do like about winter—snuggling up with my sweetie in those early morning hours when it's still dark and quiet outside. We joke, "Just five more minutes," when the alarm goes off, and I nestle back into his arms. Then, after both our alarms have sounded about twelve times, and we've said, "Just five more minutes" for an hour, Scott and I begin the day by praying. It's our morning "fix."

I never realized how important that time was—and how powerful those prayers were—until a few weeks ago, when Scott had to go in to work early. No cuddling time, no "five more minutes," and no prayers. That week, we were more frustrated, irritated, bothered, and mean to each other. "What's up with us?" I finally asked one night.

That's when we realized how much we depend on that together time to get us through the day. We realized just because we're Christians, doesn't guarantee some ideal married life. It takes work, connections, and commitment. While prayer and snuggling don't take away those daily annoyances or struggles we have with each other, they do prepare us to handle them better.

Do you and your spouse pray with and for each other? Why or why not? It doesn't have to be long, drawn-out prayer times. To get started, just ask your spouse if you can pray a short blessing over his or her day today. Then try to do that every day—and watch God work.

Melinda Schmidt

For to us a child is born, to us a son is given, and the government will be on his shoulders. And he will be called Wonderful Counselor, Mighty God, Everlasting Father, Prince of Peace.
ISAIAH 9:6 (NIV)

In *The Miraculous Journey: Anticipating God in the Christmas Season*, Marty Bullis writes, "The birth of Christ too often becomes a secondary issue amidst the busyness of Christmas. Christ understands the type of frenetic world in which we live. His early days and months were as harried as any modern life could offer. Yet this Word-made-flesh, brought stability into a tumultuous world."

Jesus understands the frantic pace most of us know at Christmas time. Enduring a long trip to his birthplace in utero, taking a toddler journey to escape the murderous king—I see the parallels to our Western world at Christmas: long trips made back to our "home" and dodging the encroaching "enemies" of the Christmas season (gift purchasing and wrapping, the many Christmas parties, family dinners with those that feel more "enemy" than anything).

Tuning in to Jesus' voice rather than the "I should do this" internal voice, I've felt Him encourage me to make changes: hosting the annual dinner with friends in a way that best expresses how God has wired me instead of like my Martha Stewart-like guests, initiating a family list with expectations for holiday activities and meeting the needs of others. This year the guys will choose a gift for a needy boy at the outreach center and my daughter and I will bake goodies for a nearby nursing home, and we'll still make time for the Christmas traditions we love. I'm listening to the Holy Spirit guide my activities according to the way the Creator made me. Calm replaces fear.

Don't be swallowed up by the holidays this year—let Jesus stabilize you as you live out of the fullness of who He created you to be!

How did God create you and how will you live that out this Christmas?

Dale Hanson Bourke

You groped your way through that murk once, but no longer. You're out in the open now. The bright light of Christ makes your way plain. So no more stumbling around. Get on with it! The good, the right, the true—these are the actions appropriate for daylight hours. Figure out what will please Christ, and then do it. EPHESIANS 5:8–13 (MSG)

Among the instant messages, pop-up ads, overnight deliveries, mobile phone calls, text messages—the average day can become a cacophony of distractions. Often I find myself mentally recalibrating: Now where was I?

There are days when I start tearing through my "to-do" list. On those days, what tends to irritate my forward movement often turns out to be the high point of the day. *Now where was I?* is then answered in humility, on my knees, in confession.

And then there are the days when I am on the lookout for any diversion that will become an excuse. I turn on the computer, keep the cell phone near, check the fax machine. I find myself jittery and easily off course. On these days I am in need of a spiritual recalibration that centers me, calms me down. *Now where was I?* becomes a plea for God-focus.

I am comforted and challenged when I look at how Jesus made these decisions.

"I can't do a solitary thing on my own: I listen, then I decide," He said in John 5:30 (MSG). Once he stopped and listened to the Father, the rest was simple.

On days when I awaken already tense with worries I find it helpful to pray the prayer of St. Augustine:

Father, you are full of compassion, I commit and commend myself unto you, in whom I am and live, and know. Be the Goal of my pilgrimage, and my Rest by the way. Let my soul take refuge from the crowding turmoil of worldly thoughts beneath the shadow of Your wings; let my heart, this sea of restless waves, find peace in You O God. Amen.

Victoria Saunders Johnson

... Oh God, protect me ... Psalm 69:29 (NIV)

When Mr. Cute Guy in the Red Mustang drove up I instantly showed interest. We rode around laughing and talking. My lingering good night farewell at my dorm door spoke clearly, "I'd like to see you again." I had no idea our next meeting would be so soon and so life-threatening.

The next day, I'm in my bathrobe, sprawled in front of Saturday homework—and Mr. Cute Guy in the red Mustang knocks. "No brotha'," I laughed, "I study during the day. I'm like a vampire, I only come out at night."

I started to close the door and—swish! He grabbed me. Pushed me into the laundry room across the hall and threw me against murky green wall. "You don't tell me NO!" My back stung. My head bounced.

"Oh no!" I said under my breath. I'm a strong woman. "He will not get away with this." I snatched up a steel clothing iron. "This is going upside brotha's head."

At that moment my dorm manager and a couple other guys came bursting in. "Vikki, put it down.

"Make him leave first." I wouldn't let go of the iron until I heard the front dorm door slam shut.

After this incident I understand what the phrase "He put his hands on me" means. I've never forgotten my feelings of fear, anger, and confusion. I realize now, I could be in a prison cell after putting Mr. Cute Guy to rest with a fatal blow. Or worse, feeling like I had no other choice but to slave dance in unhealthy relationships, loving men who think women are property.

But thank You Lord, You were there, protecting, shielding, and working out other plans.

If you are in an abusive relationship, there are people ready to offer you help. The domestic violence hotline phone number is 1.800.799.7233. The rape hotline number is 1.800.656.4673.

Adele Calhoun

I wait for the Lord, my soul waits, and in his word I put my hope. PSALM 130:5 (NIV)

Life is about waiting. No matter how disciplined and organized and prayerful you are, you will still wait: in lines, in traffic, for doctors and children and parents. Waiting is part of being human. There is no perfect life where people don't wait.

What are you waiting for?

- A circle of friends, relationship, a spouse
- A career, job, a letter of acceptance
- An answer to prayer
- Your finances to turn around

And how good are you at waiting? We want instant access and quick results. Fast food, fast lanes, fast delivery, fast recoveries, fast weddings and fast divorces. We hurry our meals, our reading, relationships, our prayers, our bodies, and hurry our souls. Waiting can throw our entire system into an internal state of emergency. We would rather do anything than wait.

But without waiting we will not know God. Waiting reveals what is in our heart. Waiting unearths desires, compulsions, temptations, and limitations. All the biblical characters that are on intimate terms with God waited: Abraham, Sarah, Moses, Hannah, David, Jesus, Anna, Simeon, Paul. The list goes on and on. I am glad that every year Advent reminds me of one central, unchangeable, universal truth: waiting is part of life. Waiting doesn't mean you are doing something wrong or that God hasn't heard you.

As you anticipate celebrating the coming of Jesus this Christmas season, would you invite him to come into your stressful rushing and bring new life? What does your impatience as you are waiting reveal about your heart? What are you waiting for right now? Picture yourself waiting with Jesus by your side. Let him draw you into His arms as you wait.

Lois Evans

God has not given us a spirit of fear and timidity, but of power, love and self-discipline" 2 TIMOTHY 1:7 (NLT)

Perhaps there was a time when you experienced the touch of Jesus, but slowly worries and tensions crept in and you allowed them to choke you and make you forget that God is sufficient for all your needs. Please don't believe that all is lost. Rejoice with me for we belong to a God who loves us in spite of our faltering steps.

Even if you detoured from the paths He wanted you to take, when you hand your life afresh into His hands, He will restore you with new energy and hope and refuel you for your onward journey.

Give your sorrows and tears, doubts and fears to Jesus. March on, my friend, because "He who began a good work in you will carry it on to completion until the day of Christ Jesus" (Philippians 1:6b NIV). Let the Master touch you today . . . and every day!

What is causing you to be fearful? Timid? Write those things out. Pray about them with the Lord. What is it that you need from Him—renewed power, love, self-discipline? Ask Him for what you need. Confess your faltering steps. Now, go and live your day! And when you need to, repeat these steps.

Miriam Neff

The angel of the Lord found Hagar near a spring in the desert; it was the spring that is beside the road to Shur. And he said, "Hagar, servant of Sarai, where have you come from, and where are you going?" "I'm running away from my mistress Sarai," she answered." GENESIS 16:7–8 (NIV)

Hagar is the first African woman who appears in Scripture. She was the Egyptian slave of Sarah, probably intelligent, strong, and attractive. She was selected by Sarah to be the birth mother of her child. When life got tough, she thought God had a blind spot, and she was in it.

Some of my sisters feel they are invisible. While we all feel unseen at times, my black and Hispanic friends find this especially troubling. They feel unnoticed, unheard, and unimportant. I relate more to that feeling of being invisible since I have become a widow. We often feel invisible when we don't see answers to our prayers. Hagar had reason to feel the same way. Read her story in Genesis 16. God hears her cry. She is the first person mentioned in Scripture who is led to water by God and enabled to give it to another. Water, in Scripture, symbolizes spiritual life. Hagar, this slave, was a noticed and blessed woman!

Hagar was transformed. She was willing to meet God in a new way, to adventure back to circumstances I personally would have avoided. No wonder she gave God a special name: "You are the God who sees me" (v. 13).

In God's eyes there are no invisible women.

Amy Norton

The Lord is faithful to all his promises and loving toward all he has made. Psalm 145:13b (NIV)

In my thirteen years of visiting orphanages, there are several children the Lord used to touch my life. One of those was Katya from Russia. I first met her when she was nine. She was young and innocent and never left my side from the moment I entered the orphanage. I took a photo with her that I gave to her on my next visit that same year. I found out that her mom was a prostitute and her dad was in prison. She was doing well in school and was a leader at the orphanage. I would visit Katya each time I went to the orphanage, usually getting only a few minutes with her but I would always tell her I was praying for her and that I loved her.

There were several years when I visited and Katya wasn't there. I found out her mother had become a bad influence on her and that Katya was not showing up at school. She had become a problem child at the orphanage. I thought I would never see Katya again and she would surely be forever lost to the Lord. I prayed for her after each trip but would forget to pray as time went on.

Years had gone by and I had not seen Katya. I was surprised and overjoyed to walk in the door of the orphanage on my next visit and find Katya waiting for me. She was making good grades and had taken on the sole responsibility of caring for her father who was dying of tuberculosis. In talking to her, I asked if she remembered the photo we had taken on my first visit. She told me the photo was hanging above her father's bed and she knew I was praying for her. She told me she wanted to know the Lord. The Lord had been faithful to Katya even though I had not.

Be encouraged that the Lord is faithful and will not forget those he loves.

Leigh McLeroy

For a child has been born—for us! The gift of a son—for us! He'll take over the running of the world. His names will be: Amazing Counselor, Strong God, Eternal Father, Prince of Wholeness. His ruling authority will grow, and there'll be no limit to the wholeness he brings. ISAIAH 9:2–7 (MSG)

It's the stuff of fairytales for a tiny baby to be left on a doorstep and cared for by another. In these stories, a frightened mother leaves a child she cannot keep in a place where it is sure to be found and nurtured. Almost always, good things happen as a result.

How desperate must a mother be to abandon her defenseless child with nothing but the hope of someone else's mercy? What awful kind of pain might cause her to break the bond of blood and walk away with empty arms?

I read stories of babies found in dumpsters and in public restrooms, and babies left at police stations and on porches. They make my heart hurt. Who in heaven's name leaves a baby on a doorstep? What could they possibly be thinking?

Then I read another old, familiar story. It doesn't begin "once upon a time." It begins, "in the fullness of time." This perfectly-timed baby was born to a young, unwed mother. But *she* didn't leave him in a strange place. His Father did. On purpose. On earth's doorstep—far from His true home.

But this baby wasn't left on the doorstep *hoping* for mercy. Mercy was what He brought with Him when He came. And the hurt that caused Him to be left in the care of two young Nazarenes was the bone-breaking, hope-crushing weight of a world of sinners. The baby on the doorstep was delivered for people like me. Like you.

Sometime during the Christmas season, listen to a recording of Handel's *Messiah*. Let the music inspire you to celebrate the child born "unto us."

Christa March

But why am I so favored, that the mother of my Lord should come to me? LUKE 1:43 (NIV)

The Christmas story has always intrigued me. The mystery of God coming to earth in the form of a newborn is by far the most miraculous part of the story, but other aspects fascinate me as well. For example, Mary, a teenage girl about to be married and she now has to tell her parents that she's pregnant. Her parents must have been devastated. They think the best thing they can do for her is to send her to stay with her older cousin Elizabeth.

What did Mary think about on her way to Elizabeth's home? Was she fearful of having to try to explain her pregnancy story one more time? Did she wonder if this older cousin was going to chastise her for getting pregnant outside of marriage or would Elizabeth just let her go through this time in peace?

Imagine the burden that was lifted off of Mary as she walks into Elizabeth's front door and she hears her cousin exclaim, "Blessed are you among women and blessed is the child you will bear! But why am I so favored, that the mother of my Lord should come to me? . . . Blessed is she who has believed that what the Lord has said to her will be accomplished!" (Luke 1:42–45 NIV)

We women need someone who just believes in us. Friends who know we're not perfect but know the intention of our hearts. Is there a woman in your life who has loved you and cared for you during a particularly hard time? Does she know how much you mean to her?

Read Luke 1:39–56. Take the time today to write that special woman a note to tell her how much she means to you. Don't just email it. Send it in the mail. Who knows? Maybe the day she opens her mailbox and sees your card is the very day she needs to know someone believes in her.

Anita Lustrea

Then Herod called for a private meeting with the wise men, and he learned from them the time when the star first appeared. MATTHEW 2:7 (NLT)

I don't know about you, but I definitely sentimentalize Christmas. I know better, but I struggle with it every year. What we usually forget, though, is that Jesus coming to this earth was an act of war.

We read in the Gospel of Matthew that Herod was deeply disturbed by the fact that the wise men came asking and looking for a newborn king so they could worship Him. Herod was not going to stand for another king encroaching on his kingdom. Herod planned to eradicate this threat. He had asked the wise men, once they found Jesus, to return to Jerusalem to tell him where they found Him, so that he could "go and worship, too!"

Yeah, right! God warned the wise men in a dream to not return to Herod. "Herod was furious when he learned that the wise men had outwitted him" (v. 16). That's why they're called "wise men"! Herod had another plan. He planned to slaughter all the Jewish children two years and under. He thought that would take care of his problem.

If you haven't figured this out yet, you can't go up against God and win. I've tried a few times. You know the story, "an angel of the Lord appeared to Joseph in a dream. 'Get up and flee to Egypt with the child and his mother,' the angel said. 'Stay there until I tell you to return, because Herod is going to try to kill the child'" (Matthew 2:13 NLT).

When I get into the meat of this story, it's hard for me to sentimentalize a death threat. We are at war with an enemy who is fighting for our souls. What will you do today to fortify your soul for the battle?

Why not read the account of Christ's birth in Matthew chapters one and two as a reminder that the Enemy is real, but God is greater!

Melinda Schmidt

For God so loved the world that he gave his one and only Son, that whoever believes in him shall not perish but have eternal life. JOHN 3:16 (NIV)

You might be reading this very early in the morning, anticipating a day of hospitality, picture taking and soon-to-be-heard squeals as wrapping paper is ripped and tossed aside and "thank-you's" are the grateful responses to lots of holiday efforts. Or you might be reading this at day's end. All the cooking, Christmas services and traditions are finished for another year and you are taking it all in.

If you are reading this Christmas morning, this could be a good time to:

- write down your expectations or concerns for the day, or remember gifts of the heart you want to make sure to remember
- find a Scripture verse to focus on today
- pray and talk with God about your feelings for the day ahead

If it's the end of Christmas Day, this might be a good time to:

- write down your impressions of the day, the good, the bad, what worked, what didn't, your feelings about how the day was spent (and before you put your Christmas decorations away, tuck appropriate suggestions and ideas for next year in one of your holiday storage boxes)
- find a Scripture that sums up your feelings tonight
- pray and talk with God about how you felt about today

You live in one of the wealthiest parts of the entire world—most of the world will not celebrate Christmas Day as richly as you—so give thanks to God for all that you have and all you have experienced, (even if it wasn't exactly as you wished it to be). Thank Him for sending His Son, for "... whoever believes in him shall not perish but have eternal life" (John 3:16 NIV).

Carol Ruhter

He makes me lie down in green pastures,
He leads me beside quiet waters,
He restores my soul.
PSALM 23:2–3 (NIV)

The similarity between trails and trials is more than a transposed letter. Are you on a difficult stretch of life's trail?

• God will give you rest. "He makes me lie down in green pastures, He leads me beside quiet waters, He restores my soul" (Psalm 23:2-3 NIV).

• When you're lost on a trail, God can lead you to His high rock above yourself and your circumstances enabling you to glimpse the "path" from His perspective. ". . . I call as my heart grows faint; lead me to the rock that is higher than I" (Psalm 61:2 NIV).

• Life trials, like nature trails, can be confusing. He guides us through His Holy Spirit and the trail map of his Word. ". . . your ears will hear a voice behind you, saying, 'This is the way: walk in it'" (Isaiah 30:21 NIV).

• God enables you to ascend steep paths. ". . . He makes my feet like the feet of a deer, He enables me to go on the heights" (Habakkuk 3:19 NIV).

• Exchange *your* hiking pack for *Jesus'* backpack. Replace worry with peace. Unpack guilt for forgiveness. Choose God's power over your own. "Take my yoke upon you and learn from me . . . for my yoke is easy and my burden is light" (Matthew 11:29–30 NIV).

• Even the most sure-footed will stumble. Yet, God is right there. "When I said, 'My foot is slipping,' your love, O Lord, supported me" (Psalm 94:18 NIV).

• You help lead others to Christ by the triumphant way you walk life's tough trails. ". . . thanks be to God, who always leads us in triumphal procession in Christ and through us spreads . . . the knowledge of Him" (2 Corinthians 2:14 NIV).

Are you trusting God as your trail guide?

Kendra Smiley

In everything give thanks: for this is the will of God in Christ Jesus for you. 1 THESSALONIANS 5:18 (NKJV)

I have always encouraged my sons to write thank you notes. In the era of electronic mail, I have tried to remind them that email, as wonderful as it is, does not replace a handwritten note of thanks to someone who has done a kindness or given a gift. For the most part, I have been successful in convincing my kids of the importance of a note of thanks.

Through the years I have saved special thank you notes that I have received. I have notes from friends and acquaintances and I even have one or two from each of our children (a testimony to the success of my teaching on thank you notes!).

When was the last time you received a special note of thanks? How did it make you feel? When was the last time you sent a thank you note? More importantly, have you ever written one to God? That is probably not a bad idea. By journaling your thoughts and feelings about God's wonderful blessings in your life, you are, in a sense, writing Him a note of thanks. Those written words can be read over and over to remind you of God's goodness.

Take some time today to write a note of thanks and praise to God. That is what the psalmist did. "Praise God in his sanctuary. Praise Him in his mighty heavens. Praise Him for his acts of power. Praise Him for his surpassing greatness. Let everything that has breath praise the Lord. Praise the Lord" (Psalm 150:1–2, 6 NIV). Thanking and praising God . . . the Next Right Choice!

Sharon Hersh

Come! Is anyone thirsty? Come! All who will, come and drink. Drink freely of the Water of Life!
REVELATION 22:17 (MSG)

"Why doesn't God give us what we want?" I'm not smart enough to answer that question. But I am learning that God knows the context in which I am most likely to develop an intimate relationship with Him. For me that has been learning in some humbling, humiliating places that God really does love me when I am good for nothing. His love for me has compelled me to begin to want Him. In other words, I want Him when He is not acting like a vending machine in my life (giving me everything that I ask for) because I love Him.

I sat with a group of women and listened as one of them, having unexpectedly lost her husband of thirty years to a heart attack, said with honesty, "Well, if this is God's context for me, then 'No thank you.'" It's scary to believe that He is wooing us—loving us—in life's most painful circumstances, to Himself.

Believing we were all desperately searching for God, my experience of redemption in the broken places of my story has taught me a deeper truth—God is searching for us.

We begin our adult lives with many ideals for how life ought to be. When the real crowds out the ideal, we turn in our dreams for a few schemes of how we can get what we want. I had tried to fix my life, save my life, create my life, keep my life on track—all bringing me to the resolution that I couldn't set myself free. Jesus waits patiently for thirsty women—like us—to discover that He is the true longing of our hearts.

Anita Lustrea

As for those who were considered important in the church, their reputation doesn't concern me. God isn't impressed with mere appearances, and neither am I. And of course these leaders were able to add nothing to the message I had been preaching. GALATIANS 2:6 (MSG)

Women. We are the great comparers. We like to size other women up. We might not say it out loud, but we are looking to see who is fatter or thinner, has better hair or skin, better makeup and clothes.

Years ago I was the worship leader and special music at a women's retreat, and Gail MacDonald, wife of Gordon MacDonald, was the speaker. The retreat was for a very prosperous church. Back then, it used to be the norm to dress up to go to women's retreats. Now Gail had done something I'd never seen done at a women's retreat. To this day it is the best thing I've ever witnessed happening at a women's retreat. She wore the exact same outfit two days in a row. I remember thinking, "Did she know? Was that on purpose? Did any other women notice?"

I was seated next to her at dinner on the second night of the retreat and I leaned over and said, "Gail, I noticed you wore the exact same outfit today." She said, "Yes, I did." I said, "Was that on purpose?" She said, "Yes, it was." She went on to say that she often does that at women's retreats. That was the extent of our conversation, but my respect for Gail shot through the roof. She had the guts to confront an affluent system in a way that spoke louder than any words she could have used.

It's one thing to compare our outward appearance. What about when we start comparing our own personal journeys with others? Is that a help or a hindrance to our spiritual growth? Read Psalm 139:1–16 out loud and pay attention to the language God uses to describe the wondrous creation that you are!

Mary Whelchel

Show me, O Lord, my life's end and the number of my days; let me know how fleeting is my life. PSALM 39:4 (NIV)

For those of us who are very busy people, we can easily start thinking that the world revolves around our schedules. In leafing through one of my journals, I noticed one entry where I wrote: "The world does not revolve around my schedule. God's eternal plan is not dependent upon my to-do list. If I fail to achieve my goals, if I cannot perform like superwoman, if my best-laid plans are never accomplished, it will not change God or his love for me."

Now, I know why I wrote that. I live by a schedule, planning to do more than I can usually get done. It certainly is good to be organized and goal-oriented, but when we think that everything depends on our performance, or it will be a real tragedy if we don't finish the to-do list, then we become slaves to that drive and schedule.

Here's a line from a hymn that I had written in my journal:

"Heaven and earth may fade and flee,
Firstborn light in gloom decline,
But while God and I shall be,
I am His and He is mine." (*I Am His and He Is Mine,* George W. Robinson, 1876)

We frequently need to get off our treadmill, put away our to-do list for awhile, and get some perspective on our schedules. You know, everything in this world will fade and flee someday—everything except the Word of God and people.

Think of your schedule, those things you think you have to do in order to keep the world spinning! Ask God for his perspective of that schedule, and remember the important things are those that last forever.

Marcia Ramsland

The Lord be exalted, who delights in the well-being of his servant. PSALM 35:27B (NIV)

I love new calendars! Those clean, white squares for a new year represent a fresh start. A chance to being anew. A change to leave the old behind and have a better life this year.

So how can we create that lifestyle of well-being and fullness? Start with your calendar. It is the place we say "yes" to let people and events into our lives, and "no" to keep out things that distract or discourage us. Here are some calendar tips to create a fulfilling lifestyle you like and enjoy this year:

1. Choose a theme verse for the year. For example, if you chose John 15:18, "This is to my Father's glory, that you bear much fruit . . . ," ask yourself if signing up for a new commitment will accomplish that.
2. Pray for wisdom at the moment of invitation before writing an event in your calendar. Or wait overnight for things requiring more than ten hours of your time.
3. Place a check mark at the end of each week when four nights have been committed. That is the maximum number that will allow you to be on top of things in your home and outside your home.
3. Remember a "balanced" woman fills only 70 to 80 percent of her day. A frown on your face and the "pedal to the metal" feeling all day long are red flags that you need to schedule some "down time" soon.

Today review your calendar for ways to lighten up your schedule, remembering "the Lord delights in the well-being of His servant." Look for ways for God to delight in you and your time choices.

Biographies

NANCY ANDERSON

Nancy C. Anderson's marriage almost ended because of her affair (twenty-five years ago) but through Christ's example of forgiveness and restoration, her marriage was healed. Nancy's book *Avoiding the Greener Grass Syndrome*, (available in Spanish) tells the story of the death and resurrection of her marriage. Nancy and her husband have a speaking ministry called "Joyful Marriage." They bring hope and practical teaching, combined with humor and personal examples, to couples of all ages. Ron and Nancy's story has been featured in national media including *Midday Connection*, *The Montel William's Show*, *The 700 Club*, and *FamilyLife Today*.

Web sites:

www.nancyCanderson.com www.JoyfulMarriage.blogspot.com

MARY GRACE BIRKHEAD

Mary Grace is an author, artist, and teacher. She has written the *Heirloom Promise* book series and she enjoys painting.

Web site: **www.marygraceb.com**

DALE HANSON BOURKE

Dale Hanson Bourke is president of the CIDRZ Foundation, supporting AIDS, malaria, and cervical cancer research in Africa. She spent twenty years as a marketing and publishing executive. She also served as publisher for Religion News Service and was senior vice president/marketing of World Relief. She has served on the boards of World Vision (US and International) and International Justice Mission, currently serving on the boards of Opportunity International and MAP International. Bourke has written a nationally-syndicated newspaper column and eight books, including *Second Calling: Finding Passion and Purpose for the Rest of Your Life* and *The Skeptic's Guide to the Global AIDS Crisis,* and most recently *The Skeptic's Guide to Global Poverty*. She earned an M.B.A. from the University of Maryland and a B.A. from Wheaton College.

KATIE BRAZELTON

Katie Brazelton, Ph.D., M.Div., M.A., is the bestselling author of the *Pathway to Purpose for Women* series, with her anchor book translated into ten languages. Her most recent book is *Character Makeover: 40 Days with a Life Coach to Create the Best You*. For years, Katie was director of women's Bible studies and at the purpose-driven Saddleback Community Church. Now, as the founder of Life Purpose Coaching Centers International®, the global training hub for Christian coaches, she is fulfilling her godly dream of opening two hundred coaching centers worldwide. She is also a professor for Rockbridge Seminary.

Web site: **www.LifePurposeCoachingCenters.com**

DEE BRESTIN

Dee first became known in the early '80s when *The Friendships of Women*, the book Dr. Dobson said "every woman should read," was released. It has sold more than a million copies and Dee went on to write many bestselling Bible study guides. She speaks internationally and is a frequent guest on Focus on the Family and Moody Radio's *Midday Connection*. Dee was blessed with a wonderful marriage, but lost her fifty-nine-year-old husband Steve to colon cancer. She has five children and five grandchildren, is a member of the conservative branch of the Presbyterian Church of America. She lives in Kansas City, Missouri, and Door County, Wisconsin.

Web site: **www.deebrestin.com**

JILL BRISCOE

Jill Briscoe has an active speaking and writing ministry that has taken her to many countries. She has written more than forty books. Jill is executive editor of *Just Between Us*, a magazine of encouragement for ministry wives and women in leadership. She serves on the board of World Relief and Christianity Today, Inc. A native of Liverpool, England, Jill and her husband, Stuart, now live in Wisconsin. They have three children and thirteen grandchildren.

Web site: **www.tellingthetruth.org**

NICOLE BROMLEY

Nicole (Braddock) Bromley is a professional speaker and the author of *Hush: Moving from Silence to Healing after Childhood Sexual Abuse* (Moody Publishers, 2007). She is the founder and director of OneVOICE enterprises and a national spokesperson on the issue if sexual abuse and assault. She speaks to thousands of students each year. Nicole and her husband, Matthew, live in Columbus, Ohio.

Web site: **www.onevoiceenterprises.com**

ADELE CALHOUN

Adele's passion is God's dream for this world. This dream led her to missions work. Adele and her husband, Doug, have worked in South Africa and the West India. They also have led mission teams to Latin America, Europe, Appalachia, Africa, and China.

Adele is a spiritual director and has taught as adjunct faculty at Wheaton College and Northern Baptist Theological Seminary. She currently serves on the board of the Pierce Foundation at Gordon Conwell Theological Seminary. She wrote *Handbook of Spiritual Disciplines: Practices that Transform Us.* Adele's hobbies include painting, gardening, reading, hiking, and traveling. Adele and Doug have a daughter who is traveling Europe and a son in New York City.

MINDY CALIGUIRE

Mindy Caliguire is founder of Soul Care, a spiritual formation ministry. She serves as a frequent speaker and leadership consultant, working with local churches and national groups such as the Spiritual Formation Alliance, Renovare, The Upper Room, and the Willow Creek Association. Her books include the new *Soul Care Series: Discovering Soul Care, Spiritual Friendship, Soul Searching*, and *Simplicity*, and *Write for Your Soul: The Whys and Hows of Journaling* (with Jeff Caliguire). She and her family are all active members at Willow Creek Community Church and make their home in Algonquin, Illinois.

Web site: **www.soulcare.com**

CAROLYN CASTLEBERRY

Carolyn Castleberry is the author of *It's About Time!—10 Smart Strategies to Avoid Time Traps and Invest Yourself Where it Matters*

(Howard Books, October, 2008). She has also written two business books for women including *Women, Take Charge of Your Money: A Biblical Path to Financial Security* and *Women, Get Answers About Your Money: Because There are No Dumb Questions about Personal Finance* (Multnomah Publishers, 2006). She is also a cohost on a program called *Living the Life* on ABC Family Channel, produced by the Christian Broadcasting Network.

Web site: **www.carolyncastleberry.com**

ROBIN CHADDOCK

Robin Chaddock is an insightful speaker, internationally known author, and seminar leader. Also a certified life coach, Robin helps others grow deeper in their spirituality, successfully navigate transitions and life changes, and discover what they are meant to do and to be in this world. As an author, Robin has written *Being a Wise Woman in a Wild World, Come to Your Senses, 12 Great Choices Smart Moms Make, How to Get a Smart Mouth,* and *How to Find Your Personal Path to Success.* She also has a weekly "Soul Snack" that you can receive via email.

Web site: **http://robinchaddock.com**

LINDA CLARE

Linda Clare is the coauthor of three books, *Lost Boys and the Moms Who Love Them* (Waterbrook, 2002), *Revealed: Spiritual Reality in a Makeover World* (Revell, 2005), and *Making Peace With a Dangerous God* (Revell, 2006). She grew up in Phoenix, Arizona, graduated from Arizona State University, and taught art for more than ten years. A teacher of writing at the college level since 2000, she is a sought-after writing mentor. Linda and her husband, Brad, and their adult children, live in Eugene, Oregon, along with four wayward cats, Oliver, Xena Warrior Kitty, Paladine, and Melchior.

Web site: **http://godsonggrace.blogspot.com**

ROSALIE DE ROSSET

Rosalie de Rosset is a professor of literature and communications (English and Homiletics) at Moody Bible Institute where she has been for thirty-eight years. She has a B.A. in English from Bryan College in

Dayton, Tennessee, an M.A. in English from Northeastern Illinois University, an M.Div. from Trinity Evangelical Divinity School, and a Ph.D. in Language, Literary, and Rhetoric from the University of Illinois at Chicago. Rosalie speaks at conferences and in churches around the U.S. as well as in New Zealand, Hawaii, Russia, and South America. She was born and raised in Peru, South America, where her parents were missionaries for forty-two years. Before becoming a teacher, she worked for WMBI AM and FM as a script writer.

JANICE ELSHEIMER

Janice Elsheimer is an enthusiastic and entertaining speaker and author with a message that creativity is a pathway to personal and spiritual growth. Writers, visual artists, musicians, actors, and folks who simply want permission to start exercising their creative muscles fill her workshops, seminars, and classes. They leave with a new sense of what is possible: a conviction that they can enrich their lives by developing God-given talents. She has written *The Creative Call*, and *Grounded in the Garden: the Wisdom of Growing Things*. Janice's presentations leave her participants refreshed, encouraged, and ready to reawaken the sleeping artist within. Janice and her husband, Seth, live in Winter Park, Florida, and they have one son. She enjoys writing, playing music, and gardening.

Web site: **www.jelsheimer.com**

LOIS EVANS

Dr. Lois Evans is senior vice president of The Urban Alternative and founder of The First Lady Ministry. She serves in the office of the senior pastor at Oak Cliff Bible Fellowship Church, National Religious Broadcasters Board, Dallas Baptist University Woman's Auxiliary Board, Dallas Mavericks Board, and The Urban Alternative Board of Directors. Dr. Evans has traveled throughout the United States, Caribbean, China, India, South America, Europe, and West Africa. She is a sought-after speaker for conferences and churches around the globe, and an accomplished singer. Married to her favorite pastor/teacher and best friend, Dr. Tony Evans, senior pastor of Oak Cliff Bible Fellowship, Lois has four children, two granddaughters and four grandsons.

Web site: **www.loisevans.org**

PAM FARREL

Pam Farrel is a relationship specialist, international speaker, and author of more than twenty-five books, including bestselling *Men are like Waffles and Women are like Spaghetti*. Pam has experience as a pastor's wife, director of women's ministry, and is president of Seasoned Sisters. Other books include: *Red Hot Monogamy, 10 Best Decisions a Woman Can Make, 10 Best Decisions a Parent Can Make, 10 Best Decisions a Couple Can Make, Woman of Influence, Devotions for Women on the Go!* and *Got Teens*? The Farrels have a newspaper and magazine column on relationships and are frequent guests on shows like *Focus on the Family* and *Midday Connection*.

Web site: **www.farrelcommunications.com**
www.seasonedsisters.com

MARGARET FEINBERG

Margaret Feinberg is a popular speaker at churches, colleges, women's retreats, and leading conferences such as Fusion, Catalyst, National Pastors Convention, and LeadNow. Recently named by *Charisma* magazine one of the "30 Emerging Voices" who will help lead the church in the next decade and one of the "40 Under 40" who will shape Christian publishing by *Christian Retailing*, she has written more than a dozen books including the critically-acclaimed *The Organic God* (Zondervan) as well as a dozen Bible studies including *The Organic God DVD Study Kit*. Her most recent title is *Sacred Echo*, published by Zondervan.

Web site: **www.margaretfeinberg.com**
Email: **margaret@margaretfeinberg.com.**

SHAUNTI FELDHAHN

Shaunti Feldhahn is a nationally syndicated newspaper columnist, public speaker, and a bestselling author whose books include *For Women Only*. After working on Wall Street and Capitol Hill, this mother of two now applies her analytical skills to illuminating surprising truths about relationships.

Web site: **www.shaunti.com**

SANDRA GLAHN

Sandra Glahn, Th.M., teaches writing and women's studies at Dallas Theological Seminary (DTS), where she edits *Kindred Spirit* magazine. She is also pursuing a Ph.D. in Aesthetic Studies at the University of Texas at Dallas. In addition she serves on the board of the Evangelical Press Association and the women's leadership team for bible.org. Glahn's books include a medical suspense novel, *Informed Consent,* and the six-title Coffee Cup Bible Study series. She has also coauthored works on reproductive technologies and on marriage as well as three medical novels—the Christy fiction finalist, *Lethal Harvest;* its sequel, *Deadly Cure*; and *False Positive*.

Web site: **www.aspire2.com**

DANNAH GRESH

Dannah Gresh is a nationally recognized expert on teen culture and sexuality. Her ministry in North America and in Zambia, Africa, a nation ravaged by HIV/AIDS, is marked by deep Bible teaching wrapped in humorous and sometimes tear-provoking transparency. She is a sought-after speaker for women and teens. Her best-known literary work is *And the Bride Wore White* as well as her coauthorship with Nancy Leigh DeMoss of *Lies Young Women Believe*. She is the creator of the *Secret Keeper Girl* brand, a collection of resources and events for moms and their eight- to twelve-year-old daughters that teach biblical womanhood in an age-appropriate and fun way. Dannah lives in State College, Pennsylvania, with her husband, Bob, and their children, Robby and Lexi and Autumn.

Web site: **www.purefreedom.org**

TRACY GROOT

Tracy Groot is a part-time writer, a full-time mom, and co-owner of JP's Coffee and Espresso Bar, in Holland, Michigan. She loves reading, writing, backpacking, family time, Thai food, scandalous amounts of coffee and equally scandalous amounts of sweets, and Great Britain. Her predominantly male family consists of her husband, Jack, her three sons, Evan, Grayson, and Riley, and a manipulative Jack Russell named Murphy.

Web site: **www.tracygroot.com**

SARA GROVES

Before singer and songwriter Sara Groves debuted in 1998, she was a high school teacher in her hometown of Rosemont, Minnesota. Through God's directing and leading, Sara left that job to pursue what had been a joy and a passion of hers since she was a little child. Sara is very involved with International Justice Mission, a team of lawyers and law enforcement officials who help women who are trapped in human trafficking. Her husband, Troy, is her manager and percussionist. Sara and Troy have three children, Kirby, Toby and Ruby.

Web site: **www.saragroves.com**

SHARON HANBY-ROBIE

Sharon has been an interior designer and member of the American Society of Interior Designers (ASID) for more than thirty years. Since 2003, she has been the resident home décor expert for QVC Inc. Her career spans television, radio, and print media, to conference speaking and even leadership and mentoring workshops. As a best-selling author, her books include *Beautiful Places Spiritual Spaces* from Northfield Publishing, the *My Name Isn't Martha* series of books from Pocketbooks, *The Spirit of Simple Living*™ series, from Guideposts Books: *The Simple Home, A Simple Christmas,* and *A Simple Wedding.* Sharon's most recent book is *Decorating Without Fear*, from Rutledge Hill Press.

Web site: **www.sharonhanbyrobie.com**

LISA HARPER

Rarely are the terms *motorcycle mama* and *Bible scholar* used to describe the same person . . . but then again, Lisa Harper is anything but stereotypical! She has been lauded as a master storyteller whose writing and speaking overflows with colorful pop culture references that bridge the gap between the Bible era and modern-day life. Lisa's resume includes directing Focus on the Family's national women's ministry, working on a large church staff, and recently becoming a regular columnist for *Today's Christian Woman*. She has a Masters of Theological Studies from Covenant Theological Seminary and is the author of several books including *Relentless Love*, *Every Woman's Hope*, *Holding Out For A Hero* and *What The Bible Is All About For Women.*

Web site: **www.lisaharper.net**

JOANNE HEIM

Joanne Heim is the author of several books, including *Living Simply: Choosing Less in a World of More* and *Misplacing God: Creating Space for Him in a Busy Life*. She has been a guest on numerous programs, such Moody Radio's *Midday Connection*, *Focus on the Family* with Dr. James Dobson, and *Home Word* with Jim Burns. As well as speaking to groups of women and teaching Scripture, Joanne is primarily a wife and mother. She and her husband live in Denver with their daughters, Audrey and Emma.

Web site: **www.thesimplewife.typepad.com**

SHARON HERSH

Sharon A. Hersh is a licensed professional counselor and the director of Women's Recovery and Renewal. She is the author of several books including the bestselling *Breavehearts: Unlocking The Courage to Love With Abandon* and her most recent release *The Last Addiction: Why Self-Help Is Not Enough*. She is an adjunct professor in counseling at several seminaries and is a sought-after speaker for conferences and retreats. Sharon lives with her family in Lone Tree, Colorado.

Web site: www.sharonhersh.com

KIM HILL

Kim Hill is a Grammy-nominated, multi-Dove award winner. She's had the opportunity to lead thousands of women across America in worship as well as in Nairobi, Kenya. Juggling the responsibilities of recording artist, worship leader, and single mother of two very active boys, Hill has found comfort and clarity in worship and encourages others through her music to do the same.

Web site: **www.kimhillmusic.com**

LYNNE HYBELS

Lynne married Bill Hybels and in 1975 they started Willow Creek Community Church in a rented movie theatre in Palatine, Illinois. She is the author of *Nice Girls Don't Change the World*, and coauthor of *Rediscovering Church* and *Fit to be Tied*. She most recently collaborated with the Willow Creek Association to develop *Hope and*

Action, a DVD and participants' guide that helps churches and small groups begin to address the AIDS pandemic. Bill and Lynne have two adult children, Todd and Shauna, a son-in-law, Aaron Niequist, and one grandson, Henry.

Web site: **www.lynnehybels.com**

KRISTEN JOHNSON INGRAM

Kristen Johnson Ingram is the author of twenty books, including *Wine at the End of the Feast: Embracing Spiritual Change as You Age* and *Beyond Words: 15 Ways of Doing Prayer* and more than a thousand articles and short stories. She collaborated with Linda Clare on *Revealed: Spiritual Transformation in a Makeover World* and *Making Peace with a Dangerous God.* Kristen has grown children and five grandsons, and with her husband, Ron, lives at the edge of the woods in Springfield, Oregon.

CAROLYN CUSTIS JAMES

Carolyn Custis James (M.A. in Biblical Studies) is an author and international conference speaker for churches, colleges, seminaries, and other Christian organizations. She is a new voice in Christian publishing with a strong, affirming message for women. Her ministry organization, Whitby Forum, challenges women to go deeper in their relationship with God and to serve Him alongside their brothers in the faith. She is a consulting editor for *Zondervan's Exegetical Commentary Series on the New Testament* and president of the Synergy Women's Network, Inc.—a national network of women active or emerging in vocational ministry. She and her husband, Frank, president of Reformed Theological Seminary in Orlando, have one grown daughter.

Web site: **www.whitbyforum.com**
www.synergytoday.org

VICTORIA SAUNDERS JOHNSON

Victoria L. Johnson is mother to three beautiful children, Lydia, Candacee, and Andre. Her desire is to inspire and teach women to study the Bible. She is a writer, speaker, and social worker based in Milwaukee. She has a Bachelor's degree in counseling psychology. Victoria started an initiative called Protecting Innocent Children, Inc., which is committed to helping and offering the hope of Jesus Christ to children and their families affected by childhood sexual abuse. Victoria's last three publications, *Restoring Broken Vessels, In-depth Bible Study for Sisters* and *Children and Sexual Abuse* are available through InterVarsity Press.

Web site:**www.protectinginnocentchildren.org**
Email: **victoriasaundersjohnson@yahoo.com**

JOY JORDAN-LAKE

Joy Jordan-Lake's professional experience has included working as a college professor, writer, journalist, waitress, director of a food pantry for homeless families, freelance photographer, and the job title that remains her favorite—head sailing instructor. Having taught at universities in Massachusetts, North Carolina, and Texas, Joy Jordan-Lake currently teaches at Belmont University in Tennessee. In addition to her writing and teaching, she is a frequent speaker at retreats, workshops and conferences. Joy and her husband, Todd, are enthusiastic advocates for microenterprise loans that assist the impoverished in developing nations. Residing near Nashville, they love sharing life with their three children, Julia, Justin, and Jasmine, as well as the family's two dogs and two cats.

Web site: **www.joyjordanlake.com**

NANCY KANE

Nancy Kane is an associate professor in the department of educational ministries at Moody Bible Institute. Kane is also the codirector of Grace Family Counseling Center in Northbrook, Illinois, and is a licensed clinical professional counselor. She is a frequent conference speaker and radio talk show guest and was a contributor/reviewer for the *Family Foundations Study Bible*. Kane also wrote *From Fear to Love: Overcoming Barriers to Healthy Relationships* with her husband, Raymond.

ELLIE KAY

Ellie Kay is the bestselling author of eleven books including *A Tip A Day With Ellie Kay* (Moody Publishers). She is a popular international speaker, presenting at arena events with up to eight thousand people. As a media veteran, she has appeared on more than six hundred radio/TV stations including CNBC, CNN and *Fox News.* She is an international radio commentator and a national columnist as well as a spokesperson consultant for clients such as Wal-Mart, Procter & Gamble, Washington Mutual, Visa, and MasterCard. Ellie and her team have been on a speaking tour from coast to coast in the USA and to China, Germany, France, Italy, and England. Ellie Kay is married to Bob, a test pilot, and they have seven children.

Web site: **www.elliekay.com**

CAROL KENT

Carol Kent is a popular international public speaker best known for being dynamic, humorous, encouraging, and biblical. She has been a featured speaker at Women of Faith and Extraordinary Women Conferences. She is the president of Speak Up Speaker Services and the director of Speak Up With Confidence seminars. Carol holds a master's degree in communication arts and a bachelor's degree in speech education. Her books include: *A New Kind of Normal, When I Lay My Isaac Down, Becoming a Woman of Influence, Mothers Have Angel Wings, Secret Longings of the Heart, Tame Your Fears,* and *Speak Up With Confidence.*

Web site: **www.CarolKent.org** **www.SpeakUpforHope.org**

VIRELLE KIDDER

A full-time writer and conference speaker for more than twenty-five years, Virelle Kidder's passion is encouraging women on their faith journey at all stages in life. She is funny, transparent, highly relatable, and solidly biblical. Moody Publishers released her fifth and sixth books in 2008: *The Best Life Ain't Easy, But it's Worth It,* and *Meet Me at the Well—Take a Month and Water Your Soul.* The Kidders have four grown children and eight grandchildren, and reside in Sebastian, Florida.

Web site: **www.virellekidder.com**

KATHY KOCH

Dr. Kathy Koch is the founder and president of Celebrate Kids, Inc., of Fort Worth, Texas. Dr. Kathy is a public speaker who addresses the discouragement dilemmas that affect everyone. Her practical and relevant ideas and vibrant teaching style are appreciated by teachers, parents, and kids of all ages in school, church, and convention settings. They appreciate her strategic, detailed solutions that encourage them to make appropriate changes. In addition to creating other helpful products, she has written two books, *Finding Authentic Hope and Wholeness—5 Questions That Will Change Your Life* and *How Am I Smart? A Parent's Guide to Multiple Intelligences.*

Web site: **www.CelebrateKids.com**

GINGER KOLBABA

Ginger Kolbaba is editor of *Marriage Partnership* magazine. An accomplished book author, Ginger was coauthor/collaborator of *Refined by Fire*. She has written several other nonfiction books, *Dazzled to Frazzled and Back Again: The Bride's Survival Guide* and *Surprised by Remarriage: A Guide to the Happily Even After*. She has collaborated on several books including *The Five Sex Needs of Men and Women* and written two *Secrets from Lulu's Café* novels with Christy Scannell. Before becoming an editor/writer, she worked as a professional actress/singer/speaker. She lives in the Chicagoland area with her husband, Scott, and her Doberman puppy, Bella.

Web site: **www.gingerkolbaba.com**

SUSIE LARSON

Susie Larson has spoken to thousands of women locally, nationally, and internationally. Susie is the author of several books and many articles and works as a freelance writer for Focus on the Family. She's been interviewed on many stations and absolutely loves Moody Radio's *Midday Connection*! Susie partners with recording artist Sara Groves as co-chair for International Justice Mission's annual fundraising banquet in Minnesota. Susie and her husband, Kevin, have been married twenty-three years and have three (almost) grown sons. Her happy places are: riding the bike trails as fast as she can, sitting on the deck with her Bible and morning coffee, and anyplace when she's with

her husband and sons.
Web site: **www.susielarson.com**

ELLIE LOFARO

Ellie Lofaro's message is a wonderful blend of plainspoken truth, common sense practicality, and disarming humor. A serious student of Scripture and a keen observer of culture, Ellie has developed a unique teaching style that touches the heart, stimulates the mind, and nourishes the soul—thus inspiring her to found Heart, Mind, & Soul Ministries. Completely convinced of God's love and His mandate to "go and tell," Ellie has committed her life to sharing the Great News. She speaks nationally, has authored six books and teaches a weekly interdenominational Bible study. Ellie and her husband, Frank, CEO of the Christian Leadership Alliance, reside near the nation's capital. They have three almost-grown children.
Web site: **www.ellielofaro.com**

LESLIE LUDY

Leslie Ludy is the bestselling author of *Authentic Beauty—the Shaping of a Set-Apart Young Woman.* She and her husband, Eric, have written numerous bestselling books, including *When God Writes Your Love Story, When Dreams Come True,* and *Teaching True Love to a Sex-at-Thirteen Generation.* They have toured extensively, speaking around the U.S. and abroad. Their poignant perspective on the spiritual climate of contemporary culture has made them a respected voice around the country. Sharing their message and music on numerous media platforms, they were among the top ten Focus on the Family radio broadcasts in 2002 and 2006. Leslie is the director of *Authentic Girl Ministries,* providing resources and inspiration for young women seeking to be fully set-apart for Christ.
Web site: **www.authenticgirl.com** **www.setapartlife.com**

ANITA LUSTREA

Authentic. That's the word women often use to describe Anita. She is a popular speaker at women's conferences and retreats, and co-host of the award-winning *Midday Connection* radio program. Her deep desire is to communicate freedom to women and help them nurture and care for their souls. Anita has her roots in Maine. She grew up in a singing family, toured with the New Disciples during her college days, then overseas with The Internationals before recording her first solo album, *Joy in the Journey*, which received national airplay. Anita and her husband, Mike, a pastor, along with her son John, live in the Chicago suburbs.

Web site: **www.anitalustrea.com** **www.middayconnection.org**

TAMMY MALTBY

Tammy Maltby is a compelling speaker, author, Bible teacher, and cohost on *Aspiring Women* with a heart for helping real Christian women live richly and fully in the real world. Her book *Confessions of a Good Christian Girl* applies the Bible's grace-filled, healing message to painful issues such as suicide, sexual brokenness, divorce, addiction, and mental illness. She is also the author of *Lifegiving: Discovering the Secrets to a Beautiful Life* and *A Discovery Journal to A Beautiful Life* and *Confessions of a Good Christian Guy* written with Tom Davis. Tammy lives near the Rocky Mountains in Colorado. She has four children, two of whom are adopted internationally. She is also grandmother to Cohen.

Web site: **http://tammymaltby.typepad.com**
www.Aspiringwomen.tv

CHRISTA MARCH

Christa is the founder of Teen Mother Choices and TMCInternational. She was born into a strong Christian home. She is married to Jim and mother to TJ and Loran.

There are four things she knows with absolute surety and these four things will last for eternity: (1) She is a child of the God of the universe because of what His Son Jesus Christ did for her on the cross, (2) She was put on this planet to be Jim March's wife, (3) She was placed on this planet to be TJ and Loran's mom, and (4) She was put on this planet to serve parenting teenage mothers.

Web site: **www.tmcint.org** **www.teenmotherchoices.org**

LISA MCKAY

Lisa McKay was born in Canada to Australian parents and was raised in Australia, Bangladesh, the States, and Zimbabwe. She has also lived in Indonesia, the Philippines, and Croatia. Lisa trained as a forensic psychologist at the University of New South Wales in Sydney, and also holds a masters degree in international peace studies from Notre Dame. She is currently living in Los Angeles and working as the director of training and education services for the Headington Institute, a nonprofit that provides psychological and spiritual support services to humanitarian relief and development workers around the world. Lisa's first novel is *My Hands Came Away Red.*

Web site: **www.lisamckaywriting.com**

LEIGH MCLEROY

Leigh McLeroy writes and speaks with a passion for God and a keen eye for his presence in everyday life. A former ghostwriter with seven previous books to her credit, Leigh's first solo effort, *Moments for Singles*, was published in 2004, followed by *The Beautiful Ache: Finding the God Who Satisfies When Life Does Not* in 2007, and *The Sacred Ordinary: Embracing the Holy in the Everyday* in 2008. Leigh is a frequent conference and event speaker, and the creator of *Wednesday Words,* an email devotional. She makes her home in Houston, Texas.

Web site: **www.wednesdaywords.com**

NANCY SEBASTIAN MEYER

Nancy Sebastian Meyer vulnerably and passionately shares hope. Her words—based on God's Word—shift paradigms and challenge perspectives. Her speaking and books motivate people to renew their minds and adjust their actions. Her two solo albums bring renewed joy and comfort to listeners' hearts. Married more than twenty years to a pastor-turned-agnostic who gives her permission to share their story, Nancy connects intimately with audiences as she shares the zigs and zags of her life and the God who meets her at every turn. Lancaster, Pennsylvania, is home to Nancy, her husband, their teenage daughter, and Wrangler, a golden retriever.

Web site: **www.nancysebastianmeyer.com**

LINDA MINTLE

Known for her humor and practical advice, Dr. Linda will motivate you to get real and get moving. A national expert on marriage, family and eating issues, her no-nonsense approach to everyday life and conversational style will inspire and uplift. She is the resident expert on ABC Family's *Living the Life* television show and has authored fourteen books. Dr. Linda received her Ph.D. from Old Dominion University in Urban Health Services and Clinical Psychology, a master's degree in social work and bachelor's degree in psychology and communications, both from Western Michigan University.

Web site: **www.drlindahelps.com**

CONNIE NEAL

Connie Neal is sought by secular and Christian media as an expert on the intersection of Christianity and pop culture. She is a Bible teacher, author, and popular speaker in secular venues, Christian colleges, churches, and at library and literacy events. Connie has authored, written, contributed to, and ghosted dozens of books. Most recently she is widely known for her book *MySpace for Moms and Dads: A Guide to Understanding the Risks and the Rewards.*

Web site: **www.connieneal.com**

LORI NEFF

Lori Neff is the senior producer for the award-winning national radio program, *Midday Connection*. Lori grew up in a small town in Ohio—spending more time outside in nature than inside. Her interests include art (looking at it and creating it), music, literature, humanitarian aid efforts, cooking, gardening, coffee, traveling, thinking, learning, and spending time with her husband and best friend, John (Miriam Neff's son). Her lifelong goal is to glorify God by being a godly woman who is fully alive.

Web site: **www.lorineff.com** **www.middayconnection.org**

MIRIAM NEFF

Miriam is an author, speaker and founder of Widow Connection. She is the widow of Robert Neff, former vice president of Moody

Radio. She has twenty-six years of counseling experience in public high schools. Miriam is the mother of four adult children and grandmother of three very active boys.

Web site: **www.widowconnection.com**

SHAUNA NIEQUIST

Shauna Niequist lives in Grand Rapids, Michigan, with her husband, Aaron, and their son Henry. She grew up at Willow Creek Community Church, then studied English and French literature at Westmont College, in Santa Barbara, California. She worked in student ministry at Willow Creek for five years and as the creative director at Mars Hill for three years. Shauna's first book, *Cold Tangerines*, is a collection of essays about the extraordinary moments in our everyday lives. Her very favorite things are throwing dinner parties, taking full advantage of Michigan summers, and reading great books.

Web site: **www.shaunaniequist.com**

AMY NORTON

Amy received a doctor of jurisprudence from Texas Tech University in 1992. In addition to private practice, she worked for two years as a guardian ad litem for children and as a court appointed special advocate for abused children. She developed and managed an international nonprofit ministry serving orphan children including adoption for twelve years. She helped begin a new nonprofit organization, Orphan Outreach, dedicated to providing orphan and underprivileged children with a Christian education. She is married and has three children: Johnathan, who was adopted from Russia, Madeleine, and David Allen.

Web site: **www.orphanoutreach.org**

SABRINA O'MALONE

Sabrina is an author, speaker, and businesswoman in sales and marketing. She is the former Mrs. New Jersey and the author of *Moms on the Job* and president of WorkingMom.com. With unwavering support from her husband, Daniel, WorkingMom.com has become a veritable online powerhouse, saving time, energy, and money for thousands of families daily with free resources, coupons, and inspirational articles. Sabrina is the mother of four children.

Web site: **http://sabrinaomalone.com** **www.workingmom.com**

LESLIE PARROTT

Dr. Leslie Parrott is a marriage and family therapist and codirector with her husband, Dr. Les Parrott, of the Center for Relationship Development at Seattle Pacific University. She is the author of *God Made You Nose to Toes*, and coauthor with her husband of several best-selling books, including *Trading Places, Love Talk*, and the award-winner *Saving Your Marriage Before It Starts*. Leslie has been a columnist for *Today's Christian Woman* and has been featured on *Oprah, CBS This Morning, CNN*, and *The View*, and in *USA Today* and the *New York Times*. Leslie lives in Seattle with her husband and their two sons.

Web site: **www.RealRelationships.com**

KATHY PEEL

Kathy Peel is called "America's Family Manager" by journalists and millions of women. The author of nineteen books that have sold more than two million copies, she has appeared extensively on television and radio and in video productions. In her upbeat and entertaining style, she delivers reality-based solutions for creating a smoothly running home and living a saner, satisfying life. She is an engaging, but relaxed Everywoman who makes it clear that you can have fun and take charge of your life and your home at the same time. Her accessible, no-nonsense strategies are a road map to a balanced life.

Web site: www.familymanager.com

BETHANY PIERCE

Bethany Pierce was born in Mount Vernon, Ohio, to parents who encouraged the reading of books by storing the television on a microwave stand in the hall closet. At eighteen she enrolled in Miami University's College of Art to study painting, staying a fifth year to complete a master's degree in creative writing. Her artwork has been exhibited in Cincinnati, Indianapolis, and Austin. *Publisher's Weekly* named her first book, *Feeling for Bones*, one of the top Christian books of 2007. Presently, she lives in Oxford, Ohio, where she supports her writing and painting by teaching English at the university.

Web site: **http://bethanypierce.typepad.com**

MARCIA RAMSLAND

Marcia Ramsland is well known as "The Organizing Pro" for her practical skills and tips to manage busy lives. As a professional organizer and international speaker, she is also the author of the *Simplify for Success* book trio, *Simplify Your Life*, *Simplify Your Time*, *Simplify Your Space*, and the booklet *Ages and Stages of Getting Children Organized*. Marcia appears on TV and national radio shows like Martha Stewart radio, and her tips appear in national magazines like *Better Homes and Gardens* and *Real Simple* magazines. Marcia believes anyone can get more organized with enough motivation and easy-to-follow solutions.

Web site: **www.OrganizingPro.com**

PAULA RINEHART

As a marriage and family counselor, Paula enjoys the opportunity to offer encouragement and insight in the everyday struggles of life and relationships. The author of the widely acclaimed books, *Strong Women, Soft Hearts* and *Better Than My Dreams* (both published by Thomas Nelson), Paula speaks frequently on topics of personal growth, intimacy with God, and sexuality. She and her husband, Stacy, served on the staff of *The Navigators* for twenty-four years. They live in Raleigh, North Carolina, and are the parents of two grown children.

Web site: **www.paularinehart.com**

JANE RUBIETTA

Jane Rubietta is an award-winning author of ten books, including the critically acclaimed *Come Closer: A Call to Life, Love, and Breakfast on the Beach* (Waterbrook). She speaks internationally, writes on assignment for various well-known periodicals, and is associate coordinator of the Write to Publish writers conference. She is a pastor's wife and mother of three. Together, she and her husband, Rich, codirect Abounding Ministries in the Chicago area.

Web site: **www.janerubietta.com**

CAROL RUHTER

Carol Ruhter is passionate about helping women rediscover intimacy with God by spending time outdoors, learning about the Creator through His creation. Her company, Trailbound Trips, offers women's week-long hiking trips and retreats in such places as Maine's Acadia National Park and Montana's Glacier National Park. Trailbound also conducts day-long hiking and bicycling trips in Northern Illinois' wild places. Carol is a freelance writer and editor and is currently collaborating with Marty Ramey on a devotional inspired by God's creation. She and her husband, Don, live in Barrington, Illinois, and have two college-age children, Dave and Emily.

Web site: **www.TrailboundTrips.com**

MELINDA SCHMIDT

As a child, Melinda was eager to grab the mic of her family's Wallensak tape machine and record make-believe news broadcasts and imaginary radio shows. What seems to have been an inevitable career in broadcasting began at KLJC-FM (Kansas City) in 1978. She has enjoyed hosting various programs at Moody Radio since 1980, cohosting the award-winning *Midday Connection* there since 2004. Residing in suburban Chicago with husband, David, and young adult kids, Kelly and Kevin, she enjoys reading or writing in front of a fireplace, traveling to the woods or palm treed-beaches, and good conversation with friends. She aspires to be a lifelong learner.

Web site: **www.melindaschmidt.com www.middayconnection.org**

JAN SILVIOUS

Jan has been a featured speaker at Women of Faith arena events as well as for WOF preconferences. She has been a plenary speaker for Precept Ministries' National Women's Conventions, Moody Women's Conferences, Moody Bible Institute's Founder's Week, and Balancing the Demands of Life Women's conferences. Jan has written nine books over the past twenty years. Two of her favorites have been readers' favorites as well—*Big Girls Don't Whine* and *Fool-Proofing Your Life*. Ongoing reader response to these books has spurred Jan to immerse herself in finding biblically sound, psychologically positive answers for women's challenges. Jan gives high priority to her family, which includes Charlie, her husband of more than forty years, three grown sons, two wonderful daughters-in-law, and five precious grandchildren.

Web site: **www.jansilvious.com**

ERIN SMALLEY

Erin Smalley earned her bachelor of science degree in nursing and worked as a labor and delivery nurse for several years. She also holds a master's degree in clinical psychology.

Erin has written several articles for *Parent Life* and *Marriage Partnership* as well as published work with her husband, Dr. Greg Smalley. They are both on staff at the Center for Relationship Enrichment at John Brown University. She coauthored her first book, *Grown Up Girlfriends*, with Carrie Oliver. Her second book, written with her husband, is *Before You Plan Your Wedding, Plan Your Marriage*.

Erin and Greg reside in Siloam Springs, Arkansas, with their two daughters, Taylor and Madalyn, and son, Garrison.

Web site: **www.smalleymarriage.com**

KENDRA SMILEY

Kendra Smiley, 2001 Illinois Mother of the Year, is the mother of three grown sons. She and her husband, John, live on a working farm in East Central Illinois. She has written eight books, including *Do Your Kids a Favor . . . Love Your Spouse*, and hosts a daily radio program, LIVE LIFE INTENTIONALLY! Kendra speaks nationally and internationally.

Web site: **www.KendraSmiley.com**

ARLOA SUTTER

Dr. Arloa Sutter is the visionary leader and founder of Breakthrough Urban Ministries. Arloa began Breakthrough when she simply responded to a need and opened up an unused church meeting room and served hot coffee and lunch to the homeless. Soon she began to build relationships with those she was helping and focused her ministry on shelter, hot meals, counseling and supportive services to homeless men. Breakthrough has expanded to serve homeless women, and a youth and family program has been added. Today, Breakthrough stands as a center of home for community residents and families of

Chicago's west side.

Web site: **www.breakthroughministries.com**

BEVERLY HUBBLE TAUKE

A family counselor, speaker, and author of *Healing Your Family Tree*, Beverly Hubble Tauke collaborates with churches throughout the eastern U.S., and for years facilitated mission workshops for the homeless of Washington, D.C. She previously managed media operations in the U.S. House and Senate, taught journalism and communications in East Africa, and worked as a writer at Chicago's Moody Bible Institute. She holds graduate degrees from Wheaton College and the Catholic University of America, and a bachelor of religious education degree from Baptist Bible College, Pennsylvania. Bev and her husband, Tom, have a son in college and teenage daughter.

Web site: **www.BeverlyTauke.com**

TIFFANY TAYLOR

Tiffany Taylor and her husband, Brad Wines, had discussed early in their marriage adopting rather than have biological children. After hearing about the heart-wrenching stories of Russian orphans, they decided to adopt from Russia. In 1996, they brought home Inna, an eight-month-old girl. In 1998, Tiffany and her husband adopted another orphan, Misha, an eight-month-old boy. In early 1999, she began volunteering for an international ministry and she found her calling in full-time ministry to orphans. In late 2007, Tiffany joined several close friends from her years in international ministry to start a new ministry called Orphan Outreach. Tiffany and Brad reside in Dallas with their children, Inna and Misha.

Web site: **www.orphanoutreach.org**

JANET THOMPSON

Janet Thompson, founder and director of About His Work Ministries, also known as AHW Ministries, is a prolific author and speaker on topics relevant to today's Christian women. Janet has a bachelor of science in food administration from California Polytechnic University, a master of business administration degree from California Lutheran University, and a master of arts in Christian Leadership from Fuller

Theological Seminary. She is also a CLASS (Christian Leaders, Authors and Speakers) graduate. Janet and her husband, Dave, have four married children and nine grandchildren. They are enjoying the season of life known as empty nest, or as Janet calls it, Parents Time To Rest. Dave is a community leader in the Saddleback Church Couples Ministry and a helpmate partner with Janet in AHW Ministries. They make their home in Lake Forest, California.

Web site: **www.womantowomanmentoring.com**
www.janetthompson.blogspot.com

ELLEN VAUGHN

Ellen is a *New York Times* #1 bestselling author and inspirational speaker. Her books include *Time Peace* and *Radical Gratitude*, and collaborative works *The God Who Hung on the Cross*; *Rags, Riches, and Real Success*; and *It's All About Him*. Former vice president of executive communications for Prison Fellowship, Ellen speaks frequently at Christian retreats and conferences, and has been featured at writers seminars in the U.S. and Canada. Her articles have appeared in *Christianity Today, World,* and *The Dallas Morning News*. Ellen holds a master of arts from Georgetown University and a bachelor of arts from the University of Richmond. She and her husband, Lee, live in the Washington, D.C. area with daughter Emily and twins Haley and Walker. Ellen has an enormous dog named after C. S. Lewis, and a small pup named Gus. She enjoys reading, walking, drinking coffee, and staring pensively at the ocean.

Web site: **www.ellenvaughn.com**

LESLIE VERNICK

Leslie Vernick DCSW, LCSW is a licensed clinical social worker with a private practice in Pennsylvania. She is a sought-after speaker and the author of five books, including the popular *How to Act Right When Your Spouse Acts Wrong* and *The Emotionally Destructive Relationship*. Leslie writes a column for *Today's Christian Woman* magazine answering relationship questions and is a regular guest on Moody Radio's *Midday Connection* program. She received her MSW from University of Illinois and received post-graduate training in cognitive therapy and biblical counseling.

Web site: **www.leslievernick.com**
Email: **leslie@leslievernick.com**

JOANNA WEAVER

Joanna Weaver is a pastor's wife and mother of three kids, ages twenty-two, nineteen, and five! She and her husband, John, have been in full-time ministry for more than twenty-six years. Joanna loves speaking to women and speaks at conferences and retreats around the country on various topics geared to a woman's heart. The author of the bestselling books *Having a Mary Heart in a Martha World: Finding Intimacy With God in the Busyness of Life* and *Having a Mary Spirit: Allowing God to Change Us from the Inside Out*, Joanna has also written the award-wining gift book *With This Ring: Promises to Keep*, and a series of children's picture books called the *Attitude Adjusters*.

Web site: **www.joannaweaverbooks.com**

MARY WHELCHEL

Mary Whelchel is the founder and speaker of *The Christian Working Woman* radio program, heard internationally on more than five hundred stations. In addition, she is director of women's ministries for the Moody Church in Chicago, and the author of several books, including *Why Do I Always Feel Guilty?* She is single and lives in Glen Ellyn, Illinois.

Web site: **www.christianworkingwoman.org**

GLYNNIS WHITWER

Glynnis Whitwer is on staff with Proverbs 31 Ministries as the senior editor of the *P31 Woman* magazine. She is a speaker for women's groups across the country, and is the author of *work@home: A Practical Guide for Women Who Want to Work from Home,* and coauthor of a Bible studies series entitled *Kingdom Living*. Glynnis and her husband, Tod, run a home-based business (www.roselanecottage.com), have five children, and live in Glendale, Arizona.

Web site: **www.GlynnisWhitwer.com.**

CHRISTINE WYRTZEN

Christine Wyrtzen is the founder and director of Daughters of Promise. Known as a recording artist, author, inspirational speaker, creative Bible teacher, and storyteller, she hosts the radio program *Daughters of Promise*, heard daily on more than stations. Christine's passion is to awaken women to the extravagant love of God, equipping them to live as children in His kingdom. Known for more than thirty-two years as a musician with fourteen albums and two books to her credit, she was nominated for a Dove Award. Christine has been a storyteller since age four—when she wore red glasses and animatedly wove stories by the hour. Nowadays, she offers herself to audiences as a friend and wounded healer. Married for thirty-five years to Ron Wyrtzen, youngest son of evangelist Jack Wyrtzen, she has two adult children and two grandsons, Gabe and Andy.

Web site: **www.daughtersofpromise.org**

KAY YERKOVICH

Kay Yerkovich has journeyed with Jesus for thirty-six years. She is a licensed marriage and family therapist in California and has been counseling people for more than twenty years. She has four grown children and four grandchildren. Recently, she and her husband Milan coauthored *How We Love*. Together Milan and Kay speak all over the United States on their book which helps the reader discover their love style and form deeper emotional connections in their most important relationships. Their ministry also focuses on helping pastors, missionaries, and Christian leaders finish well.

Web site: **www.howwelove.com** **www.relationship180.com**

Index

June 24
August 12
October 4

Rosalie de Rosset
September 20

Janice Elsheimer
www.jelsheimer.com
January 31
August 30
September 5
October 19
November 20

Lois Evans
www.loisevans.org
April 4
May 30
August 2
November 27
December 19

Pam Farrel
www.farrelcommunications.com
April 27
July 1
October 6

Margaret Feinberg
www.margaretfeinberg.com
February 24
August 6
November 16

Shaunti Feldhahn
www.shaunti.com
May 3
October 1

Sandra Glahn
www.aspire2.com
November 11

Dannah Gresh
www.purefreedom.org
March 1
June 2
October 5

Tracy Groot
www.tracygroot.com
January 24
September 14

Sara Groves
www.saragroves.com
March 3
June 7

Sharon Hanby-Robie
www.sharonhanbyrobie.com
January 23
February 18
March 31
August 3

Lisa Harper
www.lisaharper.net
April 28
June 18

Joanne Heim
www.thesimplewife.typepad.com
January 12
May 6
July 5
October 8
November 25

SHARON HERSH
www.sharonhersh.com
May 31
July 27
October 27
December 28

KIM HILL
www.kimhillmusic.com
April 5
July 4

LYNNE HYBELS
www.lynnehybels.com
March 10
June 23
September 24

KRISTEN JOHNSON INGRAM
March 19
April 19
May 26
June 28
July 14
September 11
September 29
October 12
December 10

CAROLYN CUSTIS JAMES
www.whitbyforum.com
April 6
September 23

VICTORIA SAUNDERS JOHNSON
www.protectinginnocentchildren.org
January 25
April 14
August 18
September 22
December 17

JOY JORDAN-LAKE
www.joyjordanlake.com
January 13
August 9
October 15

NANCY KANE
January 2
February 3
April 8
May 27
September 15
October 28
November 9

ELLIE KAY
www.elliekay.com
March 9
March 28
April 23
May 9
June 27
December 12

CAROL KENT
www.CarolKent.org
March 30

VIRELLE KIDDER
www.virellekidder.com
February 17
July 18
October 29

KATHY KOCH
www.CelebrateKids.com
February 28

May 5
August 16
October 21
December 4

GINGER KOLBABA
www.gingerkolbaba.com
July 28
October 18
November 21
December 14

SUSIE LARSON
www.susielarson.com
April 16
May 19
August 29
November 23
December 5

ELLIE LOFARO
www.ellielofaro.com
March 15
April 10
July 31

LESLIE LUDY
www.authenticgirl.com
January 28
March 27
June 25

ANITA LUSTREA
www.anitalustrea.com
January 1
January 21
January 27
January 30
February 16
February 19
February 27
March 5
March 17
March 22
March 26
March 29
April 2
April 12
April 20
April 25
May 4
May 7
May 12
May 25
May 28
June 8
June 14
June 21
June 26
June 30
July 3
July 12
July 17
July 21
July 29
August 1
August 14
August 23
August 27
September 7
September 28
October 20
October 31
November 2
November 14
November 19
December 3
December 11
December 24
December 29

TAMMY MALTBY
http://tammymaltby.typepad.com
January 20
July 24

CHRISTA MARCH
www.teenmotherchoices.org
August 10
September 6
September 30
October 11
December 23

LISA MCKAY
www.lisamckaywriting.com
February 22
April 18
July 26

LEIGH MCLEROY
www.wednesdaywords.com
January 26
March 11
April 11
June 1
August 28
October 22
December 22

NANCY SEBASTIAN MEYER
www.nancysebastianmeyer.com
February 14
March 16
April 26
May 18
July 15
August 31
September 27
December 9

LINDA MINTLE
www.drlindahelps.com
May 10
June 15
July 10
August 13
September 16
November 13

CONNIE NEAL
www.connieneal.com
March 13
July 25

LORI NEFF
www.lorineff.com
January 8
February 5
March 20
April 24
May 14
June 3
July 7
August 5
September 9
October 7
November 17
December 6

MIRIAM NEFF
www.widowconnection.com
January 5
April 15
June 10
September 13
October 26
November 15
November 29
December 20

Shauna Niequist
www.shaunaniequist.com
January 6
April 13
September 8

Amy Norton
www.orphanoutreach.org
November 28
December 21

Sabrina O'Malone
www.workingmom.com
February 23
May 17
July 6
September 1
October 9

Leslie Parrott
www.RealRelationships.com
January 22
May 13
August 17

Kathy Peel
www.familymanager.com
February 6
March 8
July 9

Bethany Pierce
http://bethanypierce.typepad.com
February 26
June 19
August 20

Marcia Ramsland
www.OrganizingPro.com
March 25
June 12
July 16
August 4
September 26
December 1
December 31

Paula Rinehart
www.paularinehart.com
March 24
June 17

Jane Rubietta
www.janerubietta.com
February 8
September 10

Carol Ruhter
www.TrailboundTrips.com
January 29
August 24
October 30
November 22
December 7
December 26

Melinda Schmidt
www.melindaschmidt.com
January 15
February 11
February 25
March 14
April 17
April 30
May 2
June 9
July 19
August 11
September 2
September 18

October 14
November 6
November 26
December 15
December 25

Jan Silvious
www.jansilvious.com
February 21
August 19

Erin Smalley
www.smalleymarriage.com
January 18
June 16
October 10

Kendra Smiley
www.KendraSmiley.com
January 10
March 21
May 29
June 4
July 23
August 22
October 25
December 2
December 27

Arloa Sutter
www.breakthroughministries.com
February 12
April 9
June 20
August 8
November 24

Beverly Hubble Tauke
www.BeverlyTauke.com
January 11
March 12
May 16
July 22
September 19
November 12

Tiffany Taylor
www.orphanoutreach.org
March 18
April 21

Janet Thompson
www.womantowomanmentoring.com
February 1
July 13
August 26
October 3
November 30

Ellen Vaughn
www.ellenvaughn.com
February 2
May 20
June 29
September 25
October 23

Leslie Vernick
www.leslievernick.com
January 9
June 11
November 10

Joanna Weaver
www.joannaweaverbooks.com
February 4
August 25

Mary Whelchel
www.christianworkingwoman.org
April 1
July 8
October 2
November 1
December 30

Glynnis Whitwer
www.GlynnisWhitwer.com
January 3
March 7
May 8
July 11
September 12

Christine Wyrtzen
www.daughtersofpromise.org
February 15
March 4
May 23
June 22
July 20
September 17
October 17
November 18
December 8

Kay Yerkovich
www.howwelove.com
February 20
April 3
June 13
August 21
October 13
November 8

ISBN-13: 978-1-881273-90-5

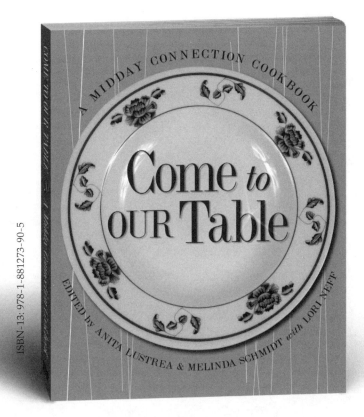